Kate Field

Writing American Women
Carol A. Kolmerten, *Series Editor*

Kate Field

*The Many Lives
of a Nineteenth-Century
American Journalist*

Gary Scharnhorst

 Syracuse University Press

Copyright © 2008 by Syracuse University Press

Syracuse, New York 13244-5160

All Rights Reserved

First Edition 2008

08   09   10   11   12   13   6   5   4   3   2   1

The paper used in this publication meets the minimum requirements
of American National Standard for Information Sciences—Permanence
of Paper for Printed Library Materials, ANSI Z39.48–1984.∞™

For a listing of books published and distributed by Syracuse University Press,
visit our Web site at SyracuseUniversityPress.syr.edu

ISBN-13: 978-0-8156-0874-5   ISBN-10: 0-8156-0874-8

Library of Congress Cataloging-in-Publication Data

Scharnhorst, Gary.

Kate Field : the many lives of a nineteenth-century American journalist / Gary Scharnhorst. — 1st ed.

p. cm. — (Writing American women)

Includes bibliographical references and index.

ISBN-13: 978-0-8156-0874-5 (hbk. : alk. paper)

ISBN-10: 0-8156-0874-8 (hbk. : alk. paper)

1. Field, Kate, 1838–1896.   2. Journalists—United States—Biography.   3. Authors, American—19th
century—Biography.   I. Title.

PN4874.F435S33 2008

070.92—dc22

[B]

2008005785

Manufactured in the United States of America

To the medical staff of Oak Park Hospital,
Oak Park, Illinois

GARY SCHARNHORST is Distinguished Professor of English at the University of New Mexico, editor of *American Literary Realism,* editor in alternating years of *American Literary Scholarship,* and the author of biographies of Horatio Alger, Jr., Charlotte Perkins Gilman, and Bret Harte.

Contents

Illustrations

Preface

THOUGH KATE FIELD (1838–1896) LIVED only to the age of fifty-seven, she was born early enough to study Latin with Walter Savage Landor (1775–1864) and she lived long enough to laud the Harvard commencement address of W. E. B. Du Bois (1868–1963). She was so famous during her life that she was a model for characters in novels by both Henry James and Anthony Trollope, though almost no one these days has ever heard of her. During her life the *New York World* once referred to her as the "brainiest woman in the United States"; at her death the *New York Tribune* memorialized her as "one of the best-known women in America" and the *Chicago Tribune* averred that she was "perhaps the most unique woman the present century has produced."[1] She was ubiquitous in late-nineteenth-century America, appearing Zelig-like in the background of some of the most significant literary and historical events of the period. As one of the first celebrity journalists, before Nelly Bly and Dorothea Dix, she both reported the news and was the subject of news reports. During her career she interviewed such figures as the archeologist Heinrich Schliemann, theatrical impresario Dion Boucicault, explorer Henry Stanley, composers William S. Gilbert and Arthur Sullivan, pianist Anton Rubinstein, and President Grover Cleveland, and in turn she often sat for interviews while on play or lecture tour. She was sufficiently well known a generation after her death that she was included among the prominent figures whose lives were sketched in the *Dictionary of American Biography*. Yet she has not been the subject of a book-length biography in more than a century, and her life has largely been lost in a biographical blind spot. An unorthodox feminist, she advocated neither prohibition nor universal suffrage, which may begin to explain why she has been neglected if not ignored. A self-described mugwump,[2] she hewed no party line, criticized men and women who tailored their views to fit the fashion, and refused to truckle to convention.

The primary sources for a new biography of Kate Field abound, though they are located in the morgues of literally dozens of newspapers and magazines in the United States and Europe. Field wrote no formal autobiography, but her hundreds of travel essays comprise a reasonably complete story of her life. She once advised Helen Hunt Jackson, who wrote long encyclical letters to her friends, that she ought not be an "intellectual spendthrift" by sending private letters to her friends but should earn money by publishing them. Ironically, according to her most recent biographer, Jackson expressed disdain for Field for offering this advice.[3] On the other hand, the manuscript sources for a biography of Field are less extensive than they might be because Lilian Whiting, her literary executor and first biographer, apparently destroyed many of her letters and diaries. So unlike many eminent modern lives, Field's life must be mainly reconstructed from published sources, interviews by and with her, and memoirs. During the course of her career Field served as the Florence, Italy, correspondent of the *Boston Courier,* the Newport correspondent of the *Boston Post,* the Boston correspondent of the *Springfield Republican,* the New York correspondent of the *Chicago Tribune,* and the London correspondent of the *New York Herald.* For five years near the end of her life, she edited, published, and wrote most of the contents of a weekly paper entitled *Kate Field's Washington.* The recovery of her life is in no small part a bibliographical project, a listing of the many hundreds of articles, essays, poems, and plays she published anonymously or under her signature or her initials or her various pseudonyms. For the record, some pieces she published (e.g., in the *Paris Continental Gazette*) are irrecoverably lost. But to the extent possible I have reconstructed her oeuvre.[4]

Acknowledgments

AS ALWAYS, I HAVE DEPENDED upon the kindnesses of friends and strangers for help on this project. I happily acknowledge the assistance of Beth Bailey and the Feminist Research Institute at the University of New Mexico; Virginia Shipman and the Research Allocations Committee at the University of New Mexico; Russell Cole, Joe Lane, and Frances Lopez Smith at Zimmerman Library, University of New Mexico; Paul Davis of the Department of English at the University of New Mexico; Lois Archuleta and Karen Hyde, reference librarians at the Salt Lake City Public Library; Eugene Zepp, Eric P. Frazier, Henry F. Scannell, Diane Parks, and Cindy Clark at the Boston Public Library; G. Travis Westly at the Library of Congress; Susanne George Bloomfield at the University of Nebraska, Kearney; Harold K. Bush at St. Louis University; Nicolas Witschi at Western Michigan University; Sue Hodson at the Huntington Library; and Joleen Muñiz, Hazel Scalia, Katie Hill, Lawrence I. Berkove, Sam Gonzales, and Roy Horton. I am also grateful to Carol Kolmerten of Hood College, Denise Knight of SUNY-Cortland, Glenn Wright of the Syracuse University Press, and Jill Root, my copyeditor, for the care with which each of them read the manuscript and offered suggestions to improve it.

I am also grateful for permission to reprint excerpts from or abridged versions of several essays about Kate Field I have published over the years, as follows: to the Newport Historical Society for parts of chapters 3, 5, and 12 in *Newport History*, vol. 72 (Spring 2003); the editors of *American Periodicals* for excerpts of chapters 3, 4, 5, and 6 in their journal, vol. 14, no. 2 (2005); the Johns Hopkins University Press for a page of chapter 4 first published in the *Henry James Review*, vol. 22 (2001); and the Oscar Wilde

Society for a section of chapter 8 in the *Wildean,* vol. 28 (January 2006). Part of chapter 10 first appeared in the *Journal of San Diego History,* vol. 51 (Summer–Fall 2006); and of chapter 11 in *Alaska History,* vol. 21 (Fall 2006). A version of chapter 2 appeared in *Browning Society Notes,* vol. 31 (March 2007); and a passage in chapter 3, in *Victorian Newsletter,* vol. 109 (Spring 2006). Part of chapter 5 is reprinted from *Legacy: A Journal of American Women Writers,* vol. 18 (Spring 2002) by permission of the University of Nebraska Press, © 2002 by the University of Nebraska Press. Part of chapter 11 appeared in *Blue Pencils and Hidden Hands: Women Writing Periodicals, 1830–1910,* © 2004 by Sharon M. Harris, reprinted by permission of University Press of New England, Hanover, New Hampshire.

Albuquerque, New Mexico

Kate Field

1

Beginnings

KATE FIELD WAS DESCENDED, if not from noble stock, at least from a performer in a distinguished stock company. Nathan Field was a late Renaissance playwright and actor, his name listed in the 1623 Shakespeare First Folio as one of the King's Players.[1] In 1798, her Irish Catholic ancestors lost their property during the "Hibernian turmoil" and immigrated to England.[2] Kate's father, Joseph Field, was born in 1810 in the village of Stockton, near London.[3] To escape further "the sight of British oppression," as he noted in a memoir, his family immigrated to America in 1815 shortly after the birth of his brother Matthew. Joe Field was educated in the public schools of New York and later reminisced that he had been a rowdy young man "sore given to carnal pleasantries" such as smoking and drinking.[4] He was once jailed overnight merely for smoking a cigar in public.[5] But he soon channeled his energy into acting, debuting on stage at the age of seventeen at the old Tremont Theater in Boston.[6] At twenty he was a regular member of the Park Theater company in New York, and at twenty-three he was hired by Noah Ludlow and Sol Smith to star in their string of theaters across the South and West, particularly in New Orleans, Mobile, Montgomery, Cincinnati, and St. Louis. He arrived in the Crescent City in 1833 just in time to escape the cholera epidemic there. It became the topic of his first important poem, "In the Cemetery at New Orleans," one of the few serious verses he ever wrote.

Of necessity, Joe Field became an indefatigable playwright, a theatrical manager, and a remarkably versatile actor. During a single season he sometimes played over fifty different roles—from Hamlet, Lear, Othello, Iago, Prince Hal, and Richard III in Shakespeare to Sir Benjamin Backbite in Sheridan's *The School for Scandal* and Puff in *The Critic* to Jeremy Diddler in James Kenney's *Raising the Wind*, Flutter in Hannah Cowley's *The Belle's Strategem*, Claude Melnotte in Edward Bulwer-Lytton's *The Lady of Lyon*, and Rover in John O'Keeffe's *Wild Oats*. To judge from his reviews, he was adept at tragedy and melodrama, but most skilled at farce. He preferred dramatic roles, but his managers chose to cast him most often in comedic parts. According to Sol Smith, most audiences "liked his comedy better than his tragedy."[7]

In the fall of 1835, the young star Eliza Lapsley Riddle visited St. Louis, and he was smitten. So was his brother Matt, who had moved west to join his brother's company the year before. "Miss Riddle," as she was known in the playbills, had also been a theatrical prodigy. Her mother, Mary Riddle, literally ran away from home at the age of fifteen to join a troupe of actors. According to a rumor that circulates in Newport, Rhode Island, to this day, Eliza's sister Cordelia was the "love child" of Mary Riddle and the actor Junius Brutus Booth—which, if true, means Kate Field's Aunt Corda was the half-sister of Abraham Lincoln's assassin John Wilkes Booth and the tragedian Edwin Booth. (Field publicly commented in 1893, albeit obliquely, on this alleged family association: "Had Edwin Booth been endowed with his father's genius without his father's failings, he would still be the bright particular star of our dramatic firmament.")[8] Born in Philadelphia, Eliza began her acting career at the age of sixteen and became a star in her mid-twenties under the management of Edwin Forrest.[9] The theater historian James E. Murdoch has declared that she was "one of the most beautiful and accomplished actresses on the American stage."[10] She played Juliet to Charlotte Cushman's Romeo in a celebrated "breeches" or all-woman production of Shakespeare's play, and she supported the elder Booth, William Macready, and Charles Kean during their U.S. tours. Kate Field once quoted her father to the effect that her mother "acted Lady Macbeth (the sleep-walking scene) like one inspired. Mother was a person of inspiration, and if she had been brought up in the French school, she would have had equal art. . . . Personally very attractive many a man has told me how much they were fascinated by her."[11] Eliza Riddle was most famous for her role as Julia, the female lead in Sheridan Knowles' *The Hunchback*, at the Arch Theater in Philadelphia during the 1831–32 season, and she had toured the United States in the role opposite Knowles in 1834. Ludlow and Smith had hired her to reprise the part in St. Louis, where she opened on September 28, 1835. During her engagement she also played Juliet opposite Matt Field's Romeo—and declined his offstage proposal of marriage. By November, brother Joe was performing in the male lead opposite her in *The Hunchback*—and they were soon betrothed.

Fortunately, neither brother bore a grudge. Joe and Matt Field and Eliza Riddle all acted in the same Ludlow and Smith company during the 1836–37 and 1837–38 seasons, occasionally even in the same plays. In a production of *King Lear,* for example, Joe played Lear, Matt the chameleon-like Edgar, and Eliza the virtuous Cordelia. Joe played Richard III opposite Matt's Richmond and Eliza's Queen Elizabeth. The brothers and Eliza also performed in Knowles' *The Wrecker's Daughter,* first staged in St. Louis on September 21, 1837. Joe and Eliza also performed together as Benedick and Beatrice in *Much Ado About Nothing* and as the Duke and Duchess in John Tobin's *The Honeymoon.* Two days after the end of the season, on November 6, 1837, Joseph Field and Eliza Riddle were married at the home of Joe's friend Charles Keemle, a local businessman, and they left on a wedding journey through the South. Two months later Eliza Riddle Field was pregnant with their first child. Ever the professional, she opened the next season in St. Louis in early June and continued to perform through early July. Or as one decorous historian of the St. Louis stage explains, she "was seen a few times in suitable roles until approaching motherhood forced her retirement."[12] Their daughter was born on October 1, 1838, and christened Mary Katherine Keemle (aka Mary Kate in infancy, aka Kate) Field.

Joe Field could not adequately provide for his family on the salary of a stock player in the American provinces. So he took a second job: that of poet. In fragile health, Matt Field had quit the stage soon after the 1838 season opened and traveled to Mexico and to the Sangre de Cristo mountains around Taos and Santa Fe in a vain effort to recover. He returned to New Orleans in the fall of 1839 and joined the editorial staff of the *New Orleans Picayune.* Joe Field moved his family to New Orleans to perform in the St. Charles Theater during the 1839–40 theatrical season and began to pepper the columns of the *Picayune* with satirical dramatic monologues in dialect over the signature "Straws" ("straws in the wind" are ephemeral, but they also show the direction the wind is blowing). The poems were wildly popular and widely copied across the country—as in the *Philadelphia Spirit of the Times* and the *Boston Notion*. Perhaps his most famous "straw" was "The Loafer's Soliloquy," with its opening stanza:

> O when I think of what I am
> And what I used to was,
> I think I've throwd myself away
> Without sufficient cos.[13]

Joe Field became the local if unofficial poet laureate. When Andrew Jackson, the former president and hero of the Battle of New Orleans, visited St. Louis in January 1840, Joe declaimed a poem he had written for the occasion and, according to contemporary news reports, it "drew thunders of applause from three thousand citizens and tears from the aged chieftain." Jackson was "very sensibly touched" and asked "to shake that young man by the hand."[14] Field also delivered a dedicatory poem at the groundbreaking of the Missouri Pacific railroad.[15]

He also became a playwright of modest accomplishments. He wrote as many as twenty plays during his career, mostly farces for his own company, virtually all of them lost. But they were undeniably popular where audiences knew him by reputation. To judge from plot synopses in reviews, *Travelers in America* skewered British tourists. The leading characters in *Victoria* were the Queen of England and James Gordon Bennett, the publisher of the *New York Herald,* supported by the Duke of Wellington and the Duchess of Kent. His play *Amalgamation; or, Southern Visitors* scorned the work of Northern abolitionists. (Sadly, Joe Field was not particularly advanced on the "race question.") His most successful play was *Gabrielle, or the Hazards of the Night,* which he translated from the French of the elder Dumas. Also entitled *Mademoiselle de Belle Isle,* it premiered in New Orleans on May 6, 1840, with Joe and Eliza in the starring roles. The next morning a reviewer in the *Picayune* hailed "the decided and unequivocal success of this piece last evening. Scene after scene was received by the audience with rapturous and enthusiastic applause, and at the fall of the curtain long continued cheering drew forth the talented translator. . . . Mr. Field has expunged the objectionable part of the French plot and woven a new thread of interest in the piece." He planned to travel to "the principal cities of Europe" that summer, "and with him will go the warm good wishes of a large and intelligent circle of friends and admirers," the *Picayune* averred. "Take care of yourself, Joe; don't forget your old friends; and remember that you are wanted again at the St. Charles next season."[16]

Joe Field turned his growing celebrity to advantage by guest-starring in brief theatrical runs or contributing to newspapers in towns across the country—for example, in both Pittsburgh and Boston in June 1840. He and Eliza—leaving baby Kate with family near Boston—sailed for Europe in early July. In his poem "To Mrs. Straws," published in the *Picayune* in mid-July, Joe assured Eliza that she was "the best of mothers" and signed it "with respect and duty." He carried letters of introduction to Dickens, Bulwer-Lytton, "and the chief literary lions of Paris and London," though there is no evidence he met any of them. He also agreed to write "straws" for the *Picayune* and the *Knickerbocker* while in England and he was as good as his word. He mailed a few dozen poems back to the United States over the next few weeks with such titles as "Old Trinity," "Newgate Prison," "Warwick Castle," "Stratford Church," "The House of Lords," and "Queen's Chapel." Joe, Eliza, and baby Kate returned to New Orleans by way of Boston on October 30. "Sea air, six months rapid traveling, and the roast beef of old England have made Joe look fresh and hearty and ten years younger," the *Pic* reported.[17]

He returned to the Ludlow and Smith company in New Orleans during the 1840–41 season, acting opposite the former child star Fanny Elssler in April, at a salary of $80 a week.[18] By late May, however, he and Eliza were performing in Buffalo and by July they had landed for the summer in New York. Joe published a long comic poem, "La Déesse; or, The Elssler-atic Romance," satirizing "the fashionable follies of Gotham" in general and his former acting partner in particular. In the fall the Fields moved to Boston, where they starred at the Tremont Theater during the winter season 1841–42. In the course of an eight-hour public dinner for Dickens at Papanti's Hall in Boston the evening of February 1, 1842, in fact, Joe sang a comic song entitled "Boz," another of his occasional lyrics in high Victorian style, in honor of the guest. It begins:

I name thee, and I see a gentle spring
Gushing in joy amid sweet herb and flow'r
Of May Day! Birds unto their *young ones* sing!
Bud, blossom, leaf, sunshine and sunny show'r
And sighs of the sweet south wind, murmuring
Of summer beauty—ev'ry pleasant thing
Salutes me![19]

There is no record that, like Andrew Jackson in New Orleans, Dickens wiped away a tear.

He spent much of the next year earning a living as an actor while trying to succeed as a playwright. He was paid a salary of twenty-five dollars a week, plus a third of a "benefit"—the highest income in the company—at the Olympic Theater in New York, though he also was obliged to assign rights to his new plays to management.[20] Fittingly, he debuted a pair of social satires, *Nervo-Vitalics; or, What Next?* and *Such as It Is,* in New York in September 1842 to dismal reviews and brief runs. No more successful was his burlesque version of *Anthony and Cleopatra* at the Olympic in March 1843. Back in the Crescent City the next month, he produced and starred in his farcical forecast *1943; or, New Orleans a Century Hence.* The winter season at the new St. Charles Theater opened in mid-November with Joe and Eliza in *The Hunchback* and *Gabrielle.* Meanwhile, Matt Field's health was rapidly deteriorating. He had become assistant editor of the *Picayune* in the fall of 1839, with an income that enabled him to marry Noah Ludlow's daughter Cornelia in Mobile in February 1841, but he was best known for the poems he published in the paper under the pseudonym "Phazma." He returned to the West in the expedition led by Sir William Gordon Stuart in May 1843, but the trip merely postponed the inevitable. He died in September 1844 at the age of only thirty-one en route from Boston to New Orleans and was buried at sea. Brother Joe tried for years to find a press that would issue a collection of Matt's occasional verse. "'Phazma' has passed away, but his brief career was full of music,"[21] as he wrote to potential subscribers. But the volume never appeared.

On his part, Joe decided to abandon all the vagaries and risks of the peripatetic life of an actor, settle down, and earn a living as a writer and journalist. A second child, a son named Joseph Matthew Field, Jr., or "little Joe," had been born to the Fields in February 1843. Papa Joe moved his family to St. Louis and, with the financial help of his old friend Charles Keemle, he started a daily newspaper, the *St. Louis Reveille.* The first issue appeared on May 14, 1844, and it was an immediate hit. The paper featured not only local news and advertising, but sketches by some of the best humorists in the Southwest, including its editor, Sol Smith, and John S. Robb. Joe Field in the editor's chair became one of the main progenitors of legends about Mike Fink, "the last of the keelboat men." He became so prolific that he assumed a second pseudonym, "Everpoint," which he reserved mostly for his prose articles. Samuel Clemens's older brother Orion briefly served as the Hannibal correspondent of the *Reveille* in 1847. Joe reprinted some of his brother Matt's sketches of New Mexico, written in 1838–39 and originally published in the *Pic.* He also published some of the sermons of the local Unitarian minister, William G. Eliot, future chancellor of Washington University and the grandfather of T. S. Eliot. He reviled Mormonism, which was centered in northwest Missouri until 1838; and he reprinted poems by the abolitionist John Greenleaf Whittier from the *National Era,* an antislavery paper. In truth, however, the paper took no well-defined editorial position on slavery. A loyal southern Democrat, Joe Field endorsed the Compromise of 1850 and the Fugitive Slave Law, asserting that "resistance to the law, not the law itself, would provoke bloodshed."[22] At least he denounced lynching. For the record, his daughter Kate grew to adulthood in a rigidly segregated South where all black Americans, slave or free, were denied the opportunity to attend public theaters.

He was a devoted father, to judge from all available evidence. In one of his "straws" for the *Pic,* published when daughter Kate was eighteen months old, he asks

Where is the baby? Bless its heart,
   Got sweety chicky honey?
Stop, wipe its handsy-pandsys, now
   Its face—so, that's a honey.
Now, just one kiss—there run along,—

Well, really now, I do think
There ever *was* so sweet a child![23]

He alluded seven years later in a poem in the *Reveille* to his

children, twain, whose accents sweet
    To words I loved to frame;
Nor less for that they loved the first
    To name their mother's name.[24]

Like many another doting father, he carried locks of his children's hair with him when he traveled.

And he continued to travel east every year or two. He was apparently present at the Boston Lyceum on October 16, 1845, for example, when Edgar Allan Poe recited "Al Aaraaf" under a different title. Certainly he was among the group to whom Poe "confessed" that evening "over a bottle of champagne" to "the soft impeachment of the hoax" of reading an old poem to the "Frogpondians," his derisive term for the Transcendentalists.[25] Poe wrote Joe Field on June 15, 1846, to enlist his help in rebutting scurrilous allegations about his physical appearance that were spreading across the country. As Poe explained in his letter, "You have seen me and can describe me as I am."[26] Joe rallied to Poe's defense in the June 30, 1846, issue of the *Reveille*. The following summer, Joe again traveled east alone, taking the so-called "lake route" through Chicago, the Great Lakes, and the St. Lawrence River, to Montreal, Quebec City, and finally to Boston and New York, returning to St. Louis in mid-October 1847 after an absence of over two months.

All the while Joe Field continued to write for his bread and butter. His plays *Oregon* and *Foreign and Native* premiered in Mobile on January 26, 1846. His play *Family Ties* received a prize of $500 from Dan Marble and was staged at the Park Theater in New York on June 19. Once again anointed the poet of the day, he composed an "Ode to Saint Louis" to commemorate the twenty-fifth anniversary of the incorporation of the city in February 1847. A collection of his humorous short fiction first printed in the *Reveille* entitled *The Drama in Pokerville and Other Stories* was issued by

Carey and Hart of Philadelphia later the same year—virtually his only writing to appear in a format more permanent than fragile newsprint. Both Bernard De Voto and Walter Blair have suggested, moreover, that *Pokerville* may have influenced the style of Samuel Clemens,[27] who at the time was twelve years old and playing hooky in Hannibal.

But Field was not destined to remain a writer and journalist. The offices of the *St. Louis Reveille* near the riverfront were destroyed in the great St. Louis fire of May 17–18, 1849. The newspaper suspended publication for a week, then returned to circulation. But only temporarily. The fire bankrupted the local insurance companies, and the city slipped into economic depression. Hundreds of residents died in a cholera epidemic the following summer. Joe Field and his partners closed the *Reveille* permanently on 6 October 6, 1850.

Among the victims of the epidemic was "little Joe," Kate's brother. He was not yet seven when he died.[28] Under the circumstances, Joe Field chose the path of least resistance: he returned to the theater to earn a living. He leased the Mobile Theater, moved to Alabama with Eliza and twelve-year-old Kate, and opened its doors on November 27. Within a month he and Eliza had performed *Gabrielle* for the first time in years. By the end of December the *Mobile Register* commended him for catering "to the public taste with that tact and ability for which he is so renowned." But the bloom was off the rose. His play *Married an Actress* premiered at Burton's Theater in New York on December 19, 1850, and closed not with a bang but a whimper. The following June he accused one of his actors in Mobile of stealing from the theater wardrobe, and the actor sued him for "malicious prosecution." The judge found in favor of the plaintiff and fined Joe six hundred dollars[29]—as much as he had earned in half a year when he was starring in New York.

So he surrendered his lease and returned to St. Louis with his family with a bold, ambitious, and desperate plan: he would build his own theater in the city where he was best known. The population of the city had tripled, to over a hundred thousand souls, over the previous decade. He raised a subscription among the business leaders in town and built a modern facility on the south side of Market between Fifth and Sixth streets that seated nearly twelve hundred people. He christened it "the Varieties

Theater," and it opened on May 10, 1852. His old managers Noah Ludlow and Sol Smith had recently ended their partnership, so he hired the best actors who remained in the two companies. During the season he performed, appropriately enough, in John Morton's farce *Where There's a Will There's a Way*. He also staged a play of his own, *Job and His Children*, the sentimental story of a stern parent and a disobedient daughter—and the only one of his many plays that survives. Nevertheless, after a modestly successful first season the theater lost money in the second, according to Ludlow because Joe was a poor manager. Field closed the building in December 1853.

He again tried to recoup his sagging fortunes by returning to Mobile to manage the theater there, but without much success. He also began to suffer from consumption. He performed in eastern theaters in the fall of 1854 as his health continued to fail. He returned to Boston to produce and star opposite Eliza in Tom Taylor's new play *Still Waters Run Deep* at the Howard Athenaeum in the fall of 1855, and according to his daughter he "made so tremendous an impression as Hawksley as to crowd the theatre for six weeks."[30] Eliza Field never again appeared on stage and, as it happened, neither did Joe. Nor would Kate Field ever again see her father alive. He retired to Mobile, and in late December 1855 the *New Orleans Picayune* reported that he had "somewhat improved" in recent days but "is still feeble. We hope to hear accounts of his entire restoration." He died a month later, on January 28, 1856, at the age of fifty-five in his hotel room in Mobile. His seventeen-year-old daughter was attending school near Boston, and Eliza insisted that the body be sent east for burial in the Mount Auburn cemetery in Cambridge so that Kate might "look once again" before its interment on "that face she loved so much."[31]

She was a precocious child, a bookworm from an early age. She published her first poem, "A Child's Muse," in her father's newspaper in St. Louis when she was only nine. She wrote a pair of poems on the deaths of schoolmates the same year. Her literary gifts were apparent even in her juvenilia, as "Ecce Homo," published a week before her tenth birthday, may suggest:

1. Kate Field in adolescence. Courtesy of Boston
Public Library.

Morning advancing, high on the mount
Sunbeams are dancing o'er the clear fount;
Music is swelling loud on the breeze,
Zephyrs are stirring the leaves on the trees;
List to the burden that mingle along
With the rippling of water, that sweet matin song.
Ecce Homo.[32]

"All the mental discipline I received," she would reminisce, "was between the ages of eight and twelve. But for a woman by the name of Smith,"
who ran a private school in St. Louis, "I should not have that."[33] Kate discovered Dickens at the age of eleven and, because she often visited her
extended family in New Orleans, she learned French—and learned it so
well that before the age of twelve she had translated some passages in

Molière and Racine. At thirteen she was so advanced on the piano that she practiced three hours a day and she began to keep a diary, a habit she maintained for the rest of her life.[34] She also read *Uncle Tom's Cabin* soon after its publication and, as she confided to her diary, she "cried for half an hour" over the death of little Eva. Among her other favorite reading in adolescence: *Hiawatha,* the poetry of Robert and Elizabeth Barrett Browning, and the novels of George Sand.[35]

At the age of seventeen, she began to contribute occasional pieces to the *New Orleans Picayune.* In the fall of 1855 she was sent east to Cordaville, Massachusetts, to live with her Aunt Cordelia and her millionaire husband, Milton Sanford, a horse breeder and Southern sympathizer, and to attend Lasell Ladies' Seminary in Auburndale. "The *Picayune* came to us regularly," she explained long years later, "and I felt an interest in the paper because my father and uncle had written for it; and so I thought I would write, too, and began to send some letters from Boston." Signed with the pseudonym "St. Bernard," after her dog rather than for the pious church leader, these letters mostly discuss the weather and holiday business. "I can recall the great delight which I experienced upon reading the first letter which was published," Field recalled. "I was an anonymous correspondent, and my secret was, for a time, carefully guarded. I do not know how my uncle discovered it, but upon a certain morning, when I went into the library, I heard him reading one of my letters aloud to his only auditor, our pet dog. Then I realized that my contributions had been recognized, and I fled precipitately from the room."[36]

She boarded at the school, wrote her mother religiously, and commuted to Boston "almost daily in the cars on the Boston and Worcester road." Her course of study included geometry, rhetoric, classical piano, astronomy, French, and Italian, and she took private singing lessons in Boston from Augusto Bendelari. On the train she met Joseph Burnett, a local chemical manufacturer, at whose mansion, "Deerfoot," in Southborough she was introduced to James Russell Lowell and Oliver Wendell Holmes. Her interest in spiritualism was piqued by the death of her father and, unbeknownst to her aunt and uncle, she hoped to attend a séance in Boston conducted by the rapping Fox sisters. "I know them to be honest and truthful in themselves," she averred, and "if spiritual manifestations are true, what a source of comfort they will be to us! We shall hear from father from the Spirit world." She also took advantage of her proximity to Boston that year to attend more mundane events, such as Thackeray's lecture on "The Four Georges" or the Hanoverian kings and theatrical performances by Rachel, Edwin Forrest, and her "aunt" Charlotte Cushman, her mother's friend. "Having become excited over Miss Cushman" in spring 1858, she wrote a short ode in her honor and mailed a copy to William Warland Clapp, the editor of the *Boston Saturday Evening Gazette,* where it soon appeared under the pseudonym "Fritz," apparently the name of her St. Bernard. More to the point, the poem questions the conventional gender roles of women. "What are thou? Creature rare," asks the poet in the first line. There follows a series of alternative answers: "Art fiend by Satan sent," "Or man?" or "a hag / Fearful in age, yet bold?" or "are thou *woman?* Born / to combat every fate, / Lively or sad, fierce, proud, love-lorn, / Real or false!—still great? / Yes, *this* thou art!"[37]

Field's mother, Eliza, had become a invalid by this time—almost blind, unable to work, yet liable for the money her late husband owed his creditors. Two months after Joe's death, she wrote Sol Smith that she hoped "to pay at least part of my husband's debts," though at present "it is *impossible*" because "I have no money." The money from Joe's life insurance policy "must go for the benefit of my child." Fortunately, most of Joe's creditors were rich, and while "I should so like to pay *all*" at least these debts "do not *oppress* me."[38] Eliza was almost wholly dependent on the hospitality of Milton Sanford to keep kith and kin together. Kate Field wrote Noah Ludlow exaltedly on June 12, 1857, to report the receipt (finally) of her father's insurance money—$389.65—and a week later to thank him again for "your assistance to Mother during last spring's trials."[39] She addressed a similar letter in September to Sol Smith, Ludlow's former partner, to tell him, too, that "Mother will never forget the kindness you so frequently extended to her last spring."[40] Though Ludlow and Smith were estranged, neither of them harbored any ill will toward Joe Field or his family.

Charlotte Cushman for a time became Kate's *femme ideal*—a successful actress widely admired for her talents. As Kate admitted in her diary, "I have sometimes thought of the stage, I love it dearly." Or elsewhere: "How

glorious to interpret the inspired notes of Mozart, Rossini, Bellini, Doni-
zetti, and even the thundering Verdi!" As her tribute to Cushman sug-
gests, even as a teenager the restrictions on her gender had already begun
to chafe. "I have always felt that I was different from the other girls with
whom I have associated, that I had a mission of some kind on this globe,"
she wrote in her diary. "I sometimes think it is a great misfortune that I
was not born a boy, for then any and every employment would be open to
me." Later she expressed this thought even more emphatically: "Oh, if I
were a man! I pity myself, indeed I do. There is not an ambition, a desire,
a feeling, a thought, an impulse, an instinct that I am not obliged to crush.
And why? Because I am a woman, and a woman must content herself with
indoor life, with sewing and babies." Prophetically, seventy years before
Virginia Woolf lectured on the topic of women's independence, Field declared that "one of the greatest delights of life to a thinking mind must be
a study,—a room religiously your own."[41]

She was paradoxically consumed with both self-doubt and vaunting
ambition, fearing at once that her uncle "does not care for me" and bragging that Bendelari gave her "every encouragement that I can become a
prima donna." But she preferred "the fame of an author" to that of a musician, whose fame dies with him.

> But the author, how different! He makes not a fortune, perhaps, his life
> may not be so great a triumph; but his brain-work is strewn all over the
> world, he is everybody's friend and companion, everybody loves him, he
> is a universal benefactor; and death, instead of ending his career of good,
> gradually increases it, until his name becomes most sacred. No fame is so
> lasting as that of a great author.

By the fall of 1858, Milton Sanford was weighing a trip to Europe, though
his niece worried that she would not be invited to join him and her Aunt
Corda, "or if I should be invited I do not know that I ought to go, leaving
poor little mother all alone." But in almost the same breath she added in
her diary, "There is nothing left me but Italy."[42] As late as September 16,
Kate worried that "the prospect of *Europe* is gradually lessening as Uncle
Milt's responsible man has 'given notice.' Of course he would. Such good

fortune as a trip to the Land of Song could not possibly befall me. No plans have been laid and we are trusting to Providence."[43] She did not yet realize that the Sanfords were planning to take her to Italy so that she could train for a career on the stage. A month later, Milton Sanford sold his house in Cordaville so that he, Cordelia, and Kate could leave for Europe.[44]

2

Florence

WITH THEIR NIECE IN TOW, the Sanfords sailed from New York for Le Havre on the steamer *Fulton* on January 8, 1859. Young Kate had arranged to contribute travel letters from Italy to the *Boston Courier,* edited by George Lunt, and she carried with her letters of introduction to the Brownings and the Trollopes in Florence and to Franklin Pierce and Nathaniel Hawthorne in Rome. They railed directly from Havre to Paris, where they registered at the Hôtel du Louvre. For the next few weeks, Field toured the museums, visited the morgue ("warranted to kill time") and the Hôtel des Invalides, attended the Théâtre Français and the vaudeville. "Gaslight is the Frenchman's sunshine," as she reported to her readers in her first travel letter for the *Courier.* She contributed a total of twenty letters to the newspaper between February 16 and August 19, all of them signed "Straws, Jr.," in tribute to her father. In mid-March she embarked with the Sanfords from Marseilles for Rome, where they took an apartment on the Via del Babuino. "Rome is a thousand times more beautiful than Paris," she noted in her diary. During her month in the Eternal City she reveled in visits to the Vatican and the Colosseum, climbed the Spanish Steps, explored the catacombs, enjoyed the carnival and excursions to Naples and Vesuvius, attended a performance of *Othello* starring the famous actor Tommoso Salvini, and reunited with such old friends as Charlotte Cushman and the sculptor Harriet Hosmer. Former President Pierce called on the Sanfords and their niece and, as Field confided to her diary, he "was very polite, but does not seem to be a man of much fun."[1] She also reported in the *Courier* that Hawthorne "has just completed a work the title of which no one knows, not even his best friends."[2] His last

16

completed romance would be called *Transformation* in England, *The Marble Faun* in the United States.

Though Cushman urged the Sanfords to take their niece to England to train for a musical career, Field was determined to study with Pietro Romani in Florence, and she prevailed. The three of them arrived in Tuscany in mid-April, and before returning to the United States the Sanfords entrusted their niece to the care of Isabella Blagden, an English writer well known among the expatriates in Florence. Blagden lived in the Villa Brichieri on a hill outside the town, and Field delighted in the view at night "from the heights of Bellosguardo." Florence "had the appearance of being set with stars; more especially was this the case with the Duomo, Campanile, and Palazzo Vecchio."[3]

By sheer chance, too, Field settled in Florence just in time to observe the opening volleys in the Italian revolution and the Austro-Sardinian War, and from the first her letters from Tuscany were filled with political news. While the regular correspondents of the *Courier* reported on the war from Leipzig, Vienna, and London, she wrote about it on the scene. "What! a real downright, upright revolution, and no powder wasted?" she wrote in her dispatch from Florence on April 28. "You tumble up stairs to your banker, whom you find tremulous with excitement and locking up valuables." So many vendors "stalked through the streets" selling red, white, and green ribbon—the colors of the Sardinian flag—that Field speculated that the "dry goods dealers probably congratulate themselves on the success of the revolution." Field clearly sympathized with the proponents of Italian independence and unification or *Risorgimento,* Giuseppe Garibaldi ("that extraordinary man") and Victor Emmanuel ("a patriot and an Italian") specifically and the Sardinians and the French emperor Napoleon III ("an instrument in God's hands") more generally. "A revolution, and not an insult to person or property offered—not even a window broken—and yet the people had the city in their power," she crowed. "Never did I see so well conducted a mob! . . . Nothing can exceed my admiration of the noble, dignified conduct of the Tuscan people during the revolution of last week."[4] She bragged that Victor Emmanuel had introduced "universal suffrage" in the Republic, which meant that men over the age of twenty-five could vote, and then she pretended to be among them: "We vote for annexation two days hence," she reported on March 9, then a few days later that "we all voted" overwhelmingly in favor of the annexation of Tuscany to Piedmont-Sardinia while a small minority of "traitors or idiots voted for a separate kingdom."[5]

Though still only twenty years old, Field proved as skillful as a seasoned journalist at unraveling the Byzantine politics of revolutionary Italy. Few readers could have guessed, from the gravity of her Florence letters, that they were written by a young American who had not yet attained her majority. She routinely corrected in her *Courier* letters the distortions and inaccuracies about wartime Florence reported in the foreign press, particularly in the London *Times*. Whereas the *Times* had declared that Tuscany is "bankrupt and altogether *hors de combat*" or out of the fight, for example, Field averred on June 3 that she had "never in my life" seen "so many happy faces" as in Florence during the war. "The tri-color is on almost every man's hat or coat, and the flags of Piedmont and France are waving from house tops and streaming from windows." While there were six thousand French troops stationed in Tuscany, they were a liberating rather than an occupying force. "Walk through the streets and you find every French soldier between two Italians," she declared. Neither timid nor sentimental, she celebrated in May the death of the tyrannical King Ferdinand II (aka "Bomba") of the Two Sicilies, apparently from the same "loathsome disease" that had killed "hundreds of thousands of Neapolitans in his filthy prisons," as a "direct judgment from the hands of God!"[6] No shrinking or submissive Catholic schoolgirl she.

Like the other English-speaking expatriates in Florence, she feared Great Britain might intervene in the war on the side of Austria. Field prayed the British government would remain neutral on "the Italian question." She was cheered to learn that John Russell, a member of the House of Lords, had advocated nonintervention. But in general she excoriated the behind-the-scenes maneuvering of British diplomats:

When in 1859 the tyranny of Austria in Italy reaches its culminating point, and Napoleon applies to his ally for co-operation, or at least countenance, in his efforts of regeneration, what does wily England do? Makes no promises on any side, coquettes with Austria, delivers sage lectures to France about their grandfathers' treaties, scolds Sardinia for desiring the welfare of tortured brothers and sisters, allows Austria to declare war while expecting assistance from across the Channel, and when the mischief is done, pronounces a neutrality.[7]

As she increasingly identified with the cause of Italian independence, Field began to refer in her dispatches to Italian government officials as "our deputies" rather than "theirs," to "Vittorio Emanuele" and "our honest king" rather than Victor Emmanuel and "their king," and to quote the patriotic slogans and songs of the revolution in the original language.[8]

In late summer the *Courier* stopped printing her columns. She was too outspoken, too partisan, too committed to the cause of Italian independence for its editors. She dismissed the snub by declaring, "I want to write in a paper which does not assert that Liberty is too good for Italy." It was merely the first of her many conflicts with editors during her career. James T. Fields, senior partner in the renowned Boston publishing company of Fields, Osgood & Co., who visited Florence with his wife, Annie Adams Fields, in January, urged Kate to contribute to the rival *Boston Transcript*. He had read her letters in the *Courier* and he spent hundreds of dollars a year to advertise his books and magazines in the *Transcript*. Its editor, W. H. Dutton, "must have you," he said. He proposed that Kate offer Dutton "twenty letters for $150." Barkus was willin'. She sent a total of twenty-three letters to the *Transcript* between January and June 1860, and she also began to contribute twice-monthly travel essays to the *New Orleans Picayune* for which she was paid five dollars apiece.[9] She again disguised her sex with aliases in both newspapers: in the *Transcript* as "Fie" (an abbreviated form of "Field") and the *Picayune* as "Semper Avanti" ("Always Advance").

Her pieces for the *Picayune* more closely resemble the fiery articles she had published in the *Courier* than the more colloquial and chatty articles she sent the *Transcript*. "The fire of the Republic is not spent, but has only been smothered" by despotism, she announced in the first paragraph of her first "Letter from Italy" in the *Picayune,* dated January 15, 1860. She had begun to shed some of her naïveté about the political endgame playing out. The Treaty of Villafranca between France and Austria, by failing to include the Sardinians, had led to an armistice that could not endure. It was, in Field's own words, "the first grief of a struggling nation." The fate of Venice had not yet been decided—whether it would be liberated or remain under Austrian domination—and republican sympathizers there had been tortured. Garibaldi, inspiring but impetuous, suffered a military defeat at Cajazzo, and the Church had refused to recognize the new government in Tuscany ("when the Holy See wishes to become unholy and occupy itself with carnal things," the Italians "become unruly") [10]

Personally, meanwhile, Field had slipped into the Slough of Despond. Her singing lessons with Romani had ended when she developed a bronchial infection in the fall of '59 that threatened to damage her voice permanently. Between October and December, she later wrote, "I did nothing except lie on a sofa and be miserable." Eliza Field, though a invalid, was so concerned for her daughter's health that she traveled to Florence early in the new year and moved into rooms with her near the Duomo and the Villino Trollope, the home of Tom Trollope, in the Piazza Maria Antonia.[11] Isa Blagden referred to Eliza Field as "a dove who has hatched an eagle."[12] Meanwhile, Kate flourished socially. Blagden introduced her to the activist Frances Power Cobbe, who later reminisced about her:

> A young American lady, tall and beautiful, with magnificent hair and column-like throat . . . [has] come to Italy to study singing and prepare herself for the stage, and has given up all prospects in America from her devotion to her art. But suddenly an attack of cold destroys her voice. She is told by the physicians she must never sing again. Does she go about despairing and thinking her life over? Very much otherwise. She engages to write as correspondent [for several newspapers,] informs herself diligently of all that is passing in Italy, goes to see whatever is to be seen of public festival or meeting, and supports both herself and her mother in comfort on the pay of some of the best letters ever sent to a newspaper.[13]

Field also befriended the Italian actress Adelaide Ristori—"a more fascinating creature I never saw."[14]

She was always a welcome guest in the Trollope home and she met such artistic and literary celebrities there as Tom's novelist brother Anthony and the artist Elihu Vedder. Anthony Trollope later modeled several

2. Elihu Vedder's painting of Kate Field in Florence, 1860.

of his heroines on Field, among them the Irish-American poet Wallachia Petrie in *He Knew He Was Right* (1869) and the Irish-American singer Rachel O'Mahony in *The Landleaguers* (1883). Field and Vedder, whom she described privately as "very talented and very poor," became fast friends. She tried to help him find a patron among the three hundred "American *temporaries*" in Florence, and when she failed she persuaded her aunt to pay him to paint her portrait. She sat for him in June 1860; she reported in July that he was "at work upon the portrait of a young lady from Boston, and is treating his subject in the happiest manner"; and he finished the painting in August, for which he received $55.[15] In the background, Vedder painted the Florence duomo and campanile. On his part, Vedder averred that Field was "the first woman of charm and intellect I had ever seen, and her bright smile and hearty laugh, combined with her innate refinement, quite bowled me over."[16]

One of the most seminal events in Field's life occurred on the last day of May 1860, when she met George Eliot and her companion George Henry Lewes at the Villino Trollope. As she wrote her aunt the next day, "there is something interesting about her, and you feel impressed with her importance. They say she converses finely, she is very retiring—and talked all the evening to Mr. Trollope." Field noted that "the Lewes" planned to winter in Florence. Unfortunately, she also described their appearance in unflattering terms. "Miss Evans, or Mrs. Lewes, is a woman whose whole face is of the horse make," she remarked. "I like Mr. Lewes, who is a very ugly man, but very charming in conversation, so that you forget his looks."[17] The same day, in a letter to the *Transcript*, Field also described the meeting and Eliot's appearance more tactfully. Her manner is "timid and retiring," Field reported, though in conversation "she is said to stamp herself as a woman of uncommon talents, without assuming the least pretension in accent or gesture." She "would be called 'ugly' by thoughtless persons, but the more discriminating pronounce her intelligent and interesting in appearance."[18] Four years later, Field embellished her account of the evening. She remembered the "kindness and earnestness" with which "Mrs. Lewes" chatted with "a young girl [i.e., Field] who had just begun to handle a pen, how frankly she related her own literary experience, and how gently she *suggested* advice. . . . We learned to respect the woman as much as we had admired the writer." More to the point, Eliot had proved that "genius has no sex" in such novels as *Adam Bede* and *Paul Ferroll*.[19]

Isa Blagden also introduced Field to Robert and Elizabeth Barrett Browning soon after her arrival in Florence,[20] and in their home she met Walter Savage Landor. The intellectual climate she encountered in Casa Guidi literally changed her life. She regarded everyone in the Brownings' circle with awe. As she wrote her mother soon after meeting them,

> Mr. Browning is the person whose good opinion I am most anxious for, and to whom I am already very much attached. He feels music, and I should like to sing before him. There is something about him that I fancy marvelously. Last night he said to me, "You are very ambitious; you are the most ambitious person of my acquaintance." I laughed and asked him how he had arrived at such a conclusion. "Oh, I can tell by your eyes," he said.

"How so?" I asked. "I can detect it in their glisten," he replied. "Well," I said, "it is no great crime to be ambitious, is it?" "No, indeed," he returned; "I admire it; I would not give a straw for a person who was not."[21]

Field referred in passing to "Mr. Browning, the poet," in one of her pieces for the *Courier* written in late June 1859.[22] She wrote her aunt at about the same time that she was reticent to show him any of her newspaper writings because "he is too great," though she also hinted at her growing friendship with his wife, with whom she shared an interest in spiritualism: "To Miss Blagden Mrs. Browning writes of me as '*dear* Miss Field.'"[23]

Early in their acquaintance, Field showed them one of her greatest treasures: the original letter Poe had sent her father in June 1846. In it, Poe had quoted a few words of praise Elizabeth Browning had expressed for "The Raven" ("This vivid writing! this power that is felt!") and pronounced her "the world's greatest poetess." "Did Poe write this of me?" exclaimed Mrs. Browning, looking up with glistening but unbelieving eyes; "he was kind." Her husband also read the letter and "expressed his gratitude for praise *from such a source.*"[24] Soon both Brownings were giving Field manuscripts to add to her autograph collection—for instance, a letter Elizabeth had received from John Ruskin—and by August 1859 they were sending their love to her from Siena.[25] As Field recalled later, the "summer of 1859 was a weary, suffering season" for Elizabeth. Dismayed that Napoleon III had failed to unite the whole of northern Italy as he had promised, she was "bent and well-nigh crushed, as by a thunderbolt," when she learned about the Treaty of Villafranca signed in early July. The news no doubt "hastened her into the grave,"[26] and her forced optimism is evident in a letter she wrote Field on August 21, 1859: "Napoleon walks under as well as on the earth. Now in Italy he is walking under, but walking surely, and we may congratulate one another in hopes again." Field and Blagden spent a couple of weeks with the Brownings in Siena the following month.[27]

The Brownings spent the winter of 1859–60 in Rome, hoping the warmer climate would restore Elizabeth's health. They were Landor's "constant correspondents," as Field reported in the *Boston Transcript.*[28] In their absence, Field looked after Landor, whom she described in one of her letters to the *Transcript* as "one of the most interesting foreigners now residing in Tuscany." Despite his age, "he seems vigorous still, conversing in his own eloquent way of times past and gone, when he was young." On February 7 she visited him in his apartment and found him "sitting at his writing table" before a "splendid" painting by the seventeenth-century baroque master Salvator Rosa. Barrett Browning was also in touch with Field, who published a corrected version of her poem "A Tale of Villafranca" in the *Picayune* in February 1860. "The great poetess" had "unintentionally neglected to send" stanza seven of the poem to the *Athenæum* prior to its publication shortly after the armistice, Field explained. A few weeks later, Field quoted the poem in the *Picayune*. "Mrs. Browning's insight into the political character of Napoleon does as much credit to her head as to her heart," she remarked.[29] For the record, Field had received the poet's permission to invoke her authority. "My dear Kate," Barrett Browning wrote, "I cant put a seal on your lips when I know them to be so brave and true at speaking truth. Take out your license then to name us as you please. . . . Love us a little, and believe that we all love and think of you."

Field also proved her mettle as an astute critic of Barrett Browning's verse with her interpretation of her "A Curse for a Nation" (1860). Most contemporary readers presumed the poem protested the failure of England to support the republican cause in Italy. But according to Field it was an attack on America for failing to abolish chattel slavery in the South. As Robert Browning wrote Field on March 29, 1860, from Rome, he had heard that she "persists that the 'Curse for a Nation' is for America & not England! . . . [I]t appears, only Kate Field, out of all Florence, can understand. It seems incredible—how *did* you find out— . . . [Y]ou are not only the delightful Kate Field which I always knew you to be,—but the perspicuous creation I am suddenly found bowing down before." His wife was no less pleased with her young disciple. "Mrs. Browning paid me a tremendous compliment the night before she left Rome" on June 4, 1860, she wrote her aunt. After the start of the Civil War, moreover, Field came to believe "A Curse for a Nation" was nothing less than prophetic ("she foretold the agony in store for America").[30] Barrett Browning was obliged to restrain Field's enthusiasm for the poem. "My dear Kate, never say that I have 'cursed' your country," she pleaded. "I only *declared the consequence of the evil* in her & which has since developed itself in thunder and flame."

She predicted that Americans "will come out of the fire purified, stainless, having had the angel of a great cause walking with you in the furnace."[31] Little wonder that, to her Uncle Milton's dismay, Field was converted to the cause of abolition during her months in Florence.

Field claimed later that she could "forget no evening" she had passed at Casa Guidi.[32] In the Brownings' home she met such luminaries as Harriet Beecher Stowe, Hiram Powers, and William Wetmore Story. When the Brownings returned to Florence in June 1860, they brought several gifts for their young friend: "a beautiful pair of Roman gold sleeve buttons," an inscribed copy of *Poems Before Congress,* and several family photographs. Kate and her mother moved to a flat on the Piazza Pitti near both the Pitti Palace and Casa Guidi in October 1860. They often took tea with the Brownings "in company with Mr. Landor," who once playfully referred to her as "Elysium Field." Elizabeth whispered to her, "I hope you appreciate the compliment, Kate." Field then asked Lander flirtatiously, "How many times does a man fall in love during his life?" "Well, every time he sees a pretty woman," Landor replied.[33] On another occasion, "just as the tea was being placed upon the table" Robert "turned to Landor, who was that evening's honored guest, gracefully thanked him for his defence of old songs, and, opening the 'Last Fruit,' read in his clear, manly voice" from the *Idyls of Theocritus. . . . I have never seen anything of its kind so chivalric as the deference paid by Robert Browning to Walter Savage Landor."[34] After another evening at Casa Guidi, as Robert "escorted my mother and myself home," he "exclaimed: 'When a young man I thought that the finest thing in the world to be was a poet, and so I determined to be one.'" Some thirty years later, Field admitted that his "confession made an indelible impression on my young mind."[35] In one of Field's last private conversations with Elizabeth, they discussed the historian John Lothrop Motley's *The Causes of the American Civil War,* an essay the poet "warmly approved," and the poet dismissed the cavils of "foreign nations with regard to America." According to Field, she asked, "Why do you heed what others say? You are strong, and can do without sympathy; and when you have triumphed, your glory will be the greater."[36]

Despite his age and failing health, Landor was obviously taken with the young American with her light brown hair, "blue, luminous eyes," and "a tongue that can talk for two hours at a stretch and advance a new idea in every sentence," as she was described later.[37] In a note to Robert Browning on April 23, 1860, his jealousy is palpable. He had remained on the terrace at Casa Guidi until 9 P.M. the evening before and there "met Miss Field in all her beauty. She was accompanied by a most *forbidding*-faced personage, *man* of course."[38] In June, as she later reminisced, "on entering the drawing-room of the villa" on the Piazza de Bellosguardo "I found Mr. and Mrs. Browning and Mr. Landor seated conversing with Miss B[lagden]. As I kissed the ladies present, Mr. Landor exclaimed: 'What! Do not my years entitle me to the same privilege?' Laughingly I went up to my dear master, who called himself 'the old pedagogue,' and kissed him, too."[39] Landor told Elizabeth the same evening that Field was "the most charming lady he had ever seen"—a comment she repeated to Field the next day with an admonition: "you know, dear Kate, that he has seen a great many." Field replied, "Dear Mrs. Browning, there is something of heaven about him." Landor later wrote a poem about the kiss forwarded to her by Robert:[40]

> Dear Miss Field, I have only a minute to say that Mr Landor wrote these really pretty lines in your honour the other day,—you remember on what circumstance they turn: I know somebody who is ready to versify to double the extent at the same cost to you, and do his best too.

To K. F.[41]
Kisses in former times I've seen,
Which, I confess it, raised my spleen;
They were contrived by love to mock
The battledoor and shuttlecock.
Given, returned—how strange a play,
Where neither loses all the day.
And both are, even when night sets in,
Again as ready to begin!
I am not sure I have not played
This very game with some fair maid.
Perhaps it was a dream; but this
I *know* was not: I *know* a kiss
Was given me in the sight of more

Than ever saw me kissed before.
Modest as wingéd angels are,
And no less brave and no less fair.

She came across, nor greatly feared,
The horrid brake of wint'ry beard.

In the spring of 1861, Landor began to teach Field the rudiments of Latin. They met several times a week. Within the first week she had learned "the conjugations of the verbs as well as the declensions," he bragged to Robert Browning. "Her quickness is equal to her sound understanding."[42] Elizabeth was also pleased: "So, Kate, you are learning Latin, & commune with W. S. Landor,—and he feels as we all do, that you are clever dear & good, & that the more we have of you the better." On her part, Field professed modesty: "Mr. Landor's praise of me is too extravagant and absurd to mention." Years later, she insisted that Landor "was very patient" and "never found fault with me, but his criticisms on my Latin grammar were frequent and severe. . . . I shall ever esteem it one of the great privileges of my life that I was permitted to know him well, and call him friend."[43]

Though he was past eighty-five, Landor flirted with Kate as if he were her young suitor. "Mr. Landor comes to see me every day, bringing me flowers, books, etc.," she wrote her aunt. "His latest donations to me are a Virgil, a fine Latin dictionary," and a copy of Aubrey de Vere's *The Search for Proserpine.* On another occasion, Landor dropped his glasses, and as Field picked them up he quipped, "Oh, this is not the first time that you have caught my eyes." Landor even asked Field to be his literary executor. He once sent her "all the manuscript scraps in his possession," she explained, "which I am to edit and publish after his death."[44] Fortunately, he soon retrieved them and "the manuscripts were not again left with me."[45] They were published posthumously under the title *Heroic Idyls, with Additional Poems* (1863). Landor also gave her at their last meeting a portfolio of about a hundred and forty valuable sketches and paintings, including a drawing of flowers by Leonardo da Vinci, a landscape by Salvator Rosa, sixteen sketches by J. M. W. Turner, and several Gainsboroughs, as well as an album of antiquarian letters, including one written by Alexander Pope acknowledging part payment for his translation of the *Iliad* and several by Louis Kossuth, the Hungarian revolutionary. She first thought of returning the gifts, but then decided to keep them lest her benefactor take offense. She wrote her aunt that "Mr. Landor is a great man, the cleverest mind I have ever encountered, as well as being the most wayward." At her own death thirty-five years later, she still owned the portfolio and album Landor had presented to her.[46]

While she lived in Florence, Field had the nearest brush with marriage she would suffer in her life. No doubt the "noble signore" who accompanied her to Pistoja in January 1860 to celebrate the dawn of the Republic was Albert Baldwin, the thirty-five-year-old scion of a wealthy American family who was studying to become a painter. No doubt the "temporary American" who rushed to Field's room on March 1 to beg her to "bolt for Paris" ahead of a rumored Austrian invasion of northern Italy was Baldwin, too. Field marveled that "a man of intelligence" could be so easily "bamboozled by newspaper reports and terror mongers."[47] No doubt Baldwin was also the "most *forbidding*-faced personage" whom Landor saw with her on the terrace at Casa Guidi in April 1860. It is clear in retrospect, however, that Baldwin was nothing more than a dilettante. Field allowed that he "will never be an artist," though she conceded that "he is a noble character and very well educated."[48] She mentioned Baldwin by name publicly only once, in a review of one of his paintings in 1864:

> Albert H. Baldwin is a new name to American art, and a promising one, if we may judge by his picture which he has sent from Venice, a view of the Grand Canal in the vicinity of San Marco. In color and composition he has done well. Conture, the great master in Paris, whose pupil Mr. Baldwin is, has pronounced him to be a born colorist (ne coloriste), and praise from such a source is as good as a diploma. Mr. Baldwin is a young man of fine intellect and culture, and is destined, we believe, to occupy a high position as an artist.[49]

Field kept "a large package" of the letters he sent her for the rest of her life, though they have since been lost.[50] For some reason, however, Baldwin failed to ask Field to marry him. To judge from Trollope's *He Knew He*

Was Right, he may have been reticent to propose because Field, like Trollope's Wallachia Petrie, planned a professional career and he preferred a more traditional wife and mother. More likely, to judge from Field's poem "From Twenty to Forty," her mother opposed the union and Baldwin chose to retreat in the face of a superior force. Narrated in blank verse by a middle-aged dowager—Field was thirty-eight when she wrote it—to a twenty-year-old girl, the dramatic monologue seems to comment on her aborted romance:[51]

At your age I loved madly—loved with all
The passion of a soul that loves but once.
I thought my love returned: his vows, at least,
Were warm enough to melt a colder heart
Than Nature gave to me. . . .
I lived for this one man—for him alone;
We plighted troth; my parents threatened then
To cast me off, to disinherit me! . . .
I loved, and so was ready to brave all.
Not so the hero of my one romance:
His face grew pallid, and his speech confused;
He kissed me hastily—said he'd return
To claim me. . . .
He wrote a cold, brief note, in which he said
That he was far too proud a man to wed
In opposition to my family. . . .
He hoped I might be happy, and then signed
Himself "sincerely" mine, etc. . . .
I sent back that man's note without remark. . . .
One day, 'mid Roman ruins, I came upon
The man I once adored. He dared to speak;
Begged me to take him to my heart again, . . .
The devil in me got the upper hand;
I lashed the craven creature with my tongue,
And sent him cringing from me.

Hell hath no fury like a woman scorned.

Baldwin belatedly realized his mistake and wrote Field in December 1867 to beg her forgiveness and to ask her to marry him. Field deigned to make no reply for five months and when she did respond she left no doubt about her feelings. "The letter you wrote last December ought to have been written in 1862," she asserted. "You were a moral coward not to have written it then," but "I shall say nothing further because I don't care. That episode has passed out of my life, and is as dead to me as if it were buried six feet under ground." She had long wondered if she had simply been a fool to expect him to marry her, but his "tardy letter assures me that I was not this idiot, and my regard for my own common sense is much greater than it has been for six years." She was grateful he had not remained "longer in Florence" (like the faint-hearted swain in her poem) "for had you offered me your hand, I should have accepted it," believing him to be a better man "than you are." The letter might have been written by Athena to Hephaestus. Five months later, thoroughly chastened, Baldwin replied that "earnest friendship" can "only exist between *equals*" and that if "I ever attain to your level" he would happily be her friend.[52]

Meanwhile, Field readily admitted in her letters to the *Picayune* that she was obsessed with the revolution, her *idée fixe,* and that "my one-idea pen hums" unceasingly "the melody of this refrain." She continued to appeal for funds from America to support the republicans. In Florence, "a 'poor widow' sends her mite," a sympathetic priest "gives a pair of boots, his only marketable private property; a young man presents a fine gold watch and chain," and apothecaries mix free medicines "for the revolutionists." Landor, though nearly destitute, removed his watch "in a burst of enthusiasm" and instructed Field to send it to Garibaldi. "Tell him," he said, "it is sent by an old man who has nothing else to give him."[53] She became by force of circumstances an apologist for both Victor Emmanuel and Louis Napoleon. When the first constitutional monarch in Italian history offered his daughter Clotilde in marriage to Napoleon's cousin "Plon-Plon" in order to cement the alliance between Sardinia and France, Field insisted that parents "have resigned their fair young daughters to roués and millionaires long ere this for far less worthy motives."[54] When Victor Emmanuel visited Tuscany the first two weeks of April 1860, Field took every opportunity to observe him and report his movements in her letters. When he ceded Nice and Savoy to France in April 1860 in order to appease Napoleon, she defended this betrayal of the revolution on the grounds that "an overwhelming majority" of the citizens of the two provinces "asserted their claim to be Frenchmen" in a plebiscite.[55] In contrast, though she had been baptized a Catholic, she repudiated the Church because the pope and his "minions" opposed the revolution. She considered Pope Pius IX not "the Vicar of Christ on earth" but "a tall, thin, stupid, obstinate old man, with a one-sided head."[56] She hoped that, rather than rule the papal states, he might "live to see his temporal power restricted to the left bank of the Tiber." The archbishop of Pisa, "the most rabid of all Papists, stands number one on the list of those to be taught" a lesson by the republicans. But not until May 1861 did she express any concern for the fragmented leadership of the revolution or pessimism about the future of the nation. She asked rhetorically whether "the world has taken leave of her senses" or "she has heretofore existed without them." Garibaldi "with his usual blind enthusiasms and mad conclusions" was feuding with Count Camillo Benso di Cavour, the first prime minister of the Kingdom of Italy, and she worried about discord in the ranks "where harmony ought to have reigned."[57]

She expressed these fears in the last letter she ever sent to the *New Orleans Picayune*. The American Civil War had erupted only three weeks before she mailed it, and the state of Louisiana had seceded and joined the Confederacy in March 1861. Though a daughter of slave-holding Missouri, Field by the age of twenty-two had become a partisan of Lincoln and abolition. From Massachusetts, Cordelia Sanford urged her and Eliza to return to the United States posthaste before its ports were closed by a naval blockade. Kate initially resisted the suggestion, explaining that she and her mother could live frugally in Florence and that she preferred the warmth of Italy to the climate of New England. The "greater part of my time is passed in an easy-chair" in any case, she explained. Besides, were she back in the States, she would agitate for the North in the Civil War much as she had campaigned for the Republic in Italy. Aunt Corda, no doubt reflecting her husband's opinion, believed the election of Lincoln meant "eternal ruin." Kate's opinion was "just the reverse,—eternal salvation." The "Union has been betrayed, government property stolen, and the flag disgraced," she wrote Cordelia Sanford on June 21, 1861, and "traitors should be punished, property recaptured, and the national flag rescued from dishonor."[58] Like a red flag to a bull, her political views were anathema to her Uncle Milton, who had planned to make her his heir.

Field and her mother might have remained in Italy indefinitely but for the sudden death from pneumonia of Elizabeth Barrett Browning on June 29 and her funeral three days later. In fact, Field's accounts of these events in letters to her aunt are the most detailed record of them known to exist. "I am sick, sick at heart, for dear Mrs. Browning is dead," she wrote. "This morning, at half-past four, she expired with the words 'It is beautiful' upon her lips. . . . Almost the last thing I did in her presence was to kneel before her, and say that when near her, I always longed to be at her feet—and she was so gentle and kind, so loving and unassuming." Barrett Browning's regular physician was away, so a strange doctor "most forbidding in physiognomy" and "said by some to be a humbug" had attended her at the end. He "began by frightening her, telling her what a fearful state her entire system was in," and then resorted to "a violent practice which her weak body was thoroughly incapable of enduring," apparently some form of purging or blood-letting. Her burial in the Protestant cemetery in Florence was hastily arranged. Field had just returned from the ceremony when she wrote her aunt on July 1. Robert Browning "seemed as though he could hardly stand," and their son Penini "stood beside him with tears in his eyes." Had she known "the service would [be] so short" Field would have taken Landor, who "ought to have been there." With the death of her friend, Field added, "My hold upon Italy has gone."[59] The next day she sent a note of condolence to the widower, who told Blagden it was "a *dear* letter."[60] He replied on stationery fringed in black on July 6: "God bless you & yours for all your kindness which I shall never forget. . . . I know you are truth's self in all you profess to feel about her—she also loved you, as *you* felt." Field also kept this letter for the rest of her life. "God bless him!" she wrote her aunt the day it arrived. "I love him more now for *her* sake. . . . It is a great comfort to have this note,—to be told again that she *loved* me." A few days later he gave Eliza Field "a favorite shawl that belonged to dear Mrs. Browning, and me a locket that she had before she was married, and of which she was very fond. In the centre is a crystal, in which is her hair shaped in two hearts. The gold around it is a serpent emblem of eternity. I cannot tell you how much I value" the memento. Within days of her death, Field had begun to sanctify the poet. "I did worship her as a glorious type of womanhood,—unselfish, suffering, loving, grand." Her "character was well-nigh perfect"; "sinless in life," she had been virtually Christ-like. No longer a contributor to any U.S. newspaper, with Baldwin absent and Robert Browning leaving, Barrett Browning's death "sundered" the "almost last link that binds me to Florence," she reiterated, "and I long more than ever to be away."[61]

Scarcely a week after the poet's death, Field began to draft a memoir of her, however unworthy she felt she was for such a task. She completed it on July 5 and submitted it to the *Atlantic Monthly,* the leading parlor magazine in America, and while she had offered it for free "as a tribute of love to the poet" she did not expect it to be accepted.[62] But her friend James T. Fields had just succeeded James Russell Lowell as editor of the *Atlantic,* and he received the piece with alacrity. The first of Field's essays to appear in its pages, and the first of her writings to appear in any venue under her own name, it was published in the September 1861 issue of the magazine alongside an installment of Stowe's *Agnes of Sorrentino.* Given the circumstances of its composition in Florence, Field's "Elizabeth Barrett Browning" predictably betrays both the merits and defects of hagiography. Field celebrated by turns the poet's saintliness, her literary genius, her learning and cultivation, and her liberal politics. "Her life was one long, large-souled, large-hearted prayer for the triumph of Right, Justice, Liberty," Field insisted. She had worn her learning lightly, and she "never made an insignificant remark." Her love for Robert Browning was perfect, their union the marriage of true minds, best expressed "in those exquisite sonnets purporting to be from the Portuguese." Her devotion to the cause of Italian independence, her "joyful enthusiasm at the Tuscan uprising," sustained her in her final years. Perhaps more than any other single essay, Field's memoir shaped Barrett Browning's contemporary reputation in America. Even the reclusive Emily Dickinson read it in her Amherst home.[63]

Over the next several months Field vigorously defended Barrett Browning, as if she were the keeper of the flame. On the first anniversary of the poet's death she reviewed a new edition of *Essays on the Greek Christian and the English Poets* for the *Christian Examiner*.[64] She occasionally invoked Barrett Browning's authority in support of feminism and women's suffrage and contested the notion that suffragists were "unwomanly."[65] Field was particularly incensed by the "monstrous libel" leveled by the London *Saturday Review* in its notice of *Poems Before Congress*, with its condescending allegations about the author's "dilettante Liberalism and dilettante art," her "delirium of imbecile one-sidedness" and "servile and seditious platitudes" in praise of the cause of Italian independence.[66] Field replied with studied if rambling remarks on Barrett Browning's sincerity, sophistication, and learning, including her facility in languages such as Hebrew. Hardly a pedant, she "had no love of erudition *per se*." Rather, "the questions of others alone made her scholarship apparent." Widely read in the classics as well as in the modern poets, she had been an astute critic of Milton, Shakespeare, Keats, Shelley, Chaucer, Spenser, Goldsmith, Cowper, Burns, Wordsworth, and Tennyson.[67] In the first flush of her growing success as a writer, Field sent a copy of this article to the grieving Robert Browning, though he seems never to have read it.[68] It was an omen of things to come in their increasingly vexed relationship.

In July, on their last day in Florence, Kate and Eliza bid Landor farewell at his home. "We sipped a final cup of tea in almost complete silence," Kate remembered, and "I tried to say merry things and look forward a few years to another meeting, but the old man shook his head sadly, saying, 'I shall never see you again.'"[69] He was prescient, of course. After leaving Florence, Kate and her mother paused a few weeks in Paris and sailed for the United States in late August. After two-plus years among the *literati* and *artistes,* no longer the adolescent young woman Milton and Cordelia Sanford had taken to Florence to train for a career on the musical stage, Field returned to a nation at war and her own uncertain future.

3

Interregnum

THE NEXT THREE YEARS in Kate Field's life are largely lost in a biographical blindspot. She and her mother lived with the Sanfords in Cordaville, and only a few events in her life during these months can be reliably reconstructed from documentary evidence. She performed in private theatricals staged at the Tremont House in Boston for the benefit of the Union Club in late February 1862, according to a playbill of the evening that survives among her papers at the Boston Public Library.[1] She addressed a pseudononymous appeal (to avoid offending her uncle) to the women of New England, "who are to suffer most and gain most from the convulsions consequent upon our civil war," for contributions to the Discharged Soldiers' Home in Boston. The Home had cared for seventy loyal soldiers during the two months it had been open, and with sufficient support from the community, "ever first in all good works," it might benefit "*hundreds* of our brave deliverers."[2] She also contributed an unsigned five-part essay entitled "What Northern Women Ask of the Government" to the *Boston Commonwealth*, a radical weekly, between late December 1862 and the end of January 1863. In this essay she solicited money for the U.S. Sanitary Commission, a forerunner of the American Red Cross; demanded that the government "abide by the proclamation of September 22, 1862," to emancipate slaves on January 1, 1863; insisted that Union soldiers "be ably led" and that "incompetent and drunken officers" be dismissed; urged the recruitment of black regiments "wherever and whenever they may volunteer"; and argued for better treatment of the wounded and the speedy discharge of permanently disabled soldiers. "This war is unavoidable," Field concluded, "and therefore must be patiently and heroically endured to the end, no matter

35

how distant that end may be, but there are sins of omission and commission in its management which ought no longer to be tolerated." Field laid the blame for "every blunder, civil or military," at the door of "that most lamentable failure," William H. Seward, the secretary of state.[3]

Anthony Trollope, who traveled throughout the United States for six months in 1860–61, wrote her occasionally. When she first met him in Florence in September 1860, Field wrote her aunt that he was "a delightful companion,"[4] and their friendship flourished. Trollope sent her a copy of *Arabian Nights* in November 1860 and joked he hoped "it will do you good mentally and morally." He visited Field in Massachusetts in November 1861, soon after she and her mother returned from Italy, and together they heard Edward Everett lecture in Roxbury on November 22 on "The Causes and Conduct of the Civil War." She asked him to critique some poetry she had written in January 1862 and his comments were blunt. "Philanthropical ratiocination is your line, not philandering amatory poetizing," he advised. He apologized for his candor and insisted "I am very fond of you, and it grieves me to pain you." After visiting her hometown of St. Louis later in the month, he reported that William G. Eliot, her father's friend, told him that Kate should marry because "it is the best career for a woman." Trollope agreed and "therefore bid you in his name as well as my own, to go & marry a husband." Field's reply to this advice is lost, though its tenor may be inferred from Trollope's next letter. "I don't in the least understand why you fly out against me as to matrimony," he protested overmuch, "or at least to what I have said on that subject in regard to you. I have said and say again that I wish you would marry. But I have never advised you to marry a man for whom you did not care." Nevertheless, Trollope was not above flirting with Field, even though she was young enough to be his daughter. In an unsigned review of Trollope's *North America* in the *Continental Monthly* for September 1862, she criticized his "extreme verbosity" and his equivocation on the subject of slavery but agreed with his indictment of the rampant corruption in American politics. In all, she concluded, she was pleased with "Trollope the writer" but "Trollope the *man* has a far greater hold upon our heart." In his next letter to Field, he seized the opening: "Your criticisms are in part just—in part unjust,—in great part biased by your personal (—may I say love?) for the author."[5]

What to make of Trollope's relationship with Field? His biographers have speculated for years. "He never made love to her," Michael Sadleir insisted as early as 1927, though "in love with her he certainly was." James Pope-Hennessey asserted thirty-five years ago that "they met whenever they could" and R. H. Super agreed: Trollope "saw her frequently." In contrast, C. P. Snow asserted that while "he loved her," he "never went to bed with her," but he "would certainly have wanted to marry her" had Rose Trollope died. In any event, they "can't have been alone together more than maybe a couple of dozen times." More recently, Victoria Glendinning has surmised that his wife "knew about her husband's infatuation, and was upset, then had her ample say about it in the privacy of the bedroom." She adds, "I cannot prove that he told her, nor that she reacted as I say, but I am sure of it."[6] Without hard evidence, the gaps in the record have been filled with guesswork and conjecture.

This much is known, however: Though Field often mentioned Landor, the Brownings, Vedder, and Tom Trollope in the articles she wrote from Italy for the *Boston Courier,* the *New Orleans Picayune,* and the *Boston Transcript,* she mentioned Anthony Trollope only once—in a piece written on April 28, 1859, before she met him, as a "son of the lady who Trolloped America."[7] Apart from her anonymous review of *North America,* Kate Field referred to Trollope in print exactly seven times in the thousands of articles she published during her career, and all of these comments are brief and innocuous. For example, she made only glancing references to him in "English Authors in Florence," also published in the *Atlantic,* while devoting whole paragraphs each to the Brownings, Landor, Harriet Beecher Stowe, Frances Power Cobbe, George Eliot, and even Frances Trollope and Thomas Trollope.[8] Field rarely mentioned Trollope even in private—only three times in the hundreds of letters from her hand that survive. They occasionally rendezvoused, as in Washington, D.C., and New York, in April, May, and June 1868. One day in mid-June, in fact, they were both photographed at Napoleon Sarony's studio on Broadway in New York, albeit not together. Field saved twenty-four letters she received from Trollope over the years, though he mailed her many more. One of them, dated July 8, 1868, concludes with "a kiss that shall be semi-paternal—one-third brotherly, and as regards the small remainder, as loving as you please."[9] Trollope apparently did not save her letters to him, but he mentions her, albeit not by name, in his autobiography, written in 1876: A woman, "one of the chief pleasures" of his life,

> has graced my later years. In the last fifteen years she has been, out of my family, my most chosen friend. She is a ray of light to me, from which I can always strike a spark by thinking of her. I do not know that I should please her or do any good by naming her. But not to allude to her in these pages would amount almost to a falsehood. I could not write truly of myself without saying that such a friend had been vouchsafed to me. I trust she may live to read the words I have now written, and to wipe away a tear as she thinks of my feeling while I write them.[10]

Field concealed the precise nature of her relationship with Trollope even after his death in 1882. He was somehow off-limits, a special case, compared to Landor, the Brownings, George Eliot, and others. Despite repeated opportunities to reminisce about Trollope, she never did so. To conclude: Their relationship was intense and intimate, though there is not the least scintilla of evidence it was ever physical. The veil over their relationship is so heavy it cannot be lifted even a century later.

On the other hand, her friendship with Elihu Vedder was perfectly transparent, not shrouded in mystery in the least. Through the agency of Kate and Aunt Corda, "the doors of society were thrown open" to Vedder when he returned to the United States in the summer of 1861. Even Milton Sanford was "disposed to help me, and he did so when I was discovered," but because he was "a fierce Copperhead" Vedder's sympathy for the Union "offended him past remedy."[11] Aunt Corda commissioned him to paint her portrait and bought several of the landscapes he brought back from Florence, which, according to his biographer, "enabled Vedder to start painting his mythical creatures." By the artist's own testimony, Kate was "a woman of advanced views" and she "always seemed bent on improving my mind," urging him to attend lectures with her. She also "gave me some sound advice as to the body, assuring me most solemnly that if I did not leave off smoking there was little prospect of a long line of progeny, in case I got married."[12] She was trying to reform him, to save

3. Elihu Vedder's painting of Cordelia Sanford, 1862. Courtesy of the author.

him from the bohemian life he had taken up at Pfaff's beer hall in the Village, where he had befriended Walt Whitman and Herman Melville. (He apparently also introduced her to Whitman's *Leaves of Grass,* which she began to quote in her writings about this time.)[13] Kate was so concerned about Vedder's health that she insisted that he join her, Eliza, the painter Charles Caryl Coleman (another acquaintance from Florence who had just been discharged from the Union Army), and his mother at Sharon Springs, a watering place in upstate New York, in the summer of 1863. There they went driving and riding.[14]

Sometime late that summer, to judge from the best circumstantial evidence, Field tumbled from a horse and the accident seriously impaired her health for several months.[15] She was an invalid in Cordaville, and she wrote nothing for publication, so far as is known, between July 1863 and the spring of 1864, the longest drought of her career. Milton Sanford was relieved, ironically, and he promised her an income of $600 a year and much of his wealth at his death if she would swear never again to hazard a public career. She did not weigh the offer long. "I would make no such promise to any human being," she replied in writing, "not even to my dear father and mother." Should her health suffer as a result, "then I must be resigned to fate, and accept poverty if necessary, but until then I want free-dom to work in whatever direction I feel called." Lest her meaning was still unclear, she added bluntly, "I don't want your money, Uncle Milt."[16] The break was not complete—they remained on speaking terms for the rest of Milton Sanford's life and Field continued to spend part of every summer with them in Newport—but he disinherited his niece and he never again offered to give her money.

When she recovered from her fall, then, she was obliged to earn her own living. She left Cordaville and moved with her mother to a modest apartment on West Twenty-seventh Street in New York in February 1864. She solicited work from George Ripley, founder of the Transcendentalist community at Brook Farm in 1841 and twenty years later the literary edi-tor of the *New York Tribune,* and while he did not offer her any assignments he did offer some advice. He suggested she contact Charles Nordhoff, the managing editor of the *New York Evening Post,* "who tells me that he would receive a series of essays or sketches on some popular subjects"; Theodore Tilden, editor of the *Independent,* to ask "to give you a chance among its saintly contributors"; and Robert Bonner at the *New York Ledger.* "If you would write some piquant paragraphs" for "the immortal Bonner," Ripley thought, "I could induce" him "to give you a niche in his famous columns." Ripley thought Field could "beat Fanny Fern, not in her own line, but in a better one." He ended his letter on an encouraging note:

> I have no doubt of your success in one way or another. I am no stranger
> to your brilliant gifts. Though we have met so recently for the first time,
> having been so much struck with the gay reports from Florence in the
> *Transcript* as to ascertain the name of the writer, which I never forgot from

that day to this. So I welcome you almost as an old acquaintance. Your beautiful musical talents may prove a better resource than the uncertain labors of the pen.[17]

On a lark, she also wrote the lyrics to a pair of songs by her old singing master in Boston, Augusto Bendelari: "Viva the laugh!" and "Tit for Tat" ("Perchè oggi none jieri").

Undaunted, Field soon arranged to become a correspondent for the *Boston Journal* and the *Springfield Republican,* a daily paper edited and published in western Massachusetts by Samuel Bowles. She inscribed on the first page of her scrapbook containing clippings of these articles the words "Beginning of my New York Life." She noted that she was paid ten dollars a letter by the *Journal,* three dollars a letter by the *Republican.*[18] Between April 1864 and September 1866, she contributed a dozen articles to the *Journal* and over fifty to the *Republican.* She also began to write for the *Boston Advertiser* in February 1865 and published nineteen articles in its pages by September 1866, in addition to a smattering of pieces in the *Round Table,* the *Boston Post,* the *Galaxy,* and other papers. Again she signed her essays to the *Republican* and the *Post* with the penname "Straws, Jr.," and her articles in both the *Journal* and the *Advertister* "Fie."

Working as a freelance, Field chose the stories she wanted to cover. The first event she picked was the "Great Metropolitan Fair," located at the 14th Street armory (aka "the Palace Garden") and in a building on Union Square, to benefit the Sanitary Commission. It raised over six hundred thousand dollars in its first five days. Field regaled her readers with descriptions of some of the exhibits, especially the art galleries that featured such canvases as Emanuel Leutze's *Washington Crossing the Delaware,* which took up "about as much space as the Delaware river occupies in nature"; Frederic Edwin Church's *Niagara* and *Heart of the Andes;* and Albert Bierstadt's *Rocky Mountains.* She also rubbed shoulders with military leaders aplenty in the crowds, among them Ambrose Burnside, Irvin McDowell, John C. Frémont, and George B. McClellan, the discredited leader of the Army of the Potomac ("such a head and face" could never "save a country"). The manuscript of Edward Everett's "Gettysburg Address"—the forgotten one—was also on display and for sale for two hundred dollars.[19]

When she once again began to write for publication, moreover, Field puffed Vedder without stint. "By far the most promising artist in America is Elihu Vedder," she wrote in a review of the annual exhibition at the National Academy of Design in New York in June 1864. "After wandering through a wilderness of mediocrity," she had come upon his painting *The Lair of the Sea Serpent,* a work of "much originality and power of execution." The following July, she publicly congratulated Vedder on his election, with Winslow Homer, to the National Academy, the forerunner of the American Academy of Arts and Letters. She also reported that, with the end of the war, Vedder planned to "go to France and study the science of his art for several years." If "done earnestly," she predicted, "he will wake up some fine morning and find himself famous." Vedder's father had promised to help support him. "I feel confident that we will find ourselves better before long," Vedder wrote Field from his studio in Boston, and he signed the letter "your affectionate brother."[20] In fact, Vedder sailed for France in December 1865 and settled permanently in Rome in 1867.

Field also became the self-appointed New York drama critic for the *Springfield Republican.* As she pointed out, she was better qualified than most of the theatrical reviewers for the New York dailies. She began to review private theatricals for the *Republican* in May 1864 and less than a year later she had graduated to critiquing the Hamlet of Edwin Booth, her aunt's reputed half-brother. Characteristically, she pulled no punches. After the hundredth performance of the tragedy starring Booth at the Winter Garden in late March 1865, Field declared that the production, "take it from beginning to end, is, with the exception of Mr. Booth, excessively bad," and

> Booth himself is only comparatively good. . . . His slips of pronunciation are strange and unscholarly . . . and many of his speeches are singularly without point. He is the old, traditional Hamlet, pleasing to look upon, showing much natural taste, refinement of character, some study, an aspiration toward what is fine in his art, but no originality, no flashes of genius, no magnetism, either personal or intellectual.[21]

She was equally ambivalent about Booth's performance as Shylock in *The Merchant of Venice.* She scorned the "insipid hero-worship" of the New York critics and bluntly expressed her own opinion: "his present performance manifests a considerable uncertainty of mind as to his conception of the character."[22] From her perspective, the emperor had no clothes.

She was no kinder to Charles Kean and Ellen Tree, her parents' old friends. They had "once patted me on the head" and "inspired my infantile veneration" by giving her toys. But when Field attended their performances in *Louis XI* and George Colman's comedy *The Jealous Wife* with her mother (the "old actor beside me") she was underwhelmed. "In *Louis XI*, as a peasant girl, [Tree aka Mrs. Kean] wore a diamond ring. Can a woman be an artist and do these things? Such carelessness is unpardonable in actors of celebrity, nor need they expect them to pass unnoticed by all Americans," she averred. "Some critics regret that Mrs. Kean has lost her fine voice," but "Ellen Tree never had a good voice." Moreover, "My old actor assures me that Kean is a better actor now than formerly, for the reason that he has changed his school, which used to be exceedingly 'stagy.'" All in all, the Keans seemed relics of a theatrical past. "They are historical personages of an era in the drama," Field concluded, "but better things than they have done can be done."[23]

Not that better things had been done by two rising stars, Kate Bateman and Christine Nilsson. According to Field, Bateman at least was "a woman whose head is not made up of rats, mice, and waterfalls that anybody can buy in Broadway for a consideration"—the referent here is to artificial hair—but if she "is better than anyone else on the American stage, it does not necessarily prove that she is good. We are simply sorry for the stage. After Rachel, after Ristori, after the many clever women to be seen nightly in Paris, it is doing the drama great injustice to accept Miss Bateman as one of its priestesses." As for Nilsson, Field publicly damned her with faint praise: she "is less satisfactory in Rosalind than in Juliet." Privately, she swore that she "wouldn't praise Nilsson to save her from purgatory."[24]

Another of her favorite topics in the mid-1860s, when she regularly vacationed in Newport, was hotel and drawing-room society there. With her mother, aunt, and uncle, Field stayed at several Newport hotels and boarding houses—the Ocean House in 1864, for example, and at other times at Mrs. Dame's boarding house on Broadway or at Mrs. Wilbur's boarding house on Washington Street. She published a total of twenty-five articles about Newport in various New York and New England newspapers between 1864 and 1868; and she wrote familiarly of balls, matinees, soirees, "hops," private dinners and theatricals, clambakes, tea parties, picnics, and dances; yacht races and horse shows; beach attire and "Old Ironsides" at anchor in Newport harbor; fashion and society at the Ocean House, the Fillmore, the Jockey Club, and the Academy of Music; events at the Naval Academy and gambling houses; as well as the social graces of such celebrities as Senator Charles Sumner of Massachusetts, the historian George Bancroft, the artists John La Farge and Hamilton Wild, and the poet Henry Tuckerman. For example, as she observed in late August 1864 after a dance at the Fillmore House, Sumner appeared "much worn by his winter's work" in the U.S. Senate.[25] Along with its founder Julia Ward Howe, the poet and author of "The Battle Hymn of the Republic"; J. G. Holland, the editor of *Scribner's;* and the radical Unitarian and abolitionist Thomas Wentworth Higginson, Field was also a member of the Town and Country Club of artists and intellectuals in Newport. She befriended the "vivacious widow" Helen Hunt (aka H.H.), later the author of *A Century of Dishonor* and *Ramona,* and Lina Warren, another summer resident, with whom she went rowing in the bay.[26]

She reminisced later about the divisions among families with Old, New, and Newer Money that fragmented the community. "Newport is many sided: it has as many phases as a well-educated politician has faces," she explained. "You can have your own cottage and live like a prince; or you can hire a cottage and live like a Christian," or you can live in a boarding house "for very little money."[27] High society in Newport "is about as difficult of access as in Boston. People who are 'in,' particularly those who have fought their way up, are suspicious of newcomers, and only welcome the presentable inordinately rich who can minister to their pleasure, and all foreigners of great or little distinction. The native American who comes here, hires a cottage and spends a deal of money, expecting in one season to penetrate the holy of holies, is doomed to defeat." Since the start of the Civil War and the absence of the old *regime* of Southerners, the newest nouveau riche of "Northern vandals" have invaded Newport and, "plethoric of pocket for the first time in their lives," they "endeavor to make money take the place of breeding."[28]

Nor did she spare from her scorn the activities of the leisure class or what she called the "moneyed aristocracy." Long before the construction of the most lavish mansions in Newport, Field observed that "Bellevue Avenue has not its peer in this country" and that a "drive on the Avenue" is "a moving panorama of stylist 'teams,' a triumphal procession of fashionable bipeds and quadrupeds. . . . People flock to the avenue as the great unwashed read dime novels, in the expectation of being astonished and having their hair stand on end, for even the most *blasé* are occasionally made to stare." "Everybody who has four horses hitches them together and trots them up and down the avenue." In fact, she added, "the Avenue is the only tolerable road" in town "in dry seasons, being the only one that is watered" to reduce the dust. Some gentlemen, including Leonard Jerome, Griswold Grey, and August Belmont, "think nothing now of giving $5,000 and $10,000 for a horse," she noted, "and of owning six or seven of these expensive beasts." And "to be pointed out as the owner of a $5000 or $10,000 horse," in a textbook example of conspicuous consumption, "is as sweet to masculine vanity as praise of her beauty is to the belle." "Every lover of show sooner or later gets to Newport," she asserted. With such gambling establishments for the wealthy as Watson's, moreover, Newport "is a Baden Baden in small, doing privately what in Europe is done publicly."[29]

Field was never loath to grind an ax on behalf of her friends or her favorite causes. Much as she puffed Vedder in her newspaper correspondence in the mid-sixties, she plugged Harriet Hosmer, the contralto Adelaide Phillipps, and the painters C. C. Coleman and W. J. Hennessy. She publicized the good work of her friend Clara Barton, the so-called "angel of the battlefield" during the war. Field wrote two glowing articles in the *Springfield Republican* on Barton and her humanitarian efforts on behalf of the Union dead and wounded soldiers.[30] She also covered a dress reform meeting at Cooper Union where she met Susan B. Anthony.[31] On another occasion, she went slumming in the Bowery and wrote up the experience for the entertainment of her readers.[32] She attended Class Day at Harvard in June 1864, which prompted her lament that virtually all young women were forbade from obtaining higher education: "The senseless, shameful, superficial system which is pursued with girls is sad enough to bring tears to the eyes of angels." She indulged her interest in Spiritualism by hearing the medium D. D. Home, whom she subsequently described in the *Republican* as "one of the illumnati," read at Dodworth's Hall.[33] As catholic as Field's interests were, the fact that she was a mere newspaper columnist earned the scorn of Robert Browning, however. As he wrote Blagden in 1865, "She is one of those disappointing people, from whose ordinary life & ways you expect something better when they shall set to work."[34]

Field repeatedly expressed her political opinions in her letters for the *Republican,* to the occasional dismay of its editor. She welcomed the new progressive magazines the *Nation* and the *Radical* to the marketplace of ideas, and she hailed the elder Henry James' lecture in New York on "Carlyle," which she heard in company with George Bancroft, William Cullen Bryant, Horace Greeley, and George Ripley. She satirized in a sarcastic voice the parade on Boston Common on the Fourth of July:

> The procession was an imposing spectacle. My heart thrilled within me as my eyes fell upon the chief of police, the board of aldermen and city clerk, the sheriff of Suffolk and registers of deeds and probate. My love of freedom rose to high water mark as the Cochituate water board passed before me, and never had my soul been so illuminated as when the superintendent of lamps and sewers turned his august eye upon me.

Her racial progressivism is evident, too, in her defense of the rights of black Americans. She condemned "negrophobia" in "this righteous city" and asked in the name of the black soldiers who fought at Fort Wagner and Fort Hudson whether "the negro be allowed rights which white men must respect?"[35]

But her coverage of Lincoln's assassination on Good Friday, April 14, 1865, and its aftermath in New York outraged Bowles, her editor. In her first column after the death of the president, she remarked on the black bunting hanging from windows throughout Manhattan. Never a champion of Lincoln while he lived, Field believed his martyrdom would serve the nation better than his postwar policies. The Emancipation Proclamation was his "most fitting monument," and much as William Lloyd Garrison famously declared that "John Brown executed will do more for our good cause than John Brown pardoned," Field asserted that "Lincoln murdered is a far greater power" than "Lincoln in the White House" would have been in dealing with the postwar South. "It is well to have 'charity for all' and entertain 'malice towards none,'" she added, invoking Lincoln's Second Inaugural Address, "but there is also such a thing as justice." John Wilkes Booth "has made a hero of the honest backwoodsman." She had attended Easter services at the Plymouth Church in Brooklyn, the day after Lincoln's death, to hear Henry Ward Beecher, the most famous preacher in the nation. "Everyone [at the Plymouth Church] expected Mr. Beecher to rise to the occasion," but "Mr. Beecher could not rise. He said so."[36] On April 24 Field watched the procession of Lincoln's cortege as it made its way through the streets of New York City to City Hall, where the body lay in state, and then, "admitted . . . by the favor of a pass," she "gazed for the last time upon the face of our martyred president. It was a dreadful shock to note the frightful changes made by death on that once benevolent countenance. Time had done almost its worst with the body, and discretion should have concealed it from view." She remarked in particular on the "dark, drawn, crumbling face." She demanded revenge on the "arch-traitor" Jefferson Davis, the president of the Confederacy, and for the sins of "slavery, Libby prison, the cruelties begotten of this war, the return of our poor, starved, idiotic soldiers, with legs and arms eaten off by disease."[37]

Bowles responded to this editorializing much like the editor of the *Boston Courier* when Field filled her Florence letters with news of the Italian revolution. "Don't write any more about Abraham Lincoln's dead body. It is too late," he insisted. Lincoln's soul might still be marching on, but apparently it was not selling many newspapers. "I can't at all like your last two or three letters. They are not 'letters from New York,' which are what we wish. If I had not known you personally, & liked you immensely, I would have sent the last one back. We don't wish political disquisitions." Instead, "I want some *New York* letters from you. Do give them to me & take $5 a piece for them. The others I do not want at any price."[38] Women were not supposed to meddle in public affairs, and Field had crossed the line. Bowles later complained about the way some "women-writers" took criticism: "they receive the unvarnished truth as if it were a red-hot bullet."[39] Not surprisingly, Field soon suspended her contributions to the *Republican,* though she insisted to the end of her life that Bowles had been her "literary father, and his trenchant criticism on the art of condensation was of great value at an early period of my career."[40]

She became an apologist for Andrew Johnson, Lincoln's much-maligned successor, much as in Florence she had defended Victor Emmanuel and Garibaldi against all criticism. To the news that Johnson had been drunk at his inauguration as vice president, she declared that "Andrew Johnson is not an intemperate man." He had simply been ill from his trip from Tennessee to Washington and had "resorted to stimulants" to endure "the ordeal of the inauguration." As a loyal Southerner committed "to an uncompromising policy," Johnson was the perfect president to oversee Reconstruction, or so she thought. She referred without a hint of irony to Johnson's "immortal" speech outside the White House on February 22, 1866, in which he claimed that "new rebels" in the North (that is, the Radical Republicans) were trying to seize power, and she added that "whatever Mr. Johnson's politics may be, he is at heart a gentleman."[41]

Much as she had gradually tempered her opinion of Garibaldi, moreover, she was compelled over time to revise her estimate of Johnson. Both Field and Senator Charles Sumner of Massachusetts were invited to dine at the home of James and Annie Fields in Boston on November 17, 1865, six months after the assassination. Sumner "opened the conversation at dinner," Annie Fields wrote in her diary, "by asking Miss Field to tell him something of Mr. Landor." Field proceeded to tell a story about Landor's anger. When she and Isa Blagden visited the Brownings in Siena during the summer of 1859, Landor was vacationing in a room nearby. One day he "fancied that the stock of tea lately purchased for his use was poisoned, and threw it all out of the window." Then Field turned the conversation by mentioning she had heard that President Johnson "was no better than a sot" and asked Sumner if the allegation was true. One of the Radical Republicans who would vote in favor of impeaching Johnson six months later, Sumner "said not word at first" and then changed the subject.[42]

When she first settled in New York in February 1864, Field had contacted George Ripley about freelancing for the *New York Tribune*, nicknamed not entirely facetiously the "Great Moral Organ." In September 1866, fluent in Italian and with a track record as a contributor to a pair of respected

New England dailies, she tried again, offering to cover the American tour of the Italian actress Adelaide Ristori, whom she had met in Italy in 1860. The drama editor William Winter acknowledged Field's "proposition to write, in my department of the *Tribune*, a series of reviews of Madame Ristori's acting. . . . I immediately assented to, and candidly advised, its acceptance."[43] Though she never held a salaried position with the paper, never was a regular correspondent for it but always an "occasional" one, Field published between 1866 and 1889 over a hundred articles, editorials, and letters in the *Tribune;* and she regarded her success as a contributor to the paper the benchmark of her achievements as a journalist. However, she is not mentioned in any of the various histories of the *Tribune,* then the most significant, reliable, and respected paper in the country, with a daily circulation of between thirty and forty thousand copies. Like many prominent nineteenth-century women, Field was erased from the record.

Her first column on Ristori—signed with her initials "K.F."—appeared in the *Tribune* five days after Winter gave her the go-ahead. The arrival of the actress from Europe, she opined, inaugurated "an epoch which will bear great results to the profession she honors, and we welcome her as an art teacher" who will elevate the dramatic tastes of her audiences and "arouse a feeling of disgust toward the degraded, sensational, morbid trash which forms nine-tenths of the dramatic staple of the American stage." Over the next two months Field contributed several more reviews of Ristori's performances to the pages of the *Tribune,* in particular her productions of Montanelli's Italian translation of Legouvé's *Medea,* Maffei's translation of Schiller's *Mary Stuart,* Giacometti's *Elizabeth of England,* and Carcano's translation of Shakespeare's *Macbeth.* Never one to gush, Field criticized the plays as much as she commended them. She asserted, for example, that "Ristori's conception of the character" of Adrienne Lecouvreur "seems to us all wrong," that her costume in the role "is awkward and ill-designed. It increases the defects of her figure, its stoutness and its want of height, and makes her look full as old as she probably is." The English translation of *Phædra* acted by the company, she averred, "is so marvelously bad as to be funny."[44] On his part, Winter was delighted by these pieces. "I have read your article on Phædra, in this day's *Tribune,* with great satisfaction," he wrote Field on October 15. "It is the best one you have written—in roundness of thought and directness of style; and it evinces literary schol-arship as well as a keen faculty of criticism." In his remarks about these early pieces, however, Winter also betrayed some of the condescension that would plague Field's association with the paper and its coterie of male edi-tors. "You might improve them," he advised her, "by greater 'compression' of style, and by more careful analysis of Ristori's intellectual and emotional nature—as you advance in the work."[45] Field later revised and collected her articles on Ristori from the *Tribune,* the *Atlantic, Harper's,* and the *Boston Transcript* for publication in her first book. Her friends at the *Springfield Republican,* among others, commended it: "It is the most authentic and com-plete account of the great actress in print, and all who see her, and many who do not, will read it with an interest which itself will feed and stimulate and hardly satisfy."[46]

The success of her Ristori reviews in the *New York Tribune* opened many doors to her, especially to the offices of other newspaper edi-tors. Between February and November 1867 she published nearly three dozen articles in the *Chicago Tribune,* most of them "New York letters." She fed her Midwestern readers a steady diet of theater and exhibition reviews as well as news and gossip about such matters as the New York Anti-Slavery Society; the Equal Rights Association, Susan B. Anthony, Lucretia Mott, and Elizabeth Cady Stanton; and the parade of Irish-Americans through Manhattan on St. Patrick's Day and prospects for home rule in Ireland. To judge from these letters, she widened her cir-cle of acquaintances during these months to include the liberal Unitar-ian minister Octavius Brooks Frothingham, the first president of the Free Religious Association; and Wendell Phillips, an eloquent orator on behalf of abolition and suffrage. Phillips "did me worlds of good when I was a young girl and helped to make me a radical," she later reminisced.[47] Field defended William Lloyd Garrison when he was still considered half a traitor for publicly burning a copy of the Constitution of the United States, declaring it "a covenant with death and an agree-ment with hell" for sanctioning slavery. More than any other American, Field contended, Garrison as editor of the *Liberator* "with the aid of a printing press" had proved "the ability of one man to excite a revolution of opinion." She also penned several travel essays about her summer cruise up the Hudson to Saratoga Springs, where "as much as a quart" of Congress water was "allowed to the acre" of dirt in the air. On her part, she preferred "claret and champagne" to the "strong waters." The Sons of Temperance had passed through town and "drank the spring nearly dry." She continued her trip to Glens Falls, where she visited Carrie Rosenkrans, Vedder's fiancé. She soon assured Vedder that "you have chosen for a wife" a wonderful young woman. "If your grandmother had had the choosing," she "could not have made a better choice." She registered at the Fort William Henry Hotel, on the southern shore of Lake George and at the site of the fort James Fenimore Cooper depicted in *The Last of the Mohicans*. The hotel kitchen served bread, she joked, "as heavy as Andrew Johnson's conscience."[48] Her trip took her north to Lake Champlain, then to Mount Desert and Bar Harbor, Maine, on the Atlantic coast north of Portland.

Slowly, by the age of thirty Field had emerged from behind the pseudonyms she had earlier chosen to disguise her gender. All of the articles she published in the *Atlantic* and in *Harper's*—"English Authors in Florence" (December 1864), "The Last Days of Walter Savage Landor" (April–June 1866), "Adelaide Ristori" (April 1867), "Ristori" (May 1867), and "A Conversation on the Stage" (March 1868) were assigned to her by name in the volume indices. Her articles in the *New York Tribune, Chicago Tribune,* and *Boston Transcript* were signed with her initials. As Field began to earn a reputation for her writing, she also became the victim of "the paragraph fiends" who spread vicious rumors and innuendo. As a talented and independent woman, she was regarded in some quarters as a harpie and a shrew. When Charles H. Webb (aka "John Paul") met her in May 1867, he was prepared "for a shock." According to "the paragraphs which had circulated through the press," he expected a "loud" woman. "On the contrary, I met a charming and cultivated lady, who discussed art and literature in a knowing way."[49] According to the *Brooklyn Eagle*, Field was "fond of boasting and of having her own way. If the truth must be told," in fact, she "is somewhat 'fast' in her style." The *Eagle* qualified this harsh assessment a month later: Field "is a strong advocate of woman's rights" and "is bound to vote, and to have every right that man has." Her "intense loyalty" to the Union during the war had caused "a serious family rupture, deeply creditable to the little lady's independence of spirit."[50] The fact remains, however, that Kate Field was controversial even before she was a national celebrity.

She had completed her apprenticeship in journalism and, in turn, she was rewarded with an unexpected break and a plum assignment: covering Charles Dickens' final American speaking tour for the *New York Tribune*.

4

New York and New England

CHARLES DICKENS was the most famous author in the world when he arrived in Boston aboard the *Cuba* on November 9, 1867. He had visited the United States before—in 1842, a trip he remembered not so fondly in his travelogue *American Notes* and his novel *Martin Chuzzlewit*. Some Americans had never forgiven him for his criticism of the Land of the Free. When asked how he would draw the American eagle, a character in Dickens' novel replies, "I should want to draw it like a Bat, for its short-sightedness; like a Bantam, for its bragging; like a Magpie, for its honesty; like a Peacock, for its vanity; like an ostrich, for its putting its head in the mud and thinking nobody sees it." On her part, Field defended Dickens months before she met him: he had not "exaggerated what [he] heard and saw" in America a quarter-century before.[1] His 1867–68 reading tour was sponsored by James T. Fields, his Boston publisher and her friend. She expected, as the *Tribune* reporter assigned to the story, unfettered access to Dickens behind the scenes.

In fact, she was invited to a dinner party at the Fields' home on Beacon Hill in Boston where Dickens was the guest of honor.[2] She stood in line on November 29 to buy tickets to his opening night in New York on December 2, when "carriage after carriage deposited its human contents on the sidewalk" and "vampires" were scalping tickets for the "very best seats in the house."[3] Among the dignitaries in the audience that evening were Longfellow, Holmes, Lowell, Fields, and Charles Eliot Norton. She attended virtually all of Dickens' readings at Tremont Temple in Boston and Steinway Hall in New York in December 1867 and January 1868. She later allowed that she was in debt to Dickens for "twenty-five of the most delightful and most instructive evenings of my life."[4] In all, she contributed seven extended reviews of Dickens' recitations to the *Tribune,* telegraphing her columns to New York when he performed in Boston. As Mark Twain reminisced forty years later, Field "made a wide, spasmodic notoriety in 1867 by some letters which she sent from Boston—by telegraph—to the *Tribune* about Dickens's readings there in the beginning of his triumphant American tour. The letters were a frenzy of praise—praise which approached idolatry—and this was the right and welcome key to strike, for the country was itself of enthusiasm about Dickens," and "Kate Field became a celebrity at once."[5] In her dispatches, Field described Dickens declaiming nine different scenes from his fiction: the "Tempest" chapter from *David Copperfield,* "Nicholas Nickleby at the Yorkshire School," "The Story of Little Dombey," "Doctor Marigold," "Boots at the Holly-Tree Inn," "Mr. Bob Sawyer's Party" and "The Trial" from *Pickwick Papers,* "Mrs. Gamp" from *Martin Chuzzlewit,* and *A Christmas Carol.* Her articles were predictably celebratory. His first reading in Boston, for example, seemed to her "full of varied power; brim-full, from end to end, of feeling, pathos, mirth, and fun, a sunlit shower of smiles and tears, not to be described in words, hardly to be comprehended by the mind." "Like all great masters in every art, Mr. Dickens shows his power in his simplicity," she noted the next week.[6] Almost overnight, at the age of twenty-nine she became a recognized authority on Dickens. Still, unlike her male counterparts, she was denied access to Dickens backstage before and after his appearances by the local press associations, particularly at a dinner for Dickens at Delmonico's hosted by the Press Club of New York, the first time she had experienced blatant sexual discrimination as a journalist.

She compensated for the exclusion in small ways, especially by exchanging messages with Dickens through his manager. When asked if he had noticed Field in the audience night after night, for example, Dickens reportedly replied, "See her! Yes, God bless her! She's the best audience I ever had."[7] On New Year's Eve, 1867, she sent a basket of violets to decorate his reading desk at Steinway Hall during his performance. Annie Fields wrote her a few days later that Dickens had "told me of the pretty basket of flowers on his desk," and on January 3 Field received a personal note from Dickens—"the most neatly worded note I ever read"[8]—thanking her for the flowers.

My Dear Miss Field—I entreat you to accept my most cordial thanks for your charming New Year's present. If you could know what pleasure it yielded me, you would be almost repaid for your delicate and sympathetic kindness.

But I must avow that nothing in the pretty basket of flowers was *quite* so interesting to me as a certain bright fresh face I have seen at my Readings, which I am told you may see too when you look in the glass.[9]

"It is very sweet of Mr. Dickens to take so much notice of my little offering," Field allowed.[10]

When they met privately for the first time, Field told Dickens she "owed him so heavy a debt of gratitude" that she would never be able "to pay even the interest on it." Dickens replied he would give her "a receipt in full" and later wrote on a "ferocious" engraving of his head "Received of Miss Kate Field all the thanks she owes me—and many more, with which I am better pleased than I appear to be in the above gloomy presentment of my state of mind."[11] The inscription became one of her most cherished possessions. While there is no record that Field mentioned her father's acquaintance with him in Boston in 1842, the thought could not have been far from her mind. She later boasted, with pardonable hyperbole, that she had been "very intimate" with Dickens during his second U.S. speaking tour.[12] But she had been on cordial and familiar terms with him.

Field fleshed out her *Tribune* columns in her second book, *Pen Photographs of Charles Dickens's Readings,* which remains even today in any of its various editions one of the most important accounts of Dickens' stage method. The original version, published in Boston in February 1868, a few weeks before Boz returned to England, was a mere thirty-eight double-columned pages long. But it was popular and well-received: the *Boston Transcript* proclaimed it "quite a masterpiece," and *Putnam's* opined that "no one can read" Field's "pen photographs" and fail to read Dickens' "novels with a more enjoyable relish." Thomas Wentworth Higginson, Field's friend from Newport, declared in the *Independent* that the "photographs" were "simply the best sketches yet written of Dickens's style of reading." He concluded that if Field, "a writer of extraordinary talent"—this the fellow who once urged Emily Dickinson to "delay to publish"—had "time to do justice to her own rare powers" she would "accomplish a great deal."[13] Before he read the pamphlet, Dickens briefly considered trying to arrange for a British edition issued by his London publishers Chapman & Hall that might earn Field £25 or £30[14]—"amazed at Dickens's proposal," Field noted in her diary—but after he read it he concluded reluctantly that it was both too short and too late to secure British copyright. Though James Fields told her that "Dickens praises my 'Photographs' very warmly,"[15] in fact Dickens objected to a couple of minor mistakes. Field had lamented some omissions from the reading text of some stories—for example, "What Mr. Dickens suppresses" from "The Trial" in *Pickwick Papers* "would not materially add to the length of the Reading, while the amount of effect lost is very considerable."[16] Dickens responded, "Can she not imagine it possible that [the omissions] are half so dear to any one as to me[?] And does she not see that such omissions are concessions to the inexorable claims of Time[?]"[17] In August 1868, Field published an expanded, fifty-eight-page version of her "photographs" for which she was paid about $200 by the Boston publisher A. K. Loring, best known today as the publisher of the early juvenile novels of Horatio Alger, Jr. "Had I foreseen its success," she confided to her diary, "I would have fought" for a royalty rather than a flat payment. Loring "will make money, and I not a cent."[18] Dickens also opposed a British edition of this version, apparently on the grounds that "No English publisher would purchase advance sheets of a second edition, however revised and enlarged."[19] Anthony Trollope, acting as Field's intermediary with Dickens in England, added, too, that "without his cooperation the publication with any good results would be altogether impossible."[20] So she put her plans for a British edition of the book on hold.

Field's snub by the Press Club of New York during Dickens' visit spurred her to organize the first women's club in the United States, a sorority of New York women with literary and artistic interests. She envisioned an organization of women with a political agenda, "a sort of woman's supplement to the Union League Club," as she said. The first meeting, on March 2, 1868, at the home of Jane (aka "Jennie June") Croly, a popular gossip columnist, was attended by Field and the poet Anne Lynch Botta, among others. Field was elected corresponding secretary of the group. She proposed to call it the "Woman's League" and, in order to open it to women of all classes, to charge very modest dues. The club was fraught with dissension from the start, however. By only the third meeting, at Delmonico's restaurant on Broadway, the members decided to hold eight social and eight business meetings a year, to consider "its work chiefly social and educational," to charge an initiation fee of two hundred dollars and so to restrict its rolls to the well-to-do, to call itself "Sorosis," denoting a fruit with many flowers, and to adopt the pineapple as the club symbol.[21]

Field was displeased by the new focus of the group. With the help of Annie Fields, she persuaded the members to change the name to the "Woman's League"—but only temporarily. "The more they thought of 'Woman's League' the less they liked it," Jane Croly wrote in the official history of the club nearly twenty years later, and at the next meeting in May the name "Sorosis was restored by an overwhelming vote."[22] Behind the scenes, Croly had lobbied for the change and had accused the headstrong Field of trying to force the other women in the club to follow her lead. Field groused that she had been accused publicly of being "Becky Sharp's superior in shrewdness and impudence." As Annie Fields reassured her on May 18, "Anything more bare-faced, slanderous, and dark than that accusation can hardly be found. Miss 'Jennie June' from whose unfledged life it sprang ought to make you the best reparation in her power."[23] But Field lost the tussle and quit the club in disgust. James R. Osgood, James Fields' former partner, who had succeeded him as owner of the Boston publishing house, agreed a week later that it was "too bad that the Woman's Club has come to grief so soon. For even if it continues to exist, it must be on a very precarious basis, after the loss of those whose membership can alone make it answer the end for which it was created. I am sure everybody—whose opinion is worth anything—will be sincerely sorry. *I* am for one, although I am not what is commonly called 'Woman's Rights.'"[24]

With her mother, Field moved to Boston in September and immediately organized an alternative group there, the New England Women's Club, more along the lines of her original idea. It boasted 118 members, including Elizabeth Peabody, Ellen T. Emerson, and Julia Ward Howe, by the end of the year; had launched a monthly journal called the *Woman's Advocate;* and had opened a "clubhouse" or reading rooms at 3 Tremont Street in the Hub. Its dues were $10 a year or $50 for life, and its object was "to become an organized social center for united thought and action." Not only were "the best women in Boston" members, Field wrote, but the club welcomed "men as well."[25] "The majority of the women composing this Club are poor," Field as secretary of the group wrote in her annual report to the membership, and "the majority of those women who are most valuable to the Club and for whom it is organized are poor; for this reason the fees have been reduced to a minimum." She urged "any wealthy man or woman of radical proclivities" to underwrite their expenses. In her diary for November 16, 1868, Louisa May Alcott noted she had visited "the Club for a change" and lunched with Field and the poet Celia Thaxter. At the club meeting three weeks later, the members heard a lecture by the elder Henry James on "Woman," and on January 12 he repeated the lecture at Chickering Hall for the benefit of the club.[26] Though Sorosis may have been longer-lived, the New England Women's Club for a few months offered Field and its other members rooms with a view of their own.

Meanwhile, Field was extending her range as a drama critic. Upon Ristori's return to the United States in early 1868, Field reviewed her stage appearances for the *Philadelphia Press*—she was in such demand that she had begun to moonlight as the drama critic for a half-dozen East Coast newspapers. She persuaded Ristori to play the lead in a four-act comedy she had translated from the Italian of Baron Cosenza entitled *Mad on Purpose*, in which a wife feigns madness to test the loyalty of her husband. It was produced at the Theatre Français in New York on June 24, 1868, and the script was soon published by the firm of Gray & Green.[27]

She had also begun to formulate the dramatic principles she would champion for the rest of her life. She advocated the "natural school" of acting, often identified with the French drama, against the more mannered or histrionic acting of the English and especially the Americans. She considered William Macready, the elder Booth, Rachel, Ristori, and Tommaso Salvini the finest tragedians in the world. She had personally seen each of them on stage either in London, Paris, or New York, though American theatrical audiences, she sniped, preferred "a fine figure" and a pretty face to a more studied performance.[28] She ridiculed what she called the "Black Crook" school of plays often staged at Niblo's Garden in the Bowery—a type of sensational melodrama written for working-class audiences by such blood-and-thunder authors as Ned Buntline. His play *The Broken Bank,* she averred, "is a model for the coming farce. It is called a farce because nobody says or does anything funny, and it is entirely new for the same reason."[29] But she was quick to attack any of the so-called custodians of culture, especially ministers, who denigrated the respectable drama. When the preacher T. Dewitt Talmage alleged that theaters demoralize the public, ruin the health of the theatergoer, attract taverns and barrooms to the neighborhood, and depress the value of surrounding property, she answered him point by point in the *New York Tribune* "to his utter demolition." She anticipated a future moment "when the profession of acting will be esteemed as one of the noblest on earth, and actor and actress will be synonyms for all that is good and great in humanity." In fact, "the noblest and best woman" and the "bravest and most generous man" she had ever known were actors—her mother and her father. "I thank God for my parents, and I honor their art."[30] Field also urged the professionalization of the job of drama critic. Reviewers should be experts or specialists, not mere reporters randomly assigned the theater beat. The job of the drama critic ought to be a "calling" no less than the work of the clergyman. "As a people we have no intellectual conscience" such as a class of professional critics might provide, she insisted. Competent theatrical reviewers were even more necessary to the growth of an American theatrical tradition than were trained actors. "I have always despised the flunkeyism of America in art matters," she added.[31]

She tried her hand at fiction too. She had been working on a short story entitled "Love and War," which she sent to Higginson in manuscript to critique for her. "It is strong, direct, & simple, with real feelings," he replied. "Whether there is quite *action* enough to make it effective as a story, I doubt. But I have no other criticism to make."[32] Field was able to place the story in *Public Spirit,* a short-lived monthly. A slight, conventional tale about a young seamstress with a drunken father whose soldier-lover dies in the Battle of the Wilderness, "Love and War" ends with the heroine a self-supporting artist and her father dead. Trollope hated it. "It has two faults," he explained to the author after she sent him a published copy. "It wants a plot and is too egoistic. . . . You simply say that a girl was unhappy in such & such circumstances, and was helped by such and such (improbable) virtues & intelligences."[33] She also placed a second story, "A Moving Tale," in *Harper's Monthly* for November 1868 after it was rejected by *Galaxy*. Higginson thought it had "many good bits & the incidental boy-talk is particularly good." Ostensibly a comic story about the risks and inconveniences of moving from house to house, its subtext is a cautionary tale about the tyranny of marriage because the narrator's husband makes so many foolish decisions.[34]

Field contributed a rich if miscellaneous mix of items to the *New York Tribune* over the months (for example, an obituary of the actor Charles Kean, her parents' friend; a puff of the singer Adelaide Phillipps, her own friend; a report on the unveiling of the statue of Matthew Perry in Newport; a review of John Forster's biography of Landor; and a piece on the American Jockey Club). She covered the New York charity balls for the paper and defended them as "a healthy tonic" for the dissipation endemic to the business class in America.[35] She published in the paper whatever struck her fancy, including a pair of articles about her summer 1868 vacation with Celia Thaxter at Appledore House on the Isles of Shoals off the coast of Portsmouth, New Hampshire. William Winter congratulated her upon the appearance of these feature stories: "I enjoyed your letters from the Isle of Shoals. That was a very pretty picture which rose before me when the last one ended. The sunset over the sea—the vesper hymn of the waves" and a "girl strolling homeward in the dusk, with her bundle of driftwood."[36]

Field spent several weeks in late summer and early autumn with her aunt and uncle in Newport, and there she met both the younger Henry James and his great good friend W. D. Howells. She recorded in her diary her impressions of James' "power and his refined charm of personality," and over the next two years they occasionally socialized in Boston. Field noted in her diary for February 8, 1869, for example, that James had called on her and remained at her home "until night. We had a good long talk about everything under the sun and some things above it." She invited James and Howells to a "Bohemian tea" at her home as late as November 1870.[37] Field and James also twice published articles in the same issue of the *Atlantic* during these months: Field's "Charles Albert Fechter" and James' unsigned review of *Selections from De Musset* in the September 1870 issue, and her "Fechter as Hamlet" and his "Travelling Companions" in the

November 1870 issue. While they may not have literally crossed paths after 1870, James continued to follow Field's career. Both published articles in the September–October 1879 issues of *Scribner's:* Field's "W. S. Gilbert" and "Arthur Sullivan," two installments of James' novel *Confidence.* They literarily crossed paths as late as October 1887, when both of them appeared in *Harper's Monthly*—Field's story "Our Summer's Outing" led the issue and James contributed an essay on John Singer Sargent.

More to the point, James would model the character of Henrietta Stackpole in his novel *The Portrait of a Lady* (1881) on Kate Field. Much as Henrietta's letters "from Washington, Newport, the White Mountains, and other places" were "universally admired," Field had been a regular correspondent from New York, Saratoga, Newport, and the Catskills. Much as Henrietta "had at one time officiated as art-critic to a Transatlantic journal," Field had reviewed plays and art exhibitions in New York and Boston for a variety of newspapers. Much as Henrietta travels to Spain in chapter 39 of the novel and her "letters from Spain proved to be the most picturesque she had yet published," Field published letters from Spain in the *New York Tribune* during the Spanish civil war of 1873–74 and collected them in her popular book *Ten Days in Spain.* Much as Henrietta becomes the English correspondent of the *New York Interviewer,* Field moved to England in July 1875 to become the London correspondent of the *New York Graphic* and *New York Herald.* An even more striking similarity: Isabel Archer's friend and confidante Henrietta "had adopted three of the children of an infirm and widowed sister, and was paying their school-bills out of the proceeds of her literary labour," much as Field helped to support the "five fatherless children in Louisiana" of her impoverished cousin Kate Wilcox, the daughter of Matthew and Cornelia Ludlow Field, whose Confederate soldier-husband had been killed during the war. Much as "Henrietta was a great radical, and had clear-cut views on most subjects,"[38] Field became a self-described "radical" and, with the elder Henry James, a member in good standing of the Radical Club of Boston. In all, Field was precisely the type of New Woman whom James characterized, if not caricatured, in Henrietta.

And make no mistake: Field reveled in her associations among the Radicals. She attended her first meeting of the Radical Club, what she called a "brain sociable," on November 16, 1868, where she hobnobbed with the likes of Bronson and Louisa May Alcott, Julia Ward Howe, the poet Lucy Larcom, Robert Dale Owen, Louise Chandler Moulton, and Ralph Waldo Emerson. (Not that she was an uncritical tyro. A month before, she confessed, she was "woefully disappointed" when she went to Boston to hear Emerson speak.) On January 4, 1869, she heard John Weiss, a radical Unitarian minister, read a paper on "Woman," which seemed to be a fashionable topic. At the meeting of the Radical Club on January 18, Higginson read a paper on "Greek Goddesses" and during the discussion Field "dared to say a word which turned out a strong blow to the pretty theorizing." She also heard her friends Julia Ward Howe speak on "Religion" on January 24 and Wendell Phillips, the "greatest of American orators," deliver a sermon on "Christianity a Battle and Not a Dream" in April 1869 at Horticultural Hall in Boston. "Never has Phillips addressed a more critical audience, and never was he greater," she noted. "Saint Wendell," as she called him in her diary, "is very sympathetic to me, and if I saw much of him I should love him." He once referred to her as "the angel who records our sins." To be sure, she considered Bronson Alcott "incomprehensible" (as did many others) and, much as Poe had remarked to her father in 1845 about the "Frogpondians," she complained that the "Concordians are too much for me." But she began a regimen of reading in protest literature, with Mary Wollstonecraft's *A Vindication of the Rights of Women* first on the docket, and the elder Henry James took her under his wing, calling at her home and addressing her as "blessed child."[39]

Her interest in Spiritualism and the occult also led her in a peculiar if not exotic direction. In May 1868 she began to experiment with "Planchette," an early type of Ouija board shaped like a heart, about seven by five inches in size, with a pencil-holder "that runs about on wheels, and thinks, writes, and swears like a trooper." The device was faddish at the time, and Field bought hers over the counter at a bookstore on Broadway. At first, she was disappointed with the results from her experiments. But soon a spirit that signed itself "J. F." (i.e., Joseph Field) contacted her and addressed her as "Mary Kate" in writing that was "a facsimile of my own." She conceded, moreover, that every word inscribed by Planchette, which/whom Field gendered as female, "enters my mind before it is written." With her mother, she began to host "Planchette parties" to which she invited such friends as O. B. Frothingham, Horace Greeley, and Anne Botta. No doubt she was sincere in her experiments. "I have seen enough of what is called Spiritualism to be convinced of the honesty of many of its 'mediums,'" she insisted. Sometimes "Planchette acted like a cross, sleepy child and very frequently verged upon ill-humor," however, and some of her "messages" were ludicrous in retrospect. Field asked the shade of George Washington his opinion of Ulysses Grant, and the Father of His Country answered from the spirit world, "I think tolerably well of him. . . . He has enough common sense to put clever men into the cabinet"—this a few years before the Crédit Mobilier and Whiskey Ring scandals. Planchette at other times revealed that the planets are inhabited, that America would eventually rule Europe, and that the Franco-Prussian War was imminent (no great revelation there). Asked if marriages exist in heaven, "she" replied, "No; once is enough."[40]

Field soon published a pamphlet about her experiments. *Planchette's Diary* was her third book, issued in New York on November 23, 1868. At a mere ninety-five pages, it was nothing more than escapist reading, and Field rarely mentioned it in later years. But she was paid a hundred-dollar advance and a 10 percent royalty, and the *Boston Transcript* predicted it would enjoy a large sale "owing to a widespread interest in this modern mystery."[41] The *Diary* was also widely and favorably reviewed by such papers as the *Transcript* ("a very curious and entertaining" book "full of surprises and occasionally dealing in wonders") and the *Philadelphia Press* ("an odd, clever, bizarre-like production, in which fancy and fact are amusingly combined"). William Winter also thought that its "revelations are strange."[42]

Field enjoyed less success in persuading many of her friends of the authenticity of the phenomena, however. Anthony Trollope was a curmudgeon on the subject, to say the least. "I don't seem to care much about Planchette," he wrote Field in June. "I should like of all things to see a ghost," but "when tables rap, and boards write, and dead young women come and tickle my knee under a big table, I find the manifestation to be unworthy of the previous grand ceremony of death."[43] Osgood, too, was a skeptic: "I should be delighted to come to see you with Planchette as an excuse; but I have no fondness for phenomena, and I can get lots of good advice from good angels in the flesh without resorting to those in the spirit." However, if Planchette could "inform me how to make a quarter of a million dollars in a quarter of a year with a quarter of the work I now have to do, I shall become the most enthusiastic of her devotees."[44] Kate and her mother visited James and Annie Fields on New Year's Day 1869, when they "talked of Planchette." Kate offered to demonstrate its powers, and "presently her hand bounded up and down instantly and she said if questions were asked she thought her hand would write as she had no longer any control over it." James Fields asked questions of Thackeray, who had died six years before, whereupon Planchette "wrote somewhat testily that he 'was finite and not infinite and could not pretend to answer such questions.'"[45] So much for the beneficent spirits in the Great Beyond.

As a prolific magazinist, newspaper columnist, and book author, Field was able to earn little more than a livelihood. Despite her literary successes, she posed the question in her diary on New Year's Day, 1869, of "where the money to live on is to come from." She decided in the spring of 1869 to capitalize on her celebrity—not for the last time—by lecturing for a living. The lyceum "pays better than anything else, and I am tired of grubbing along," as she explained.[46] "Comparatively speaking, the writer has all work and no pay; the lecturer, supposing him to be moderately successful, has all pay and no work."[47] Her first lecture was a defense of women lecturers—hardly a bold or controversial subject. Such speakers as Olive Logan and Anna Dickinson had already toured the country before Field took to the hustings. But Field's "Woman in the Lyceum" was both more learned and less polemical or confrontational than their addresses and her delivery was more restrained: she typically spoke before her audiences while sitting at a desk or table. The gist of her argument was that "genius has no sex." Field invoked the authority of the classical tradition by reminding her audiences that Aspasia had taught rhetoric to Socrates, a point she had gleaned from Landor's "Pericles and Aspasia."[48] (On his part, Anthony Trollope ridiculed this notion in a letter to Field. "That Aspasia taught Socrates I doubt much. . . . Had Aspasia taught Socrates what would that prove, seeing that Socrates was never eloquent as far as we know[?]")[49] Still, she insisted, "there is no more reason why a woman should not lecture than that she should not sing or act."[50] She also frankly admitted that she had entered the lecture field to earn money. It was "the best and safest way for a woman of brains to churn them into bread and butter."[51] She rehearsed the ninety-minute lecture on the afternoon of March 15 before the New England Women's Club, and it was heard "with interest and pleasure by all who were present," according to the *Boston Advertiser.*[52] She debuted the lecture on March 31 to a crowded house at Chickering Hall in Boston. The elder James apologized to Field for missing it. "I am suffering from a most prostrating attack of influenza," he explained, "and nothing short of necessity robs me of the pleasure I had expected in hearing you."[53] Those who were present were impressed by the novice speaker. In her diary, Annie Fields wrote that while Field "looked very pale," her lecture was both "a great struggle" and "a great success. As in the old days of Greece the beautiful Aspasia again exhorted the people. She pleaded her case well and applause and approbation greeted her on every hand."[54] James Fields told Kate "it was the most successful début he ever saw." William Lloyd Garrison remarked that "it was worth the admission fee just to see Miss Kate Field on the platform."[55] Frothingham congratulated her on "a brilliant success"; E. P. Whipple thought her manner "refined, graceful, self-possessed, and ladylike"; Edward King in the *Springfield Republican* praised the "witty" lecture and her "admirable" delivery; and Oliver Wendell Holmes signed a petition asking her to repeat it.[56]

And she did so, on April 12, again in Chickering Hall, with Lowell, Julia Ward Howe, and John Greenleaf Whittier in the audience.[57] Whittier wrote a friend a day or two later that the address was "very bright and sensible, and read with grace and spirit."[58] A critic in Newton, Massachusetts, on April 24 compared her to Wendell Phillips.[59] On May 3 Field read "Woman in the Lyceum" in the lecture room at Plymouth Church, Brooklyn, where she was introduced by Henry Ward Beecher to an audience that included Harriet Beecher Stowe, Elizabeth Cady Stanton, and Theodore Tilden. "When Beecher introduced me to the combined intellect of Brooklyn, I felt like a fool, but the feeling seemed to agree with the occasion, as the verdict passed was in my favor," Field mused.[60] A week later she delivered the same lecture at the Union League Theater in New York—to unstinted praise in the papers in both cases.[61] E. L. Godkin, the founder and editor of the *Nation,* accorded her "first place on the Lyceum platform."[62] The poet E. C. Stedman composed one of his most popular lyrics after hearing the lecture. He compared Field to Hypatia of Alexandria, a fourth-century Hellenic philosopher and teacher. One evening the poet "found her lecture-hall" and joined the "throng that watched the speaker's face / and on her accents hung."

> No civic crown the sibyl wore,
>   Nor academic tire,
> But shining skirts, that trailed the floor
>   And made her stature higher. . . .
>
> Her hair was coifed Athenian-wise
>   With one loose tress down-flowing

and "Apollo's rapture lit her eyes." She spoke not about the classics "but searched historic years, / The sisterhood to scan / Of women,—girt with ills and fears."

> Their crosiered banner she unfurled
>   And onward pushed her quest
> Through golden ages of a world
>   By their deliverance blest:–
> At all who stay their hands she hurled
>   Defiance from her breast.
>
> I saw her burning words infuse
>   A warmth through many a heart,
> As still, in bright successive views,
>   She drew her sex's part;
> Discoursing, like the Lesbian Muse,
>   On work, and song, and art.

The poet concludes with an apostrophe to the "Brave girl" to "let thy wild heart ripple on" through "vale and city!"[63] Field was charmed by the poem, though she later allowed that Stedman "little understood me in his concluding verses."[64]

Stedman's allusion to Field's "defiance" notwithstanding, she was re-peatedly commended in the press for her decorum on the platform. She "made no outrageous assaults on male opinions or even on the prejudices of men," the *New York Evening Mail* opined. Field "promises not to abuse men, but to turn her batteries upon her own sex," according to the *Springfield Republican*.[65] Whitelaw Reid was even more explicit in the columns of the *New York Tribune*. "Because Miss Field takes up her work with quietness and courtesy," Reid averred, "because she does not denounce, nor bully, nor demand, because she illustrates her belief that any woman, like any man, appearing as a public speaker, is bound to give her hearers the highest result of her culture," her appearance on the platform "is earnestly to be welcomed." William Winter again wrote to congratulate her on this unsigned notice and added, "You evidently have a good friend in the *Tribune*." She had learned who her "good friend" was only five days earlier at a dinner in New York with friends. "Yesterday I dined at the Bottas with Whitelaw Reid," she wrote on May 7. "He is a *young* man and a clever man; good looking and looking good—I *think* he is honest. I sat beside him at table and we 'got on' very fast. *He* is my friend on *The Tribune*."[66] Two weeks later, Reid was appointed managing editor. With good reason, she anticipated a long and prosperous association with the paper.

Reid was one of the giants of late-nineteenth-century American journalism, U.S. minister to France from 1889 to 1892, and the Republican nominee for vice president of the United States in 1892. A midwestern patrician, he became editor-in-chief and part-owner of the *New York Tribune* after the death of Horace Greeley in 1872. More to the point, he was also Kate Field's patron on the paper for several years in the late 1860s and early 1870s. From the first, she lobbied Reid to pay her more money for her contributions. "Do you expect Hood, Charles Lamb and George Alfred Townsend [to write] for $15 per column?" she quizzed him scarcely a month after his appointment as managing editor. "Let me feel that writing for *The Tribune* is easy, and I'll do much better than by feeling the weight of some terrible elephant." She insisted that "$30 is the least *The Tribune* ought to pay" for a theatrical review.[67] Reid agreed "that *The Tribune* doesn't pay enough. I think the same myself and shouldn't make the slightest objection to its doubling my salary; but there is a view of the question which in spite of my having already given, you won't look at. You forget that though our rates are below those of the magazine we can furnish you 50 times the market the magazines can."[68] Still, the *Tribune* routinely paid her less for her columns than it paid male contributors for similar articles. In April 1872 she insisted that Reid pay her "at the rate of $20 per column as you do Huntingdon [the Paris correspondent of the paper]. You pay him 100 francs per letter which is really more. Do this and I shall believe that you really care to have me write for *The Tribune*."[69] Unfortunately, her repeated arguments fell on deaf ears.

Nevertheless, they became good friends and business associates. When Reid asked her to report on the Peace Jubilee held on Boston Common in June 1869, she dutifully complied. In fact, as she wrote him, "I have written four letters in all,—one more than you suggested."[70] Rather than $45 for three essays, she was paid $60 for four—or the same sum she would have received for three at the higher rate she had demanded. In these letters, Field detailed the events of the Jubilee, and in the last of them she asserted that it had proved "men and women can work together as journalists without the slightest embarrassment or loss of prestige on the part of the latter." The press corps for the event had "gained rather than lost by the presence of women, and now that the experiment has been tried with success, let it be repeated."[71] Still, when a reporter for the *New York World* carped that "K.F." in the *Tribune* "must be a woman, because the letter is so full of exclamation points," Field was incensed. When he alleged that "K.F." would not be "in danger anywhere for where there is no temptation there is no sinning," she was outraged.[72] "That *World* man ought to be hung," she wrote Reid.[73]

On July 4, thirty-four years to the day after Henry Thoreau settled at Walden, Field left for a month-long camping trip in the Adirondacks with her mother and three friends. James Fields had introduced her to Thoreau's writings six months before.[74] She had read William H. H. Murray's *Adventures in the Wilderness; or, Camp Life in the Adirondacks* in advance and she consulted Thoreau's *The Maine Woods* while packing. "To come into the Wilderness and not camp out would be to me as unnatural as to bathe in a diver's water-proof suit," she wrote, so the five women carried their larder with them: potted meats, dried fruits, canned vegetables, maple sugar, condensed milk, crackers, and sea biscuits. They took a train past Keene, past the Connecticut River and Bellows Falls, past Burlington, past Platts-burgh to the Point of Rocks. They hired a guide for $2.50 per day and a wagon that carried them to Martin's, on the southeast shore of Lower Saranac Lake. For the next three weeks they fished, hunted, hiked, rowed on the lake, and read. "Days come, days go, and life grows richer, fuller, until the thought of old harness and bit become the *bête noire* of existence," Field wrote.[75] They slept one night in a cabin in the woods inhabited by the son of a local judge, who "from early Spring until early Winter" lived there "after Thoreau's own heart." They also fended off "black flies, musketoes, and midges."[76] In the course of the month she gained fourteen pounds.[77] She had promised to chronicle the camping trip of the "Black Fly Club" in the Adirondacks for the *Tribune,* though she did not send Reid the first of her letters until 10 August. In addition, she submitted an essay based on her Adirondack adventures and entitled "In and Out of the Woods" to the *Atlantic Almanac,* where it appeared on November 13.

Before leaving the North Woods Field made a pilgrimage to North Elba, near Lake Placid, to visit the grave of the abolitionist John Brown—the very grave in which his body literally lay "a-mouldering." She discovered that the 244-acre farm where the family plot was located, given to Brown by the abolitionist Gerrit Smith, was for sale for $2,000, and in mid-October she tried to raise the money in Boston to buy it and hold the property in pub-lic trust. Among the possible contributors she contacted was Ralph Waldo Emerson, who had helped to raise money to aid Brown's family in 1859, but who demurred on this occasion. As he replied to Field's request on October 28, "I do not know enough of the present condition of the Brown family to judge of the desireableness to them of your project." He remembered that he "once passed by the farm when it did not look attractive to a settler."[78] Much to the embarrassment of Boston, within forty-eight hours of contact-ing potential donors in New York, first among them Isaac H. Bailey, editor of the *Shoe and Leather Dealer,* Field had raised the necessary money.[79] The farm was purchased, maintained by the trust, and in 1895 was turned over to the State of New York and declared a historical site.

Returning from the Adirondacks, Field spent the first seven days of August in Saratoga and sent the *Tribune* a piece that satirized that famous watering-place: "For the variety of its mineral springs Saratoga is probably without a rival in the whole world. For scenery and general attractions it can be excelled by many a modest New England village. For dust, it stands without a peer," she added. The mothers who bring their daughters to Saratoga to find husbands are ill-informed, because the only "men who seek wives in Saratoga are fortune-hunters." Fashionable young women "attract the attention of vulgar men, who study them as they would prize animals, and use no refined language in discussing their points." And tourists beware: "Every stranger is an orange to be squeezed dry."[80] Like Mark Twain in *The Innocents Abroad*, Field parodied the formulaic travel essay. But she was attacked, nevertheless, for her gender. She had entitled her satire "Saratoga Seen with the Naked Eye [It Being a Woman's]." In a rejoinder, "Saratoga Seen with Another Eye [It Being a Man's]," a fellow tourist contended that the "dear lady" would "have seen more and seen some things differently if she had been a man" and thus a more perceptive observer. For one thing, "if she had inquired," as men do, she would not have been surprised by the extent to which the management of the fabled Saratoga race-course "is a swindle and a fraud."[81]

On his part, Reid welcomed all of these contributions from K.F.'s pen. He inserted two of her Adirondack letters in "the place of honor in eight columns of correspondence" on the first two pages of the *Tribune* for August 13, and he urged her to write for the paper as often as possible. Six weeks later, he appealed to her vanity. "Perhaps you will be glad to know that your Adirondack letters were a success, the first one particularly," he informed her. "The second happened to please the publisher of *The Tribune* and some other people who take a commercial view of such things." He admitted to her in early September 1869 that, after he became managing editor of the newspaper, "somebody warned me not to engage you. 'You never can get along with her, unless you give her her own way in everything, & that you couldn't do.' I thought we might succeed better than the false prophet predicted. After a Summer's work—of which there hasn't been half enough,—I'm satisfied. If you are not,—you ought to be!"[82]

Field was stunned by the revelation. As she replied to Reid, she was delighted to write for the *Tribune*, but

I should much like to know who advised you to have nothing to do with me, professionally. The editors with whom I have disagreed have invariably been dishonest. And I am to blame for rebelling! If you are satisfied with me I am satisfied. My only ground of complaint against *The Tribune* is that it does not pay as well as the magazines I write for. . . . I am amenable to reason, and am frank in the expression of my good will toward the present managing editor of *The Tribune*.[83]

Reid declined to reveal the name of "the person who gave me the advice about you against which you remonstrate so characteristically," because it "has proved untrue and so is not worth minding, but some time when you are here I may tell you."[84] (The culprit was almost certainly Bowles of the *Springfield Republican*.) Ever the patron(izing) editor, Reid nevertheless admired his occasional correspondent K.F.

His genteel condescension is nowhere more evident than in another pair of comments they exchanged in August 1869. After spending most of the summer traveling and camping, Field retired for a few weeks to Newport, arriving there on August 16. As she wrote Reid, "At last I have reached a haven of rest where the rest must be left out as a small mountain of work rises up to obstruct the view of pleasure. So when you ask me what my plans are 'for the remainder of the season,' I can only answer Newport. Here I propose to remain until October, unless the Winter begins in September as is likely."[85] To her dismay, her presence there became the fodder for columnists. The Newport correspondent of the *Tribune* wrote that Field appeared to be "a strange marine creature, in dark drapery of masculine style. This apparition wore an immense scoop of a dilapidated hat, and had pretty little eyes and brown tresses."[86] Predictably, Field wrote Reid the next day to protest the invasion of her privacy. "If I can't go out in a boat in bathing costume for the purpose of swimming, without seeing a badly drawn picture of myself in *The Tribune*, I shall be obliged to retire to my grave. Why couldn't the woman say I had on a bathing dress and not lead people to suppose that I went about the harbor in horrible attire? I was at my own back door," she wrote.[87] "Of course I knew, when I saw the letter ab[ou]t y[o]u[r] 'toggery' that there was something wrong," Reid replied, "but I confess I hadn't thought it deserving of quite so serious epithets as you apply to it." He then counseled her about the price of celebrity, albeit once again in a patronizing tone: "You will have to learn, my sensitive little friend, that people in public or quasi public positions get all sorts of criticism, & must quietly bear it & make no sign."[88] The question remains, however: would the *Tribune* have published such demeaning gossip about one of its featured contributors who was male?

Not that the *Tribune* was the only paper that invaded her privacy. The author Mary Clemmer Ames reported in the *Independent* in September that she had spotted Field "down at the little pier behind the Malbone house." She was tanned from rowing with her mother every morning on the bay before working every afternoon, "writing lectures and letters to earn an honest living, instead of expending her powers in inveighing some man into earning it for her. And she'll make a dear, willful little wife some day— none the less because, before she became one, she successfully paddled her own little life-canoe without assistance."[89] In fact, Field devoted her working hours in Newport that summer to preparing a new lecture and planning her next assault on the lyceums.

5

At Large

BY 1870, virtually every town and village in the country had a local organization, a library or lyceum committee or a mechanics or mercantile association, which sponsored a series of six to eight lectures between fall harvest and spring plowing. Lecturing was one of the few well-paying careers available to American women during the Gilded Age, moreover. Anna Dickinson earned an estimated $20,000 per year at the height of her popularity in the 1870s and Victoria Woodhull was paid $250 per lecture date. Some of the most popular speakers advocated social change, such as women's suffrage or world peace or civil rights. But most lectures were designed to entertain rather than edify, and most lecturers were motivated more by money than by philanthropy. Or as Mark Twain once insisted, "A sensible man lectures only when butter & bread are scarce."[1] Field normally charged a minimum of $150 plus expenses per lecture, and at that price she was in great demand—though she admonished her agent to book her into "no God-forsaken place."[2]

Field's first full season on the boards was one of her most successful. She finished a draft of her lecture for the 1869–70 season, variously entitled "Among the Adirondacks," "Life in the Adirondacks," "Out in the Woods," and "Life in the Woods" (also the subtitle of Thoreau's *Walden*) on October 15, only five days before she was scheduled to deliver it at the Boston Music Hall. It included humorous descriptions of the "Black Fly Club," the women's excursion to the North Woods, and their ascent of Blue Mountain. She carried her manuscript, with its frequent allusions to both Thoreau and Whitman, to Osgood to read and critique. He returned it the next day, "praising it highly, saying that it would go far toward making my future, but advising me, as a matter of policy," to omit the final pages, a peroration on the heroism of John Brown. Osgood's suggestion was well intentioned but, to Field's credit, she refused to take the advice. "I sobbed like a child, and wanted to die" when she read Osgood's suggestion. "Then conviction took possession of me and said, 'Retain the peroration if you die.'"[3] While the first hour and a quarter of her lecture was mostly light entertainment, she devoted the final fifteen minutes to preaching the gospel of social progress. Though no manuscript of the address survives, its final paragraphs were often transcribed in the local papers where she spoke:

> I could not leave the North Woods without making a pilgrimage to John Brown's grave. Standing beside that, plucking rose and buttercups that sprang from the giant's heart, I saw the entire history of our terrible civil war. . . . I saw John Brown come to the Adirondacks in 1849, hoping to find the nucleus of a black army in the colony of fugitive slaves. . . . I saw him at Harper's Ferry, with the fastnesses of the Alleghenies for an army, strike for freedom with the sword of Frederick the Great, that had been sent to Washington. . . . I saw him wounded and a prisoner, sacrificing himself that innocent blood might not be shed. I saw him bid farewell to his life; I saw him lying in blood-stained clothes, listening to his sentence; I heard him say with undaunted heroism, "I am persuaded that I am worth inconceivably more to hang than for any other purpose"; I saw him leave his prison door for the last time. . . . I saw him hanging dead. I saw the dark and stormy night that followed the execution, precursor of the war to come. . . . John Brown's scaffold, six feet high, twelve feet wide, fifteen feet long? It is as high as heaven, as wide as the universe, as long as time; its lessons will endure throughout eternity.[4]

She insisted on speaking these lines whatever the response they provoked from her audiences. "I close my lecture over John Brown's grave, pronouncing a eulogy upon him," she wrote Reid on November 9, even though "I dread to have horrid things said about me."[5]

As it happened, Field was rarely criticized for praising Brown, who had been hung by federal authorities in December 1859 for fomenting slave rebellion at Harper's Ferry, Virginia. The lecture was generally well received wherever she delivered it, from Boston, Salem, and Providence in

October; New York, Newburyport, Springfield, and Hartford in November; Marlboro and Lynn, Massachusetts, Troy, New York, Pittsburgh, and Cleveland in December; Fall River, New Haven, Stamford, Elmira, Rochester, Buffalo, Brooklyn, Yonkers, Newark, and Morristown, New Jersey, in January; and Chicago, Detroit, Fort Wayne, Saginaw, St. Paul, Dubuque, and Milwaukee in February. By her own estimate she "journeyed up and down the land to the extent of twenty thousand miles."[6] Journalists across the country marveled at her audacity—"how reliantly she journeys about the country unattended" while "everywhere commanding the respect and courtesy due to a lady, without in the least offending against the idea of true womanliness." Field proved "that it is actually possible for a *lady* to travel the continent over unattended and yet safe," and she was well paid for her trouble, however far-flung the towns where she spoke. She "won the hearts of a thousand people" in Chicago with "her brilliant sketch" and cleared about $500 in the process, for example. The *Chicago Tribune* remarked that in the peroration Field "became truly eloquent and stirred the hearts of her audience to their deepest depths."[7] According to the *New Haven Journal and Courier,* her lecture "threw into the shade most of the humorous lectures of Mark Twain," and the *Buffalo Courier* asserted that she was funnier than Artemus Ward when she declared that "in the woods, you take in life at every breath. First, we took in midges, then blackflies, then mosquitoes."[8] In all, asserted the Boston papers, it was "one of the spiciest and most entertaining lectures which has ever been given in Boston" with the peroration on Brown "natural and well-sustained"; and it "transfixed an audience" of thirteen hundred people in Troy with its "strain of moral earnestness." The *Troy Times* averred that Field "reached the summit of eloquence in her peroration."[9] She was rarely censured—ironically, once by the radical *Boston Commonwealth* for crediting New Yorkers with the purchase of the John Brown farm, "as though Bostonians had not expended a thousand fold as much for real practical anti-slavery purposes."[10] On occasion, the "tender-hearted" Field (in modern parlance, a "bleeding heart liberal") was also chastened for insisting that the "soul" of the "martyr" Brown was still "marching on." "Its journey is ended," the *St. Paul Pioneer* cried, "and a surfeited people are ready to exclaim '*Requeiscat in pace.*'"[11]

By her own estimate, Field earned over eight thousand dollars with her Adirondacks lecture during the 1869–70 season, the equivalent of over a hundred thousand dollars in 2008. Still, the joke went around that "Kate Field works like a beaver—with her mouth." She began to repay her uncle the money he had loaned her and her mother over the years, and she was able to move with her mother in March 1870 to a fashionable house at 21 Joy Street on Beacon Hill in Boston.[12] In early April she started to write what would be her last two essays for the *Atlantic Monthly,* a pair of studies of the French actor Charles Fechter.[13] In January she had seen Fechter on stage in New York as Claude Melnotte in Edward Bulwer-Lytton's *The Lady of Lyon* and as Edmond Dantes in the elder Dumas' *The Count of Monte Cristo* and she had been charmed. To the complaint that Fechter delivered his lines in a heavy French accent, Field replied that "he is the only actor on the stage of the Grand Opera House who speaks distinctly enough for me to hear every word."[14] But she reserved her greatest praise for his performance in *Hamlet.* "Of all his *répertoire* thus far given in this country Hamlet is the only character that has fully called out Fechter's resources," as she wrote.[15] (For the record, Field was paid $500 for her *Atlantic* article on Fechter's Hamlet.)[16] When Fechter was hired to manage the new Globe Theater in Boston and to star in its company, moreover, Field puffed the event in the *New York Tribune*. She also began to take notes for a full biography of Fechter, an elaboration of her *Atlantic* sketches, and she enlisted the actor's cooperation. "The material for Fechter's life was given me by the actor himself, when we were good friends and he was the adoration of Boston," she later explained. "He was one of the few actors who put brains into their work and was worth studying."[17]

She spent most of her working hours during the late spring and early summer of 1870 catching up on writing assignments and preparing for the next lecture season. She published the first half of her lecture "Woman in the Lyceum" in the *New York Tribune* in April 1870, but she was unable to pencil-whip the balance of the lecture into shape for months afterwards. Finally she conceded to Reid that she was "ill in body and exhausted in mind," able to sleep no more than "three hours out of the twenty four. . . . I am generally as good as my word" but in this case "I have not been. It is my misfortune, not my fault, but I shall in no way take umbrage should you decline to publish further articles on lecturing. I cannot say when I can continue them."[18] In fact, Field published the balance of the lecture in the Boston weekly *Every Saturday* a year later. Meanwhile, she began to write two new lectures, one on Elizabeth Barrett Browning and a second on "Actors and Acting." She even arranged for flyers advertising her lecture on "the great English poet" to be printed and wrote Robert Browning with a few factual questions about his wife, the answers to which she hoped to incorporate into the lecture. He declined to cooperate. "I wish I could do what you request of me," he replied on July 5, 1870,

> but it is doubly impossible: in the first place, I know next to nothing of the places, dates and circumstances you want: and, were it otherwise, my mouth would be stopped for reasons strong enough which I can't explain now. The works, and what of the life you had the opportunity of becoming acquainted with, are quite within your competency to lecture upon— and I need no assurance that the feeling with which you will treat them is as good and kind as ever.[19]

Field in fact had decided to abandon her plan to lecture on Barrett Browning a week or so before receiving this letter, probably because Robert Browning had delayed so long in responding to her queries. As she wrote on June 27, she had already "made a change in my programme. Instead of Mrs. Browning I shall lecture on Charles Dickens."[20] She also cancelled her plan to speak on "Actors and Acting" and no draft or fragment of this lecture survives.

Instead, she reread all of Dickens' novels that summer and prepared a lecture on him while vacationing in Newport. Field and her mother, aunt, and uncle so cherished their holidays in the resort town that in 1869 the Sanfords purchased a lot at 72 Washington Street, on the water near the Point a short walk from the railroad depot, and they hired the Boston architect W. R. Emerson to design a home for them. Built in 1870, Edna Villa was a showcase, one of the most expensive and luxurious homes ever constructed to that date in Newport. Though scheduled for completion in early July 1870, the builders did not finish it until mid-August. "We have actually got into the new house," Field wrote Whitelaw Reid on August 20, and her elders "have even dared to invite relations to be the first guests."[21] The cottage featured a French roof, piazzas on three sides, an entry hall open from floor to ceiling some thirty-five feet, hardwood floors, Turkish carpets, wide balconies on the second and third stories, broad staircases, custom-made furniture, bronze gas-jets, billiard and smoking rooms, as well as stained-glass windows and oiled frescoes. The green and gold paper decorating the walls cost eighteen dollars per roll, according to contemporary reports, and the "cost of the chandeliers" alone would have built "a comfortable house."[22] The parlors were finished in butternut, with ebony and gold moldings and mottled panels, and the dining room was finished in black walnut with carved wainscoting. A seawall built at great expense extended the small lot into the harbor a hundred feet. The cost of the house, even without the land, was estimated to be between fifty and a hundred thousand dollars. Kate's room on the third floor sported an "eyrie" or square bay window opening onto the Newport inner harbor and an upholstered couch framed by mirrors that enabled the occupant of the room to view a panorama out the window. "Here she can sit when the mad waves rage, dashing soft shell crabs to death on the rocks below, and write poems and things," as C. H. Webb wrote in the *New York Tribune*. "Were a ship to be wrecked on the south-east corner of the garden wall, which juts boldly and threateningly out among the wild waves, I've not a doubt but she'd put out to the relief of the sailors, for she's a capital boatwoman, and has a bonnie blue boat of her own."[23] Field wrote her lecture "An Evening with Dickens" in this room after the house was finished. In all, according to Margery Deane in the *New York Evening Post*, the Sanfords' "elegant seaside residence" was "the finest house . . . ever built in Newport," a villa "almost palatial in its appointments."[24] On her part, Field cracked that the reporters had slobbered over the house "like idiots,"[25] though she also gushed over its appointments: the interior "is artistic in construction and adornment," she later wrote, "and many a gay party of kindred souls have watched the setting sun and bade the moon welcome on the broad piazza of Edna Villa. A magnificent grand piano made the drawing-room of the Villa as attractive as the charming waterscape without, for the nimble fingers and well-trained voice of the hostess created such music as is rarely heard from amateurs." Over the next few months Field and family would host Reid,

Charlotte Cushman, Edwin Booth, Adelaide Phillips, E. P. Whipple, and the artist Thomas Ball at the house.[26]

But her friendship with Reid did not preclude serious disagreements with him. He offended her by denigrating women journalists during his visit to Newport in late September 1870 and, as she wrote him a few days later, "I began an editorial after you left, being stung by what you said of woman reporters." She also sketched a story she planned to write, a transparent critique of the male chauvinism she observed in the editorial offices of the *Tribune:*

> When I have a good digestion and a clear head and rest and time, I intend to write a story. The heroine a reporter. The hero an editor. The heroine shall fall in love with the editor. The editor shall fall in love with reporter but shall believe thoroughly in the miserable dogma that a woman lowers instead of elevates her womanhood by honest labor. Consequently the editor shall put away his best nature and marry a curled darling of Fifth Avenue whom he fancies realizes his ideal. The ideal shall open up an amount of well regulated falseness very startling to her husband, and the dénouement shall end with some sort of catastrophe (perhaps destruction by fire of editor's office) in which the editor's life is saved by the energy and magnanimous daring of the unwomanly reporter while the wife goes into the feminine swoon so indicated of the ideal character.[27]

Field never wrote the story, but this précis with its depiction of a heroic woman reporter reveals in silhouette the discrimination she suffered in all-male editorial offices and how a woman might enter that sanctum to rescue the men only in the event of a "catastrophe."

By September she had finished a draft of her Dickens lecture and, acting as her own booking agent, she had contracted to read it over a hundred times during the fall and winter.[28] It would become her signature lecture, the most popular lecture in her repertoire, one she delivered literally hundreds of times over the next quarter-century. Though she gleaned many biographical details from R. A. Hammond's *The Life and Writings of Charles Dickens* (1870), Field mostly reminisced about Dickens' performances in Boston and New York, how "he made a panorama of himself, turned an invisible crank and unwound an entire theatre." On a bare stage, without any changes of scenery or costume, "he presented a repertoire of one hundred characters" from his fiction. He championed the working reporters of London and international copyright; he assisted his friends; he wrote fiction that was true to life; and he drew women characters faithfully. Field also defended Dickens from the charges he was intemperate and irreligious, asserting that those theological fundamentalists "who represent him as the apostle of vice willfully pervert the lessons of his books." If he was a heathen, she avowed, "let us all be heathens—if we can!"[29] As innocuous as her argument may seem now, Field was sharply criticized by the Episcopal newspaper *Churchman* for rationalizing Dickens's failure to attend church regularly. Dickens's "silly eulogist" insulted "an intellectual profession" (i.e., the ministry) with "sentimental twaddle" in her speech, the paper editorialized.[30]

Field delivered the lecture for the first time at the Globe Theater in Boston on the afternoon of November 16 before an audience that included Whipple, James Fields, Henry Wadsworth Longfellow, and the humorist Petroleum V. Nasby.[31] Her performance exceeded expectations and reviewers from both Boston and New York were lavish in their praise the next day. Fields, Longfellow, "and the best people" in Boston "pronounced the thing 'tip top,'" she bragged to Reid.[32] She repeated the lecture at the Globe on November 27 and Newark on December 5 before delivering it at Association Hall in New York on December 6 and the Academy of Music in Philadelphia on December 8. Unfortunately, when Field asked Horace Greeley, the editor-in-chief of the *Tribune* and a faint-hearted friend of the woman's movement, to introduce her at her lecture in New York, he not only refused but replied with "a most outrageous message" that slurred all women lecturers and that Field believed merited "an apology. If I could once make up my mind that all men are rascals I should never get into difficulty. It is a lesson I have not yet fully learned."[33] To add insult to injury, the *Tribune* the next morning published a tepid notice of the lecture presumably written by Winter. "Her enunciation was scarcely distinct enough to be heard in all parts of the house," the reviewer complained.[34] Her lecture had been "a success," Field insisted to Reid the same day this notice appeared, "although had I not been there, and did I take my coloring from *The Tribune,* I should consider that lecture a failure and my voice a myth!"[35] More scholarly than "Woman in the Lyceum," less anecdotal than her Adirondacks lecture, Field's eulogistic "An Evening with Charles Dickens" was a reliable money-maker from the very beginning, especially each year around the holidays. She spoke before large audiences at the Fifth Avenue Theater in New York on Sunday evening, December 18, despite the proscription on Sabbath entertainments, and on Christmas Day, 1870. "I am very sorry not to be at home at Christmas," she wrote her mother, "but I must think of our business interests first."[36]

Increasingly inclined to sell her work to the highest bidder, she lamented the poor pay she received for her writings from the *Tribune* and other newspapers compared to the honoraria she was paid for her lectures. When, in December 1870, James Gordon Bennett, the editor of the *New York Herald,* offered Field fifty dollars per column to contribute to his paper, she was quick to solicit a counter-offer from Reid. "As Mr. Greeley, you say, dislikes me," she began, "it may be very unpleasant for you to receive offers of articles from me. Believe that I would not wittingly place you in a disagreeable situation, and I have no desire to contribute to *The Tribune* outside of the desire to write for a journal edited by yourself. A certain other paper gives me my own terms, and if *The Trib* does not want me, I can go over to the enemy and make money by the operation."[37] She was no longer a "penny-a-liner." In February 1871 she began to write book reviews for the *Herald*—among them, of C. V. Jamison's *Woven of Many Threads,* Elizabeth Stuart Phelps' *The Silent Partner,* and E. P. Whipple's *Success and Its Conditions*[38]—while between February and April of that year she submitted at least three articles to the *Tribune* that were declined.[39] On April 11, she bluntly asked Reid "whether *The Tribune* will begin to treat me as well" as Bennett's paper. She was increasingly offended by the editorial positions adopted by the newspaper as it drifted into the conservative camp, privately indicting it for supporting the president, whom she dismissed as "Universally Stupid Grant." She also complained that "Greeley and The Tribune should assert [that] a belief in Woman Suffrage is belief in Free Love. I can't understand it. Because adventurers take up Suffrage to win notoriety I don't see why you should denounce the honest believers in Woman's Suffrage. There never was a cause more badly managed, but that does not make the cause itself immoral."[40]

Field began 1871 with a lecture tour through New England and up-state New York, with dates in Providence, Manchester, Utica, Syracuse, Auburn, Rochester, and Buffalo. Reviews were generally favorable and audiences respectable—at least until she arrived in Buffalo, where Mark Twain resided during the brief period he co-owned and coedited the *Buffalo Express*. He did not suffer rivals gladly, especially those who wore crinoline. In early January, he had referred derisively to Field, albeit not by name, in a column for the *New York Tribune* as one "of the most courted lady-lecturers of the day" who "is soaring along on a lucrative notoriety nine-tenths of which is the result of industriously-supplied two-line per-sonal items telling how she wore her hair at Long Branch." On January 30, the day of her lecture in Buffalo, he was predictably nonplussed when he "stumbled in awkwardly & unexpectedly" on Field at a private home "& introduction followed." He attended her lecture at St. James Hall that evening, but he was not particularly impressed. His newspaper reported the next day that while Field's audience was unusually large the lecture it-self hardly deserved "as unstinted praise as we have found lavished" upon it "in many of our exchanges." As the editors of Mark Twain's letters add, he "may have written, or at least inspired these remarks, for he was con-sistently contemptuous of Kate Field's platform abilities." The same day, Twain derided Field, albeit again not by name, in a letter to the lecture agent James Redpath as one of the "ladies whose sudden rise into news-paper notice" had made her name "familiar in our mouths as household words." She "writes a smart little essay and reads it in a smart little way—without one touch of native or acquired eloquence."[41] If such a comment sounds like sour grapes, so be it: when Twain leveled such charges Field was a famous lecturer whose popularity rivaled his own. She received equal billing in advertisements with him as well as with such eminent speakers as Wendell Phillips and Henry Ward Beecher. For the record, too, Field's lecture in Buffalo was much more favorably reviewed in the rival *Buffalo Courier* than in the *Express*. According to its notice, Field, "a lady of most excellent sense, fine culture and pronounced critical ability," had spoken "eloquently of Dickens."

On her part, Field was no more impressed with the famous humorist than he with her. She wrote a friend that she had met Mark Twain in Buffalo. He is amusing but not inherently a gentleman I should say. He talks or rather drawls through his nose in an absurd manner but to marry such a voice or to connect such a voice with sentiment is to me incomprehensible. Yet this queer, original man with a disregard for things polite, has married a delicate little woman who thinks much of her upholstery and *will tolerate no smoking or drinking in her house!* He went to my lecture and I was somewhat curious to know what he thought of it, but all I heard was that he called me "an actress."[42]

Their paths would cross occasionally over the next decade. The better they became acquainted, the less they liked each other.

From Buffalo, Field launched a tour of the Midwest, with stops in Cleveland, Dayton, Columbus, Cincinnati, Indianapolis, Louisville—and then Ironton and Portsmouth, Ohio, on successive evenings in mid-February. ("Let not such rural precincts as Boston and New York outdo Ironton," the editor of its paper quipped.) Though she shoehorned dates in Chicago and her native St. Louis into her itinerary, most of her lectures in "the West" were in small cities and towns, such as Springfield and Bloomington, Illinois; Toledo, Sandusky, and Oberlin, Ohio; Titusville, Meadville, and Sharon, Pennsylvania. As she admitted six months later, "I never wish to repeat my lecture experiences in America. I loathe the life and the majority of the country audiences. I did it for money."[43] Nor did she ever revise her

4. Ad for lecture series, *Hartford Courant*, 25 October 1869, 3.

5. Kate Field in traveling clothes. Lawrence Hutton
Papers, Manuscripts Division, Princeton University
Library. Courtesy of Princeton University Library.

opinion. "I am simply staggered by the opaque stupidity of the average
villager," she told an interviewer in 1885. "In the small village ignorance
stalks on every corner in unblushing effrontery."[44] On this point, at least,
Mark Twain agreed. "A country audience is the difficult audience," he too
allowed. "A passage which it will approve with a ripple will bring a crash
in the city."[45] The western swing of her lecture tour exhausted her, by all
accounts. In Indianapolis in February, she admitted she was "somewhat
weary from travel" and "her mind was more or less disturbed by business
cares."[46] In Chicago, she wrote that she was "nearly dead with fatigue." She

had not slept "or changed my clothes for *two* nights" and had eaten "only one square meal in forty-eight hours. I earn my money."[47]

Back in Boston in March 1871, she earned a few more dollars contributing to the *Tribune,* especially for a review of the Boston premiere of *No Thoroughfare,* a play Dickens and Wilkie Collins wrote together. Reid admonished her not to "gush" over it, which only incensed Field the more: "I'd rather be accused of murder and arson. I *don't gush.* I honestly and *manfully* admire what is beautiful and I say so in strong language, giving my reasons for it." She asked Reid to pay her thirty dollars for the review, which ran a column and a half. "I want all the money I can scrape together," she explained.[48] She also finished yet another revision of *Pen Photographs.* Dramatically enlarged to 152 pages and published by Osgood, this third edition was even more successful, both critically and commercially, than the first two. The *New York Times* remarked that it was "one of the most attractive little books of its day" and was "written in a very witty and graceful style"; and the *New York Graphic* insisted that the "little book" was "indispensable to all who would study the great author in his personal relation to his writings!"[49] Field also volunteered to deliver her lecture on Dickens to benefit the North End Mission, one of Annie Fields' charities. The governor of Massachusetts, William Chaflin, introduced her at Horticultural Hall. But as Annie jotted in her diary on April 27, the day of the lecture, Kate was "looking worn and is getting sleepless, which is bad for her."[50] A month earlier, she had decided to spend the summer in Europe.[51] "My mother is ill, has been all winter," she revealed. "She must have a change, and I can devise nothing better than England."[52] In addition, she wanted to try out her Dickens lecture on English audiences; she hoped to secure British copyright on her Dickens book; and she also needed a rest.

Kate and her mother sailed from New York for England on May 17, 1871, aboard the Cunard steamer *Russia,* the same ship on which Dickens had returned to England three years before. They planned to be absent three or four months, and Kate expected to return with a new lecture or two for the fall season. En route, however, Eliza became ill with migraine headaches, nausea, and fever. The ship's doctor gave her opium on 23 May and she lapsed into a coma and died on Friday, May 26. The official cause of death was "brain fever," which might encompass literally dozens of maladies, from a stroke to encephalitis and cancer. "I can never forget those sweet features growing gradually more and more pinched," her daughter wrote, "but there was no agony on the face." Field was furious at the callousness of the crew and passengers—"there was laughing, talking and singing on deck"—as her mother lay dying. The ship's captain "never came near me," preferring to entertain "hearty, healthy, *wealthy* people, half of them young, stout men," at his table each evening. "From first to last Captain Cook never by visit or word expressed the slightest interest or sympathy in my mother's suffering or my grief. Not an officer, the kind doctor excepted, did his decent duty." No priest was on board to administer last rites. Nor was there "*a room fit for a hospital on board Cunarders.*" To her dismay, she learned that the bodies of steerage passengers who died en route were unceremoniously dumped overboard. She asked Whitelaw Reid to publicize her unpleasant experience with the Cunard line,[53] and Reid shared Field's letter with George W. Smalley, the London correspondent of the *Tribune*, who quoted it in the column he wrote on July 18.[54] Kate removed her mother's wedding ring and put it on her own left hand, where she wore it the rest of her life. "She was a faithful daughter, a loving sister, a devoted wife and mother, a loyal friend," Kate wrote privately. "She needs no prayers. Her soul is fit for Heaven." Eliza Field's body, embalmed "too late to retain the beauty," was returned to the United States on June 1 and buried next to her husband's in Cambridge, Massachusetts, on June 16. The Unitarian minister Cyrus A. Bartol, Field's friend from the Radical Club of Boston, officiated. On her part, Kate resolved to "go to London and do what my dear mother would have me do; try to take care of myself and show my love for her by endeavoring to overcome my faults."[55]

In the days immediately following her mother's death she was assisted by her friend W. J. Hennessy. He helped settle her into a room in the Aubrey House, Notting Hill.[56] She initially hoped that her aunt and uncle would join her in Europe, but Cordelia was afraid of sea-sickness and Milton planned to ship a stable of horses to New Orleans to race during the winter. "He loves me not less but horses more," as Kate grimly remarked.[57] She had at least one other friend in London to whom she might have turned in her extremity: Robert Browning. A few weeks earlier, Field had alerted Isa Blagden, who in turn informed Browning, that she was planning a trip to England. "I shall be glad to see Kate Field again: ten years will have played tricks with her, too, I fear," Browning replied to Blagden in late May.[58] They met again after nearly a decade when the poet visited Field to offer his condolences. "I am profoundly grieved at your misfortune, most sad misfortune: I shall not attempt to speak about it," he wrote her on June 5. "I should be very glad to know the time when you are most likely to be met with if I call."[59] He even offered to help her find a place to live.[60] A month later, however, he admitted to Blagden his relief that Field had not asked him for help. "I have seen next to nothing of Kate Field," who had "plunged into all sort of sight seeing" and "Women's Rights, Anti-Contagious-Disease agitation and so forth"—regrettably so, he insisted, "for I really like Kate Field and remember her kindness of old." Though she insisted, not for the last time, that "I was born to be an artist and not a reformer," Field threw herself into work as an escape from grief, and she was indignant at the "social and political rottenness here." In any event, Browning confessed he was "glad that Kate Field had no wrong notion of my indifference to her visit."[61] He need not have worried. Field was no longer an impressionable twenty-something. Nor, in truth, did she notice the snub. "Whenever I think of Robert Browning, I try to remember only the best he wrote and the best he did," she averred. "Browning in London is Browning less a poet than a man of the world. My pansy is for Browning of 'the woman country.'"[62]

After Eliza's death, Kate reconsidered her summer plans. Though she had saved $2,000 and carried a letter of credit from Milton Sanford for $2,000 more should she need it, she decided to work as much as rest. "You have said nothing about my sending any correspondence from Europe," she wrote Reid on June 11, "but ill as I am in body and mind, I see numerous things untouched by your people. Shall I ever take advantage of my opportunities?"[63] Between July 1871 and September 1872, Field published a series of eleven essays on British society and politics in the *Tribune*—and nothing, meanwhile, in the *Herald*. She repeatedly referred in these essays to Sir Charles Dilke, the "young and brave" radical MP from the Chelsea district with a "bright, fearless deportment" whom she befriended and who championed such causes as women's suffrage, the rights of labor, and the Republican movement. Such liberal topics were increasingly out of fashion at the *Tribune*. "The more I saw of Charles Dilke the better I liked him," she reminisced twenty years later. "He was an accomplished man of the world, with a keen appreciation of women. He believed thoroughly in their equality with men, and demanded the same laws for both sexes."[64] Richard Watson Gilder, the assistant editor of *Scribner's*, wrote Field about this time to commend her work: "I read your 'Tribune' letters with interest, and so do a great many people."[65] She read her Dickens lecture to "thirty critics" and a few invited friends, including Dilke, Fanny Kemble, and Frances Power Cobbe, at the Haymarket Theatre in London on July 23 "where it proved quite a hit," though she declined all invitations to deliver it in public.[66] She surrendered the lease on her house in Boston—"where I shall never live again."[67] She arranged for the third edition of her *Pen Photographs of Dickens* to be reprinted by Nicholas Trübner, who had published British editions of works by several other American writers, including Howells. It was hailed in *Every Saturday* as "a generous tribute from a large-hearted nation to the genius and nobility of nature of our great English novelist,"[68] and it sold out by early December despite the opposition of Chapman & Hall and Dickens' biographer John Forster.

After canceling all her lecture dates for the 1871–72 season in the United States, Field left in late July 1872 for the continent,[69] heading first to Paris and Hombourg les Bains, then Brussels, where she visited with Adelaide Phillipps, next Cologne, and finally the resort town of Ems, Germany.[70] Six weeks later, she was "one hundred percent better," the warm waters there "of great benefit to me."[71] "I drank twenty-six gallons of tepid water" and "took seventeen baths," but the town was "the stupidest place the imagination can conceive."[72] On September 9 she railed south with her old beau Albert Baldwin, who was at Schwalbach for his health. "Will this be tortured into a scandal?" she wondered. "I don't know what the world is made of." They dallied at Worms, Heidelberg, Baden-Baden, Strasbourg, Basel, and Lucerne, where they were joined by Lina Warren, her old friend from Newport days. The three of them lingered in Geneva, then continued to Vevey on Lake Geneva, where Field took the "grape cure" for three weeks[73] and where she was advised by doctors to linger another year or two in Europe and recuperate.[74] She traveled alone to Paris in mid-October, where she registered at the Hotel Chatham for a couple of weeks.[75] She had other plans than merely to rest and recover, however. She wanted to know the singer Pauline Garcia-Viadot and George Eliot, as she wrote from Vevey. "The latter has sent me some very kind messages and I shall meet her when I return to London. She was in the Country during the summer."[76] She returned to London on November 1 and took rooms at Half Moon Street in Piccadilly where she passed the winter—at least in part to renew her acquaintance with Eliot.

To be sure, Field waited to be asked to join Eliot's Sunday salon. "I stayed away from the Priory until invited," she recalled, "as I knew George Eliot shrank from strangers, and I had no reason to suppose that she would remember an American girl in Florence. Fortunately for me I was not forgotten, and when one foggy Sunday I entered her pleasant London drawing-room, she and Mr. Lewes warmly welcomed me." Every Sunday afternoon, "the cleverest men and women in London felt honored in being received by the quiet woman who sat by the fire with her back to the window and talked earnestly in almost a whisper, while Lewes pervaded the atmosphere, speaking first with one and then with another, always interesting and frequently brilliant, the ugliest of men who made you forget his pocked face and shaggy red hair in about fifteen minutes." Field became a fixture at the Priory on Sundays for the next several months. In early February 1872, Field wrote Reid that "George Eliot is polite to me."[77] In an undated note from this period, Lewes wrote Field that "We may be obliged to go out on Sunday, but shall be at home again a little after 4, if you think of again swelling the crowd; but I hope you will be in London on our return."[78] Field once reminisced about her visits "to George Eliot and George Lewes—she perhaps the cleverest woman living, and he a really brilliant man,"[79] and she later explained that Eliot "spends nearly all her time at home" and "is very affable, a brilliant conversationalist, and lives in a beautiful villa in North Bank, London. Every Sunday afternoon she receives her friends, among whom rank the most prominent literati and artistic people of the town. Her disposition is very lovable, and she is much liked," even though she is "the most retiring and bashful woman I ever saw. She is generally abstracted; always thinking, and her voice is no louder than a whisper." As to the exact nature of her relationship with Lewes, Field was indifferent. Asked if Eliot and Lewes were married, she replied in remarkably blunt terms, all the more surprising for the times: "It was none of my business, and I never asked. Frankly, I don't know." She also remembered that Lewes often "came to my rooms" at Half Moon Street "and delighted me with his conversation and advice, but she never came. She visited no one; all visited her."[80]

Field also crossed paths occasionally with Robert Browning, not that either of them sought the pleasure. Browning may have been the greatest living English poet, but only because his wife had died, in her view. In a wonderfully equivocal compliment, she once asked, "what can be more attractive to a cultivated person than a dinner with Robert Browning, whose conversation is as entertaining and varied as the museum at South Kensington?"[81] The poet invited her to dinner in mid-January 1872 and afterwards he wrote Blagden that she was "the same lively—and pretty— (for at first, no doubt under her recent misfortune, the prettiness was in abeyance,)—and liberal lady we used to like: she is probably primed and loaded with book-stuff about England, and perfectly ignorant of course." To his dismay, Field thought that English was ripe for revolution and "the *Commune* must cure these horrors" of social inequity. "She is sure I shall never go to America *now:* and upon my word, I incline to believe her!"[82]

Despite her increasingly hectic schedule, including singing lessons with Manuel Garcia (a former teacher of both Adelaide Phillipps and the opera star Jenny Lind), appointments with two physicians ("one for my throat and the other for nervous dyspepsia"), and work on behalf of republicanism, Field professed lethargy and indifference to her surroundings while she was still in mourning for her mother. "Nothing is pleasant to me," she wrote Reid on February 2, 1872. "I have been interested in nothing, and if any thing, become more and more indifferent. I have been to see no sights. I can't make up my mind to exert myself. I've not been to the tower [of London] even. I read the papers with ineffable disgust except when republican meetings are reported, and I heartily despise the English government." She privately predicted that the English monarchy would disappear within the next twenty years. "English society turns everything upside down and the sooner the revolution comes the better," she opined.[83] She grew very

6. Kate Field in mourning, 1871. Photograph by Charles
Reutlinger. Courtesy of the Library of Congress Prints
and Photographs Division, LC-USZ62-134817.

fond of Dilke, who, she reported, "is remarkably clear-headed—a marvel
in an Englishman." She met Tennyson, the poet laureate; Alfred Austin,
later poet laureate; George du Maurier; Lord Houghton; Wilkie Collins;
Herbert Spencer; and James Whistler. She also took a young German musician, Franz Hüffer, under her wing and, in June, she began to write a regular weekly column for the Paris *American Register* "because the editor has
begged me to help him and I am always too weak-minded to refuse."[84]

Before she returned to the United States, Field was determined to deliver her lecture on Dickens in order to gauge its appeal to British audiences.
"I want an English reputation to take the rank I desire," she admitted.[85] She

arranged to speak before a by-invitation-only audience in Willis's Rooms in the aristocratic neighborhood of St. James on Saturday, May 4, 1872. She invited Lewes to hear her and he replied with alacrity: "Ce que vous me demandez sort tout à fait de mes habitudes; par consequent (telle est la logique humaine!) I shall be there 'or perish in the attempt.'"[86] On the other hand, Browning declined the invitation on the grounds he had a previous engagement—as did his sister.[87] In the end, Field addressed a crowd of between one and two hundred "literary and political celebrities" that included Lewes; Ellen Tree (aka Kean); Robert Schenck, U.S. minister to the Court of St. James; Charles G. Leland (aka "Hans Breitmann"); the painter Hennessy; the ballerina Marie Taglioni; the Irish politician, novelist, and historian Justin McCarthy; the novelist William Black; and Garcia, who accompanied her on the piano when she sang. The lecture was a rousing success, according to the London *Daily News* ("a hearty, simple, and grateful tribute to the merits of a great man"), the London *Times* ("her manner pleasing and self-possessed"), and the *Examiner* ("a bright and attractive lecture").[88] Smalley reported in his London letter for the *Tribune* that Field "might undoubtedly have won a brilliant success in England either as a lecturer" or musical entertainer, and the London correspondent of the *Boston Globe* added that Field said "innumerable pertinent and witty things with unbroken spontaneity of expression."[89] Field referred to this experience in after years as "a revolution" in her life. Lewes and others urged her "to become an actress," and she "determined to follow the bent of my inclination."[90] Louise Chandler Moulton soon reported in the *New York Tribune* that while "the English hate being lectured to" they "went to hear our bonny Kate." Lewes, "the most awful critic in all London, was so delighted with her rendering of her Dickens lecture as to tell her she could make a fortune upon the stage. Mrs. Kean expressed the same opinion, and said that, at least, with such a voice Miss Field ought to recite."[91] On May 21, as she and Lewes were packing to leave London for the summer, George Eliot wrote Field to express her regret, not that she had missed her Dickens lecture exactly, but that she had not "seen you oftener. I was placidly looking forward to your staying in England another year or more. . . . Mr. Lewes adds his hearty wishes to mine that your future may be a bright one. We trust that your visit to England has been at least a good seedtime in your experience, and you are young enough to make each sowing all-important." Though Field later claimed that she had saved "several letters" from Eliot,[92] this is the only one that survives.

The very next day, moreover, she delivered the reply to the toast to "The Ladies" at the fourth biennial festival of the London Hospital for Throat Diseases at Willis's Rooms, and her speech was a redacted version of her old lecture on "Woman in the Lyceum."[93] Smalley reported in his "London Letter" to the *New York Tribune* that Field was already writing a new lecture for the winter season entitled "The England of Today,"[94] and she had recently traveled to Coventry, Kenilworth, and Warwick Castle—virtually her only sight-seeing during all the months she was abroad—in order to see more of the people and the countryside. With her recovery from depression and fatigue, Field had decided to return to the United States in early August. Her uncle had been urging her to return for weeks because she was running out of money—both her $2,000 savings and his $2,000 loan—but she resisted his suggestion. "I have been overworked all my life," she replied. "All that I could do for myself last summer I did do. I am better, but I am far from well. Both physicians say that in justice to myself I ought to try Ems again." Field returned to Paris in early June, where she renewed her acquaintance with Ristori,[95] and then departed for Ems a week later where, as she complained to Reid, "I am again boring myself," though she once more found the warm springs there therapeutic. She celebrated Independence Day with fifteen other Americans at the Hôtel d'Angleterre in Ems, and though she still considered the resort "a hole,"[96] the occasion was "the pleasantest Fourth of July I ever passed." The comic actor W. J. Florence presided over the festivities, which included impromptu speeches by Field and others and a "toothsome" bill of fare of "Potage républicain," "Salade de Baltimore," "Compôtes d'Horace Greeley," and "Glaces au Grant" for dessert.[97] She returned to Paris by way of Cologne on the night train, crossed the Channel to London, and sailed for the United States on August 6. She arrived at Edna Villa in Newport eleven days later after a fifteen-month absence from the country.[98]

It was not a pleasant homecoming, however. Cordelia Sanford was beginning to suffer from the mental illness that would afflict her for the rest of her life. "My aunt is in a very wretched state of health and I am very, very anxious," Field wrote Reid soon after her return. Aunt Corda was often irrational and jealous, sometimes accusing her niece of wanting to injure her. In mid-October, Milton Sanford finally asked Field to leave Newport and "my aunt as soon as possible. I shall move God knows where in a day or two." Within only sixteen months her mother had died and she had been effectively sent packing by the couple who had helped raise her. "My engagements are few, my lecture not written, and I begin life unexpectedly with a few hundred dollars in cash," she conceded to Reid. "You said you were tired. I am tired enough to commit suicide."[99]

6

"Free Lance"

FIELD RENTED A ROOM at the Everett House in New York while she planned her next move. Before leaving Newport she had consulted James Gordon Bennett, a Newport habitué, who renewed his offer of a job with the *New York Herald*. He made "no special proposition" but Field expressed an interest in writing "an independent column in Sunday's paper (headed Independent Column and signed Free Lance or something of the sort) in which the week shall be reviewed exactly as *I* please, totally regardless of the regularly expressed opinion of the paper." Bennett "would be inclined to pay handsomely" for such a feature, she speculated.[1] They reached an agreement in November 1872, and Field broke the news that henceforth she would be dividing her allegiance between the *Tribune* and the *Herald:* "I've had a fine offer here and have accepted it (for writing) and postpone lecturing until the universe is in a listening mood."[2] Her allegiance was not equally divided, however. While she continued to sign her initials to articles in the *Tribune,* she signed her pieces in the *Herald* with the mascu-line-inflected pseudonym "Free Lance" (e.g., "Free Lance Has a Tilt with His Critics") as she had suggested. She maintained pleasant relations with Reid despite her work for the rival newspaper. When Greeley died on November 29, Reid asked her to attend his funeral as a member of the Editorial Department of the *Tribune,* along with Winter, Ripley, E. C. Stedman, Rebecca Harding Davis, and Noah Brooks.[3] Three days after Christmas, she was invited to attend a banquet at Delmonico's on Broadway to celebrate Reid's ascension to the chair of editor-in-chief, and she declaimed a poem in his honor that she had composed for the occasion.[4] For the most part, Field's contributions to the *Tribune* over the next few months were unremarkable—for example, features on all five of the New York winter charity balls, a note on P. T. Barnum's circus, a proposal to provide professional medical training to all nurses, and a review of the horse-racing season entitled "The Turf" written to appease her uncle.[5] Several of these items appeared as letters to the editor, and for them she likely received little or no money.

Through her affiliation with the *New York Tribune* Field also enlarged her circle of friends. She met John Hay, the former private secretary to Abraham Lincoln and future U.S. secretary of state who had joined the editorial staff of the newspaper in 1870. She heard Hay lecture on "The Heroic Age in Washington" on January 13, 1873, at Steinway Hall in New York. A day or two after Hay's lecture, Field wrote to congratulate him (her notes on his lecture were "in the top-right hand drawer of my secretary") and to invite him to her home for dinner on February 27 with Bret Harte, who began to contribute to the *Tribune* three months later.[6] She moved in the same social set as the poet William Cullen Bryant; the author Hjalmar Hjorth Boyesen; soldier and diplomat Samuel H. M. Byers; the novelist Ann S. Stephens; and former secretary of the treasury Hugh McCullough.[7]

Meanwhile, "Free Lance" became a prolific and well-paid contributor to the *Herald*. Between June 1873 and July 1874, by her own count, Field wrote a total of fifty-seven articles,[8] most of them for the *Herald*. She courted controversy by scorning opera performed by undistinguished European artists ("Shall we continue to pay first class prices for third rate performances?"), punishing Edwin Forrest for his misinterpretations of Shakespeare ("queer is Mr. Forrest's conception of Hamlet") and Christine Nilsson for her lack of talent ("when Miss Neilson becomes most tragic she is cross-eyed"), and ridiculing the majority of lecturers in America ("not only are we deluged with the drivel of our own gifted land of gab, but England is sending us all the mediocrity she can conveniently spare").[9] She wrote an unknown number of editorials for the paper published without signature, such as her condemnation of the respectable citizens of New York who tolerated prostitution and other crimes ("The Carnival of Vice—Shall Law Be Leagued with It?")[10] and commentary on corruption in the city park commission. She refused to join the staff of the *Herald* and draw a regular salary, however, because, as she had told

7. Field lecture bureau publicity photo, fall 1872.
Courtesy of Boston Public Library.

Reid two years before, "I can't be salaried" because "I won't write what I don't believe."[11] With her income from journalism, an estimated $5,000 a year,[12] Field rented a house in November at 23 Gramercy Park South and postponed her lecturing. Louise Chandler Moulton announced in her *Tribune* column that "Miss Field will be unable to lecture in the West, at all, this season; and will be even be obliged to curtail the number of her engagements in the East. But, after the Presidential election is over, she will deliver, in various places, a lecture on 'The England of Today'" resplendent in gowns by the French fashion designer Frederick Worth.[13] Field was rumored in December 1872 to be writing a new lecture on "English History and Life,"[14] but in fact she did not speak publicly in any venue or on any topic until early in the new year, when she returned to Michigan and Ohio to talk about Dickens.

In spring 1873 Field published her best-selling travelogue *Hap-Hazard,* which collected pieces originally written for the *New York Tribune* and the Paris *American Register* the previous spring, including "Opening of Parliament," "Republicanism in England," and "The Thanksgiving Service." Moulton hailed the book as "one of the brightest, freshest, breeziest books of the season. . . . It is as unaffected and piquant as the talk of the wittiest woman; and why should it not be, since one of the wittiest women of her time wrote it?"[15] It was almost universally commended by such newspapers as the *Woman's Journal* ("a compound of Mark Twain, John Hay and Bret Harte"), the *New York Evening Mail* ("bright, snappy, and readable"), the *Boston Globe* ("irrepressible"), the *Overland Monthly* ("flippant, piquant, and declamatory"), and the *Christian Union* ("it is impossible for Kate Field to be dull").[16] With the publication of *Hap-Hazard* Field reached the apex of her fame as a journalist and travel writer, and Dilke described her from across the Atlantic as "a slightly outrageous person"—and one of his best friends.[17] More than almost any other American woman of her generation, she was adept at self-promotion. As one of her friends later remarked, "she understands the art of advertising as no other woman I have ever known understands it, and she knows that a star without satellites is only a star, and Kate's ambition was to figure as a constellation always in the zenith."[18]

Field renewed her acquaintances with Dilke, Robert Browning, and Mark Twain in June when Reid gave her another enviable assignment: to cover the visit of the Shah of Persia to England for the *New York Tribune.* Ironically, Twain covered the event for the *New York Herald.* She had hoped to summer in Newport in 1873,[19] but she visited her aunt and uncle there for only a few days before her departure because Cornelia Riddle Sanford's health was failing. She had suffered a stroke and a severe fall and, as Field later remarked, her aunt "was never the same."[20]

En route to England aboard the *Donau* on June 1, Field interviewed the eminent Russian pianist Anton Rubinstein, her seasick fellow passenger:

> He is seated at my left, and looks like the remains of former greatness. He is in a state of eclipse, and I am heathen enough to rejoice, for at sea misery likes company. I derive inexpressible comfort in beholding genius

reduced to my own level. The sea is democratic in its tendencies; it is no respecter of persons, else it would spare the great pianist who has done so much to elevate the musical standard in America, and whose great objection to our country is that it is 3,000 watery miles from Europe.[21]

Field landed at Southampton on June 4 and immediately railed to London, where she consorted with Dilke and his wife for the duration of her stay.

Less than a week later, Field and the Dilkes invited Twain and his wife to dinner, and Twain graciously accepted the invitation even while failing to acknowledge they had met before: "Dear Miss Field: I see that it isn't your fault that you do not know me, & I'm sure it isn't mine that I do not know you. Plainly, then, the party to blame is Providence, & therefore damages cannot be had in this vale. But we shall be glad to see & know you & likewise Lady Dilke." The couple dined with Field, the Dilkes, and other guests on June 22.[22] Field reported in her letter to the *Tribune* on June 24 that the dinner had lasted until well after midnight and that she had enjoyed the company of "an American by the singular name of Mark Twain" who was "endeavoring to instil civilization into the Shah by sitting on the floor and playing draw poker" with him. According to Field's report, Twain claimed "his august pupil makes wonderful progress in this great American game."[23] On his part, Twain never mentioned Field in any of his dispatches to the *Herald,* and she was conspicuously absent from other entertainments to which men only were invited. When Anthony Trollope hosted a dinner in honor of Joaquin Miller, he teased Field that "[t]wo of the wildest of your countrymen, Joaquin Miller & Mark Twain, dine with me at my club next week. Pity you have not yet established the rights of your sex or you could come and meet them, and be *as jolly as men.*"[24] Her response to the rebuff, if any, has not survived.

But she exacted revenge on Browning. When the poet invited her to hear him declaim one of his new poems prior to its publication, she privately belittled his recitation and left the party early:

> Once Robert Browning read "White Cotton Night Cap Country" to an audience of two, Lady ____ and myself. He divided the poem in twain. At the second reading the audience was reduced one-half; Lady ____ had

the poet all to herself. The monotony and hardness of Robert Browning's voice was more than my ears could endure a second time for an hour and a half. It is a mistake, it seems to me, for men and women great in one profession to attempt what demands greatness in another.[25]

Browning "killed a fine dramatic fact," she added in her diary.[26] Still, through her association with Browning, Field befriended the novelist Wilkie Collins in June 1873. "I have heard of the American lady—she is adored by everybody," Collins wrote Browning in accepting a dinner invitation where they met, "and I am all ready to follow the general example."[27]

Field's eight dispatches to the *Tribune* about the shah's visit to England were nearly as well received as her notices of Dickens' readings six years earlier. Certainly the articles she filed with the *Tribune* were more popular than the articles Twain sent the *Herald,* which were not exhumed from the morgue of the paper and reprinted until 1923. As Reid wrote Field on July 17, "You do not need to be told that most of the stuff he has done for the *Herald* is very poor, because you have seen it. It won't hurt you to know that your letters, on the other hand, have received more praise than any you ever wrote for us before."[28] In late June, Field traveled from London to Southsea to observe the queen and the shah as they reviewed a flotilla of English ships off the coast of Spithead, and she excoriated English pretension in her report:

> Here ordinary folk are called "persons," and royal folk are called "personages." I like these distinctions. They keep classes apart and foster that noblest of all traits, flunkeyism. I like to see journalists pandering to this sort of thing by publicly writing up what they privately ridicule and despise. It proves the nobility of English journalism and how little its professors merit the contempt with which they are regarded by the "personages" about whom their pens cringe and lie.[29]

Obviously, Field did not gladly suffer fools any more than Twain did rivals.

Her report "The Shah at Windsor," filed from London on June 27 and published on July 14, epitomizes the irreverence and the conversational tone of her satirical reports to the *Tribune.* Invited to accompany an MP "to

see Her Majesty's troops dance before the King of Kings" at Windsor, she
readily accepts:

> Of course I would [go]. Am I not a child of nature? Is not my home among
> the howling savages of an unlicked, untutored world, and is it not my duty
> to improve my opportunities and my manners by beholding Shahs and
> Queens? What we republicans need is the polish acquired by association
> with the "ruling families of the earth." Feeling this great want, I accepted
> the invitation with alacrity. All that I had heard of the Shah had endeared
> me to him. I can conceive of no greater pleasure than sitting beside him
> at table and receiving the contents of his plate, thrown lavishly up and
> down the inviting skirt of one of Worth's immaculate dresses.

Field's scathing satire of the shah's table manners is again reminiscent
of Twain's burlesque of all things foreign in *The Innocents Abroad*. Rumor
had it that, while eating cherries at a state dinner, the shah was unsure how
to dispose of the pits.

> At first he put them into his wine-glasses, but, after filling them up, be-
> came ashamed of the ever-increasing quantity, and, to make matters
> better, threw all upon the waxed floor. Victoria preserved her royal coun-
> tenance. The remainder of the lookers-on "tittered." "I don't object to
> the Shah's visit," said the Princess of Wales, when first informed of his
> coming. "It will be very amusing." She was quite right, but on the whole
> wouldn't a monkey from the "Zoo" be more so?[30]

While such remarks may betray Field's ethnocentrism, they are of a piece
with Twain's humor.

When she presumed to promote the Republican movement in England
at the expense of the aristocracy, however, Field incurred the wrath of more
than one newspaper editor back in the States. In her final letter from England for the *Tribune*, entitled "Royal Betrothals," she lampooned the Duke
of Edinburgh and the toadyism of his subjects. In her ridicule of social
conventions, she apparently overstepped the bounds of feminine breeding
and good taste. According to the *Brooklyn Eagle*, Field "has either fallen on
evil associations in England" (i.e., such Republican leaders as Dilke and

Charles Bradlaugh) or she has "dispensed with that sixth sense of propriety which is a constant monitor to most of her sex, and to none of them more than to those engaged in literary work." Field "and her kind" display the same "servility" toward "what they most expansively call the people" as the nobility display "toward the throne folk." A "man who flatters a Prince and a woman who flatters a mob" are "snobbish both. Miss Field, through the perverted and exaggerated perspective she indulges, seems to imagine that Republicanism in England is the cause of the people" whereas the Republican leaders are "demagogues of impurest ray obscene."[31] Similarly, the *Rondout Freeman* editorialized that Field's journalism exemplified "something which is fast assuming the outlines of a fact. That is that women as newspaper correspondents either fall into vapid inanity or run into a wretched imitation of what they seem to think is noble and leonine masculinity. Masculinity in a man is the aggregation of all commendable traits; in a woman it is the prolific seed bed of all verbal vulgarity."[32]

After Adelaide Phillipps joined Field in late July, they retreated to Goodwood near Arundel on the southern coast of England for a few days.[33] On July 31, they crossed the Channel to Paris, then to Bordeaux, before continuing to the northern Pyrenees. Field's "energy is unconquerable," Smalley testified in his London column for the *Tribune*.[34] In early September, after Phillipps returned to England, and after "walking about on the top of the Pyrenees with a glass of lukewarm water in one hand and an umbrella in the other" for six weeks, Field decided to travel to Madrid to interview Emilio Castalar, the leader of the Spanish Republic. On September 15 she left for Biarritz.[35] To reach Madrid, she had to cross the battle lines established by the Carlists or monarchists who were mounting a civil war against the Republic. "I would go to Spain and see Castelar," she insisted. "I would look a Carlist in the face, and ask him what century he was living in." She was not on assignment for the *Tribune*, however; she was "not sent on a mission by a Great Moral Organ; I was not clothed in the garb of an interviewer."[36] Rather, she embarked on impulse—and she was one of the few journalists permitted to cross both frontiers during the insurrection.

The nine essays Field published in the *Tribune* about her trip to Spain comprise, in effect, what today would be called a nonfiction novel. She invented a character loosely based on her courier and called him "the

Blinker." Field's Spain letters are unique in her career because they are not technically daily journalism, but polished essays written months after the events they purport to describe. As she recounted the trip, she railed with "the Blinker" to St. Jean de Luz, where they caught a tramp steamer for Santander on September 19. "If, as Ruskin maintains," she reported, "dirt be an element of the picturesque, *The Four Friends* would have thrilled him with delight."[37] From Santander they caught a train for Madrid, where Field registered at the Hotel de Paris at the Puerta del Sol. On her first afternoon in the capital she went to a bullfight attended by fourteen thousand other spectators and took notes for a graphic account of the event she would eventually write for the *Tribune*. "There are many variations" to the fight, she noted, "but the theme never varies, and before the act closed six horses lay stark and stiff."[38]

In the afternoon of September 23, after two days of waiting to be summoned and armed with a letter of introduction from the American Embassy, Field interviewed the "exceedingly amiable" president of the first Spanish Republic in his private apartment in Madrid. However much she admired him, she was disappointed by his comments on the issue of Spanish oppression in Cuba.

"But how is it, Señor Castelar," I asked, "that you, who throughout your public career have asserted the right to self-government, should persist in holding Cuba in spite of having buried 80,000 soldiers and a vast amount of treasure?" "Ah, I see that you do not sympathize with Spain in this matter." "Most decidedly not. I believe in Cuba Libre." Castelar looked at me. He would not argue because he could not. No man cares to eat his own words. No diet is more indigestible. "My two great ideas whose worship I shall never renounce are liberty and country," wrote Castelar in *Old Rome and New Italy*. Said he to me, quietly: "I am first a Spaniard, and then a Republican." . . . In the Spring, Castelar was out of office; in the Autumn he was dictator. I know in what a difficult position he is placed; I know that justice to Cuba means signing his own political death warrant; for all that Castelar stultifies himself. . . . In betraying the dream of his youth, Castelar makes a fearful mistake, which in exile he will rue. The Spanish Republic is not worth founding if it can only exist at the expense of colonial despotism.[39]

Field was prescient: the Republic was overthrown a few months later in a military coup.

After interviewing Castelar, Field spent successive days in San Lorenzo del Escorial inspecting the palace and monastery there ("five long hours I wandered over the great, yellow barren, gloomy building") and Toledo. "If I lived in Toledo I should go mad," she reminisced later. "The conjunction of so much history, so much live art and so much dead nature would set my brain on fire with conundrums. There is nothing more tragic than living among great things and little people." On September 28, Field caught an omnibus to Pamplona in the Carlist region of Spain, where "telegraph wires dragged upon the ground, railroad bridges were blown up, and solitary stations were torn inside out."[40] The next day she reached Bayonne, just across the French border. "I am safely through the Carlist lines," she wrote her aunt, "and in two days shall be in Paris."[41] She arrived in England a few days later and sailed for New York aboard the *Mosel* on October 15.[42]

Back home, she began to write the series of essays soon published in the *Tribune* under the title "Ten Days in Spain." They were nearly as popular as her reports on Dickens and the shah. Louise Chandler Moulton praised them without stint: the narrative, she wrote, "not only illustrates the mishaps and mistakes of travel with the light of the kindliest and brightest humor, but it is also full of sagacious observation."[43] Her Newport friend James Parton, a popular biographer and the husband of the late Sara Payson Willis Parton (aka Fanny Fern), wrote to her, "I wonder if you know how welcome to readers of 'The Tribune' are your initials and all that goes before them. . . . All your letters from Europe last year,—your Spanish, especially, . . . delighted me, and I feel grateful to you for them. I hope you will regularly join 'The Tribune' as its writing-whenever-you-feel-like-it-correspondent, at a salary that will cheer and not inebriate you." Edward Increase Mather later noted that Field's "foreign letters to the *Tribune* discussed questions of political significance and international interest."[44] For the next Christmas season, Field collected her Spain letters into a volume published by Osgood & Company and it became one of her most popular books, passing through four editions. Moulton declared it "brilliant and vivacious" in her column in the *Tribune,* and the *Boston Transcript* concurred that it was "lively" and "amusing." The poet Charles Warren Stoddard wrote her that the book was "delicious beyond expression."[45]

When Charles Bradlaugh (aka "beast Bradlaugh") came to the United States in late 1873 to raise money for the cause of English Republicanism, Field heralded his arrival with a biographical sketch of him. They had been friends for several months, and Smalley had allowed in his London correspondence for the *Tribune* that Field knew Bradlaugh "much better than I do, and is going to tell you someday what she thinks of him."[46] She began her sketch with a reminiscence of Bradlaugh when he dined with her in London. He joked she would need to have her apartment "fumigated" because "by good English people I am called the devil." In her sketch of his life, Field hailed the orator as "a man of the people" and an "indefatigable radical" on such issues as trade unionism, birth control, women's suffrage, and Irish Home Rule. More than any other Englishman, Bradlaugh made Trafalgar Square and Hyde Park centers of republican activity.[47] The essay appeared in the *Cincinnati Commercial*, moreover, edited by Murat Halstead, whom Field had befriended during her lecture in the Ohio city in February 1871.[48] Between late August and early November 1874, moreover, she published a nine-part retrospective series entitled "Republican Notes on England" in the *St. Louis Republican* in which she endorsed the movement in all its iterations. "Today, for the first time in England's history," she declared, "the working class is personally represented in parliament."[49]

In the spring of 1874, Field made at once the bravest and most foolhardy decision of her life. Despite her past successes as a writer and lecturer, with no formal training and no experience apart from private theatricals, she had long aspired to be an actor. "The one desire of my childhood," she recalled, "was to go upon the stage. It was a natural instinct, inherited from my parents. Circumstances [that is, the injury to her voice in Florence] prevented the consummation of my desire."[50] "I shall write as much as ever," she explained, but "I don't believe in literature as a profession, and never did. Literature is a charming mistress, but a terrible master. It requires much more physique to endure the strain of writing seven columns a week, the number I have often turned off, than to act nightly; yet the pecuniary reward is a tolerable living in the first case and a fortune in the second. My blood boils when I think of the many brilliant men and women who are struggling for a competency, while the successful singer and actor are showered with gold. If I had my way, journalists should be paid better than any other professional men and women."[51] Or as she would write E. C. Stedman, "Oh, how I loathe journalism! More and more I long to be out of it. To write for a living is hell—to write for love is heaven. At present, I'm in hell." Moreover, she added, "lecturing is probably the most miserable business that any woman ever engaged in." She had "merely lectured to make money," but now "lecturing has been overdone and no longer pays."[52]

She took the first steps toward a stage career by reciting Thomas Hood's "The Bridge of Sighs" at a benefit for her former manager Henry McGlennen at the Boston Theater on May 27 and declaiming Bulwer's translation of Friedrich Schiller's poem "The Song of the Bell" at the Summer Garden Hall in Central Park on June 25. Moulton declared the Boston recitation "very emotional, finely conceived, and well executed," though she did not "venture to predict" from the reading of a single poem what Field "would be likely to accomplish as an actress." Moulton added that Field wore "an immoral gown" to the reading—"immoral because it was so handsome as to tempt to wicked envy all her suffering sisters who have never crossed the seas to Paris or seen the face of King Worth. It was a black miracle of silk and velvet, suiting in hue her somber theme."[53] Field's New York performance, however, was not so well received. "I don't regret [my] Central Park reading a bit," she wrote Stedman." My enemies have had a chance to say their worst (which they have done with effusion)." The hall was crowded with over three thousand people, the windows and doors were open for ventilation, and the acoustics were miserable. Field read the poem "under such serious disadvantages" that her voice was "lost to nine-tenths of those present."[54]

Winter of the *Tribune* was underwhelmed too—a response that foreshadowed his subsequent reviews of her acting. He praised Field's "fervor and her grace" but allowed that as "a piece of elocution it was ineffective to auditors at a distance. . . . It would not be possible to draw any positive inference, as to Miss Field's powers as an actress from her performance upon this occasion."[55] Field tolerated, perhaps even appreciated, this criticism, at least initially. She wrote Winter a "kind little note" when his review appeared, and Winter replied that it was

> exceedingly welcome. I was feeling sad and anxious lest my words had given you pain. You went through that ordeal bravely and with great credit, and I should have been false to truth as well as to friendship if I had omitted to recognize your victory. The difficulty in writing was that I had to be exact as to the facts, without wounding your feelings, and kind to a dear friend and comrade, without making her appear to be the pet of the *Tribune;* and the record had to be made off-hand. I am much relieved to know that it seemed right in your eyes.[56]

Unfortunately, the matter did not end there.

Field spent months trying to select a play and place for her professional theatrical début, though both Winter and Reid repeatedly tried to dissuade her from the experiment. She briefly considered a premiere in Chicago on November 2, 1874, though she finally decided to open in New York, the theatrical capital of the world. She heard that a dramatic version of Nathaniel Hawthorne's *The Scarlet Letter* might be available in French translation and thought she might "be able to do something with it—adapting it if it be bad."[57] Bad it was. So she completed her own dramatization of the romance, a draft of which Osgood & Company copyrighted in her name.[58] This script was not satisfactory either, however, and it is now lost. Finally, she asked the impresario Augustin Daly to manage her coming out, and he selected both the role, Peg Woffington in Tom Taylor's adaptation of Charles Reade's novel *Masks and Faces,* and the venue, Booth's Theater on Broadway. On her part, Field conceded that she would have preferred to début in New York as Rosalind in Shakespeare's *As You Like It* and that she agreed to appear at Booth's "not because I liked it, but because it was the only opportunity that offered."[59] The producer Lester Wallack observed one of her rehearsals and reportedly told her that "she had ability."[60] Under Daly's supervision, Field opened in the play on November 14, 1874. Winter, Reid, Stedman, Ripley, Hay, Richard Henry Stoddard, future president Chester A. Arthur, Julius Henri Browne, Mary Mapes Dodge, and Charles A. Dana were all in attendance. "The house was not papered" with complimentary tickets, she later insisted. "There was $1000 in money and

I made several hundred."[61] Still, by her own admission she was paralyzed with stage fright before the performance and "it was not until the second act" that she gained enough self-control "to carry out her conception of the role."[62] To judge from the applause, Field's début was a remarkable success. She was welcomed by the audience upon her first entrance on stage, called before the footlights after the first scene, and in the second act, after she had sung a song and danced a jig, she was again called out for an encore and "almost buried in flowers." She also received an ovation at the end of the play.[63] Reid wrote her a short note the next morning to congratulate her "with all my heart. . . . you did not fail."[64]

The critics were not so kind, however. Field later rationalized that "they all went to see me fail and not doing so made them mad."[65] The *New York Clipper,* a theatrical weekly, concluded that Field "was completely over-weighted by the character assumed," and the *New York Times* was even more harsh: "Unhappily Miss Kate Field is neither young nor handsome; her voice is inexpressive, and the frailty of her physique makes the acquisition of power in the future at least improbable." Field's age raised a red flag for some critics, as if no woman could become an accomplished actor who did not begin her theatrical training while still in short dresses. The New York correspondent of the *Boston Transcript,* for example, sniffed that he had "little faith in the success of any woman as an actress who commences to study for the stage after she is thirty years of age," and the *Baltimore American* averred that "were she younger" Field might have eventually succeeded on the boards. In panning her performance, the *New York World* suggested that "we seem to be looking at the bouncing wench through the wrong end of a lorgnette." Both the *Clipper* ("injudiciously applauded") and the *Times* ("the lady may have honestly thought . . . that her success on the stage was real") dismissed her warm welcome by the audience as nothing more than the pity of friends. The *New York Evening Post,* in fact, asserted that despite the applause "the performance was felt by Miss Field's best friends to be a failure." Even her friends at the *New York Graphic* suggested that the performance might be regarded as a success only because "everybody expected a dead failure."[66] Worst of all, Field miscalculated the response of her friends on the *Tribune.* She presumed that Winter would review her performance favorably and, if not, that Reid would kill the article. Neither happened.

Winter praised Field's acting with faint damns. He applauded the "courageous effort of a brilliant and worthily ambitious comrade," and he asserted that "[n]o novice has appeared on the New-York stage under better auspices, and none has accomplished more, at the outset, to satisfy the anticipations of friendship, if not to meet the requirements of dramatic art." But, he added, "If Miss Field possesses the faculty for acting (and possibly she does, for she is descended from an ancestry of players), she did not largely display it upon this occasion." Most damningly, Winter compared Field, a "slight, fragile, gray-eyed New England woman, of an intellectual and not a sensuous aspect," to a wax figure adorned in white muslin.[67] Field regarded this review as nothing less than a personal betrayal. "The article in *The Tribune* almost killed me," she wrote Stedman. "I expected more generous treatment. Is Whitelaw Reid in sympathy with it? If so, what did his note to me mean? Ah, noble friend, the world is hard and I want to be out of it more than ever. I hoped to get away from myself in acting, but these attacks make me desire to bury myself. What a mistake that I was ever born!" In an interview, she complained that "a drama critic, an old friend, who, after all, does not seem to know me, stated that I am 'a New England girl of frail physique.'" Needless to say, Field disputed the characterization. She was neither a native New Englander nor frail: "I outwalk all the woman of my acquaintance, can pull a pair of eight-foot scull to the satisfaction of good male rowers."[68] She alleged a conspiracy among the New York newspapers to humble or humiliate her, though the accusation hardly held water given that, as a Baltimore reporter noted, the *Tribune* had "always been her 'organ'" and the paper hewed to the same critical line as the others.[69] She argued that theatrical critics should not be admitted to the performances of a debutante "for at least a week," whereupon one wag asked, "When should the confiding public be admitted?"[70]

The hostile reviews doomed the production. It closed after only two performances, though Field believed that "if my brothers of the quill had witnessed my second appearance they would have put less vinegar in the ink." She blamed the *Tribune* for its failure, one of the most humiliating experiences of her life. If Reid "does not let me have justice in *The Tribune*," she wrote Stedman, "he is not my friend. I shall not write to him. If you choose to tell him, I am willing."[71] As requested, Stedman wrote a letter to the editor of the *Tribune,* published on November 18, in defense of Field. He thought the "close attention and intelligent applause" the audience gave the debutante indicated her performance was "an unusual success" and he had "nothing to disturb my illusion until I read some of the morning papers."[72] Despite her avowed intention not to contact Reid, moreover, Field wrote him two weeks later to protest Winter's review. Her letter does not survive, but its substance may be inferred from his reply: "You say that I have stabbed you to the heart by writing you an opinion about your appearance on the stage and allowing the publication of another; that, in my place, you would have been burnt alive before printing 'The Tribune's' notice." Reid reminded her that, "in common with most of your friends," he had tried to dissuade her from her experiment "and that after your appearance at Thomas's Garden [in Central Park], in answer to your frank question, I said with equal frankness what true friendship required, that you had not shown a spark of dramatic power." Reid insisted the notice in the *Tribune* was consistent with his advice. In any event, if he had "changed the tone of Mr. Winter's criticism" he would be "as despicable as you describe me" for censoring the opinion of "a most capable, friendly, and conscientious critic" to spare the feelings of a friend.[73] In the end, of course, Winter and Reid pulled no punches, the same standard Field famously observed in her own dramatic criticism. Her friendships with Reid and Winter would never recover.

Field was chastened but not crushed by her failure. In early December, John T. Raymond, who was starring as Colonel Sellers in Mark Twain's farce *The Gilded Age,* "suggested something else which may be the thing" to help her recoup, as Field confided to Stedman.[74] Raymond had proposed that Field join his company in the role of the ingénue Laura Hawkins, the female lead in Twain's comedy. The play itself is an unhappy marriage of farce and melodrama: while Sellers comically schemes to reap a fortune from a corrupt Congress, Laura, betrayed by the man she loves, kills him and is tried for murder. As dramatic literature *The Gilded Age* was all bombast and "purp" stuff, and while Twain copyrighted it he never printed it in any edition of his writings. But as sensational theater it was an unqualified smash: Raymond staged it over a thousand times over a period of twelve years and it earned Twain over $100,000 in production fees. However complicated or nuanced Laura Hawkins' character may be in the novel he wrote in collaboration with Charles Dudley Warner, she is little more than a sentimental caricature in the play. Unfortunately, Field was woefully miscast in the part. In the first act, according to the script, Laura is sixteen years old, and in acts 2 through 5 she is twenty-five. Field had recently turned thirty-five.

More to the point, during the brief time she acted in Raymond's company Field foolishly tried to exploit Mark Twain's name for her personal benefit. She performed the role only a few times, all in mid- to late January 1875, in Hartford, Springfield, New Haven, Brooklyn, and Newark. The notice of her début in the *Hartford Courant* was tepid at best:

> Miss Kate Field, the well-known writer and lecturer, made her first appearance in the play last night in the character of Laura. Miss Field is as yet so inexperienced on the stage that she is entitled to charitable criticism. During the first part of the evening she was evidently nervous, and her talking savored somewhat of recitation.[75]

From here her reviews could only improve, though they did not improve much. Of her second performance in Hartford, the *Courant* observed, "Miss Kate Field's personation of Laura Hawkins was better than on the first evening. Then she labored under the disadvantages of a first appearance in the character, a position more trying to a recent debutante than to one long familiar with the stage."[76] For the record, Twain was in the audience for neither performance. The next evening, Raymond's company performed in Springfield, Massachusetts, where the play was favorably reviewed by her former editor Samuel Bowles.[77] The following day, January 14, Field sent a list of blurbs about her acting to the *Newark Register* and the *New York Tribune*. As she noted to Jeanette Gilder of the *Register*, "I've made a success and here are my vouchers which you can use. Have acted the part three times and improve nightly. Great house."[78] The *Tribune* published the "vouchers" in its January 19 issue under the title "Miss Kate Field in the Country." Two of the three of them—those attributed to Bowles and the *Springfield Republican*—were gleaned from the same source, Bowles' review on January 14. Only the other blurb was new: "Miss Field played her part admirably and made a most happy success—[Mark Twain]."[79]

8. Notice in the *New York Tribune*, 19 January 1875, 5. Collection of The New-York Historical Society, negative #79963d.

Field's attempt to legitimate her performance in *The Gilded Age* by invoking Twain's authority was a foolish mistake by any standard. Simply put, how could she claim that Twain had approved her performance in his play if he had never seen her act? In fact, Field had excerpted a sentence from a private note, now lost, that he sent Raymond's wife in Hartford. The same day his ostensible testimonial on Field's behalf appeared in the *Tribune*, Twain wrote a note objecting to the unauthorized use of his name. "This woman is the most inveterate sham & fraud & manipulator of newspapers I know of," he complained. "I didn't think she would ever be smart enough to get a chance to use me as a lying bulletin board to help her deceive the public, but . . . she really has got the best of me, after all."[80] Field was spared a major embarrassment when she simply left Raymond's company a week later. The Brooklyn papers had ignored her performance entirely, and the *Newark Advertiser* allowed that the quality of Field's acting was "debatable ground." She was perhaps "too closely allied to the naturalistic school" and so relied "too much upon the quietude of her action."[81] After she left Raymond's company, her acting experiment again a failure, she dropped from sight for two months. She registered at Barnum's Hotel in New York and laid low.[82]

She surfaced in late March 1875 in the cast of yet another company. Over the next six weeks she performed in Providence, Springfield, Buffalo, and Cleveland as Mademoiselle de Belle Isle in *Gabrielle,* her adaptation of her father's translation of the elder Dumas' play, and as Madame de Liria in the afterplay *The Opera Box,* her own translation of a one-act French comedy. In effect, Field tried out these plays in the provinces before appearing once more before a New York audience. Both scripts treat sexual themes in remarkably uninhibited ways, moreover. In *Gabrielle,* set at the Palace of Versailles during the reign of Louis XV, the heroine is suspected of infidelity by her lover and must foil a conspiracy to discredit her in a series of complications worthy of a modern screwball comedy. Just returned from a romp in Paris, a promiscuous marquis wagers his friend the Count D'Aubigny a thousand sous that he can bed the fair Gabrielle, played by Field. "The lady whom my Lord Marquis is to dishonor before midnight," the count explains, "I am to marry in three days." The first act ends as the marquis enters Gabrielle's chamber in the dead of night where the marchioness is asleep, though he does not know it. Both the marquis and the count presume he has deflowered Gabrielle—by the end of act 3 the count is pledged to "blow his brains out" in despair the next morning. But in act 4 the marquis learns that he slept not with Gabrielle but with his own wife ("'Twas you I met that night?") and both couples are reconciled in the dénouement.[83]

In *The Opera Box,* a rich widow played by Field is wooed by two suitors, the fop Duvivier and the cad D'Arsay, each of whom tries to finagle an invitation to attend the opera with her that evening. Unfortunately, only an incomplete prompt copy of the script survives among Field's papers at the Boston Public Library, so it is impossible to recreate all of the dialogue of the play. The fragment that survives, however, is filled with risqué scenes and sexual innuendo. Duvivier explains, for example, how once in a "love-chase" one of his friends ("pardon me the expression, dear madame") only "distanced his rival by the length of a head!" He begs to accompany Madame de Liria to the opera, where three of the seats in her box will be filled with "your flounces—one for you—and two for me and my hat, if you will suffer us to enjoy your society." Elsewhere, Duvivier jokes that when drafted during the Franco-Prussian War he "bought a substitute who was wounded at Gravelotte. This is the extent of my military service." Meanwhile, D'Arsay, pretending to be blind, joins Mme de Liria in her chamber while she is dishabille—an act of voyeurism that disqualifies him as a suitor, however much it must have piqued the interest of the audience. The pompous but chivalrous Duvivier is also an aficionado of the cigar: "It is the opium of the East transformed to suit the customs of the West; it is the intoxication of wine idealized for the man of fashion—a cigar! It is a benefactor—a friend always at hand—the phoenix of friends—rising always from its ashes!" As the play ends, Duvivier laments that "the fondest hopes in life seem destined to end" as Madame strikes a match, lights his cigar, and says "in smoke, Monsieur Duvivier?"[84] The sexual symbolism of this tableau would not have been lost even on nineteenth-century audiences.

During the weeks the company toured New England and the upper Midwest, Field was acclaimed in the roles of Gabrielle and Mme de Liria. As an ingénue she "gave pleasing proof of a careful study of her part," performing with "much artistic power," according to the *Providence Journal*.[85] Still, Field was unhappy with the initial productions of *Gabrielle:* it "ought to have been killed, for I only had two performances, the actors did not know what they were about and I was as nervous as a witch. The papers spoke well of the play and me after first performance, extremely well [after the] second."[86] Years later, she allowed that *Gabrielle* was "out of my genre."[87] By the time the ensemble reached Cleveland in early May, the actors were more polished in their roles. According to the *Cleveland Leader,* Field proved "that she possesses a remarkably high order of talent for society plays" and the *Cleveland Plain Dealer,* while more restrained, was still complimentary ("she may not be classed among the great actresses" but she is "certainly above the average").[88] She was ready to test the waters in New York again.

The critics there were lying in ambush. The New York reviewers "write like men envenomed with personal spite" toward Field, as an out-of-town paper put it. She wheedled an invitation to appear on June 9 from a group of influential New York friends, including Stedman, Reid, Bayard Taylor, Frothingham, and Vincenza Botta.[89] She rented the Union Square Theater and, on June 9, played the leading roles in her drama and comedy. The audience was again peppered with celebrities, among them Winter, Stedman, Frothingham, Bayard Taylor, J. G. Holland, Mary Mapes Dodge, and the actors McKee Rankin, Rose Eytinge, and Stuart Robson. Again Field was warmly applauded throughout the evening and, according to the *Graphic,* "several times recalled" after her songs "by the hearty plaudits of an audience of a decidedly critical character." William Winter, once burned and twice shy, was the epitome of tact: Field's performance had been "thoroughly competent," which augured well for her future as "a good actress in light comedy." The other reviews were savage. The *Times* expressed sympathy for the actors "who appeared with Miss Field" because "their presence, unlike that of the audience, was not optional." The *Brooklyn Eagle* went even farther, accusing Field of fraud: "she had no more moral right to accept money as an actress than a man who has never studied medicine or law would have to take fees."[90]

So long as she performed in the United States, she realized, she would never receive a fair hearing from the critics. Yet she refused to surrender her stage ambitions. The solution to her dilemma was a characteristic one: she would both change the venue in which she performed and assume a stage name in order to prove her talent. "It seems to me I must go to England," she wrote Stedman. "It will be dreadful, but then I'm used to tragedy."[91] After agreeing to become the London correspondent of the *New York Herald,* she sailed for Liverpool aboard the *Republic* on June 26.[92] "When I came here it was with the intention of sinking K. F. and becoming somebody else so as to be judged impartially on my merits," she explained to Stedman on August 7 from London. "I had had enough of disgraceful jealousy and unfair criticism." She chose to make her début on the English stage "as an utterly unknown friendless person."[93]

7

England

KATE FIELD LIVED for the next four and a half years in Europe, mostly in England. These years proved to be the most successful and rewarding in her life. She became a genuine international celebrity—a London correspondent for three newspapers, a renowned lecturer, an aspiring actress and playwright, author of a serial novel in a popular London weekly, publicity agent for the Bell telephone in England, and a fundraiser for the Shakespeare Memorial Theatre in Stratford-upon-Avon. Her fame in fact rivaled that of Henrietta Stackpole in fiction. She was often in the news, either as a journalist reporting it or as a person making it, and her movements were tracked in gossip columns on both sides of the Atlantic.

In order to pay the bills, she sent London letters regularly to the *Louisville Journal-Courier,* the *New York Herald,* and the *New York Graphic* during her first months abroad. Henry Watterson, the mugwump owner and editor of the *Journal-Courier,* engaged Field "on very good terms," she reported to Stedman, "to write whenever I please on whatever I please—preferring music and the drama."[1] Between mid-July 1875 and May 1876 Field sent twenty-eight articles signed with her full name to Watterson, who promised $30 for each of them, although he was invariably late in sending the money. She reviewed exhibitions of paintings at the Royal Academy, American actors on the London stage, and debates in the House of Commons ("It is an axiom to speak well of the dead. On that ground the recent Parliamentary session should be taken up tenderly"). She commented on the recent purchase by Britain of stock in the Suez canal, the sensational Whitechapel murder and mutilation, and of course the English winter ("these are the times that try men's soles").[2] She continued to send articles to Watterson despite his dilatory habits. "Not a paper or a dollar have I got from him yet, and he owes me $400, enough to keep me alive four months," she complained to Stedman in December 1875. Two months later, she was still waiting: "It seems impossible to get money from *The Courier-Journal.*" Watterson had apologized for the delay in December and promised she would receive a check soon, perhaps "in time to buy myself a Christmas turkey. No draft from that day to this."[3] Pressed for cash, she offered the sketches in her "Landor album" or "portfolio of immortals" for sale "en gros" or separately "from $200 to $500." She eventually received the money Watterson owed her, but after the spring of 1876 she never again contributed to the *Courier-Journal.*

Her articles in the *Herald* and *Graphic* were similar in style and substance to her contributions to the Louisville paper, and she was paid on the same scale for them. She commended the American expatriate painters Hennessy, Coleman, and James McNeill Whistler; defended Whitman and Swinburne from accusations of libertinism; announced a new novel by her friend Anthony Trollope; detailed events at a centennial Fourth of July banquet for Americans at the Westminster Hotel; interviewed the playwright Dion Boucicault; covered the reception for the explorer Henry M. Stanley at the Royal Geographical Society and the concerts of Patrick Gilmore's band at the Crystal Palace; and reported on the display of the Cesnola collection of Cypriot antiquities recently acquired by the Metropolitan Museum of Art in New York. (Forty years later, this collection of the "recovered fragments of Ilium" would figure in Edith Wharton's novel *The Age of Innocence.*) She reported to Stedman that she was "confined to social subjects" else she "could hammer away on politics."[4] Elihu Vedder visited her in London and she "bushwhacked" him "almost every night" into "seeing a new play." As his biographer remarks, "They went to the Olympic to see *The Ticket of Leave Man,* to the Alhambra to see 'one of the most wonderful ballets,'" and to "another theatre to see *The Corsican Brothers.*"[5] She attended productions of Tennyson's *Queen Mary,* Dumas' *L'Etrangére,* and Wagner's *Der Fliegende Hollander* and praised the acting of the American expatriates Hermann Vezin, Joe Jefferson, and Gencvièvc Ward. "It *riles* me to be told by fools that I am giving up literature for the stage," she wrote Stedman.[6] "I never wrote as much as I do now," she maintained, "and I never was so actively attached to the stage."[7]

As if to prove the point, she opened on August 30, 1875, in Liverpool in a "new musical burlesque" under a stage name, Mary Keemle, a version of her birthname. The "buretta" or burlesque operetta played to her strengths as a singer and she again began to take private voice lessons. "If I had had a musical piece to cut my teeth on in America, what a difference it would have made! It was what I wanted," she allowed.[8] The notices of her performance in the *Liverpool Post,* the *Era,* and the satirical weekly *The Porcupine* were uniformly favorable, and within a week she was engaged to perform a "folie musicale" in Middlesboro in October and to sing pantomime in London as well as Dundee, Aberdeen, Edinburgh, and other cities in Scotland over the Christmas holidays. "So far so good," she wrote Stedman.

> Of course I shall have a tug. I expect it; but if my health is preserved and my money holds out until I can command my own terms, I'll not complain. I can live on my salary and my letter writing but of course if I buy plays and dress well I must draw on my very small capital which can't last very long. However, I've made a beginning, have succeeded and am in a fair way to get the experience I want in as easy a way as possible, without any compromise of dignity or position.[9]

She pledged the Americans in Liverpool and her fellow workers in the theater to secrecy. While she earned her living by sending travel letters to the *Courier-Journal,* the *Herald,* and the *Graphic,* she began her acting career over again by playing supporting roles on the English provincial stage where no one knew who she was. As the *Boston Globe* remarked some months later, "she has shown her courage and persistency of purpose in going back to the beginning and learning the alphabet of the art."[10] Under her stage name, she "won plaudits at the hands of her audiences and from the British journalists by her spirit and versatility."[11] No less a luminary than Wilkie Collins was privy to the secret. When Field insisted that she had never met a woman who had fallen in love with a man "utterly unworthy of her," Collins replied, "Oh, Miss Keemle, Miss Keemle, have you still to discover one of the brightest virtues of the sex?"[12]

Early in January 1876 she traveled to Newcastle to lecture on Dickens under her own name. The *Newcastle Chronicle* commended her "capital mimetic powers," and Smalley reported in the *Tribune* that "she appears to have turned the hard heads of the Tynesiders."[13] In February she allowed that "I don't send articles to W[hitelaw] R[eid] because I think I'm not wanted." In March she asked Stedman to ask Reid on her behalf "how often *The Tribune* would care to hear from me, whether if I wrote twice a month my letters would be welcome. I naturally incline to *The Tribune* but if I'm not wanted there, tell me what you'd do in my place." Nothing came of the overture. "I have known for a long time that *The Tribune* cared nothing for my writing—a fact that would make me shed tears if [I] ever allowed myself the luxury of crying," she admitted later. "I couldn't make up my mind to be the one to break all connexion with the paper" to write for "a rival that would pay me far better but the time has come." Her failure to place her writing with the *Tribune* caused her to "fear that I really am a failure as a journalist, else why would my letters not be in demand? What does it all mean? The public read what I write and I stand begging to get printed. Oh if I only were a dressmaker or a cook, how quickly I could find a place!"[14]

On April 27, her stage identity still a secret, she opened in the role of Volante supporting her friend Geneviève Ward in John Tobin's *The Honeymoon* at the Gaiety Theatre in London. It had been one of the staples in the repertoire of Field's parents forty years earlier. In the comedy, a man impersonating a duke woos and marries a young girl. Instead of escorting her to a palace, however, he takes her to a hovel and reveals that he is nothing more than a peasant. The audience is expected to revel in her gradual acceptance of her womanly duty to love him through thick and thin—hardly a plot that would be popular today. Field appeared in the play after only two rehearsals, the second an hour before the initial performance. Still, she made a hit in the part. At the end of the second act, her friend Vezin came backstage "and shook me warmly by the hand. Then I knew that I was all right as he is a severe and honest critic. The stage manager said 'very good,' the dresses said 'wonderful for a first time,' and the stage carpenters crowded the wings and led the applause." After the final curtain, she was thrown three bouquets; and Moncure Conway, an American minister and the London correspondent of the *Cincinnati Commercial*, congratulated her "and said he was surprised and pleased."[15] In his next letter to the paper

Conway praised "Miss Keemle" without stint.[16] The day after her début, the London *Times* commended "Miss Keemle," a "young actress of distinct power and remarkable intelligence," whose "performance was bright and vivacious," the *Athenæum* her "intelligence and vivacity," and the London *Globe* her "bright, animated, and intelligent" personation.[17] Smalley acknowledged that "she was nervous at first, but at no time lost her self-possession, or forgot her part." Not only was Miss Keemle's first appearance in London a triumph, "it left no doubt upon the minds of the audience that the young American will be heard of in the future." Smalley promised to follow the career of the debutante, though he was "not now free to make public" the reasons for his special interest in her.[18] The play enjoyed a run of twenty-six performances before it closed. As soon as she debuted on the London stage, however, the *Era* in London and the *New York Herald* blew her cover. "I did my best to keep the matter quiet," she wrote Stedman. "I'm awfully sorry for I'm not ready to be talked about and I'd like you to make people understand that it isn't my fault if I don't quietly pursue my dramatic career until the right play gets written."[19] A month later, Smalley broke his silence about her. "I ought to have said long since that Miss Kate Field" was performing "under the odd stage name of Mary Keemle, and has been kindly spoken of" by the local theatrical journals.[20] She was so successful that, after she sang "the Spanish muleteer's song" at a benefit at the Gaiety Theater in late May, she was offered but declined a role on the operatic stage beginning in the fall.[21] Instead, she sang light opera at the Westminster Aquarium in London that autumn "with marked success"[22] and hosted a salon in her rooms at 15 New Cavendish Street, Portland Place, near the Langham Hotel.

Field's theatrical successes in London prompted her to go "into plays as well as playing," as she put it. Over the next two years she both wrote plays and acted in them. In October 1876 Stedman urged her to return to the United States and she replied, "No, my friend, not until I stand better in my own estimation—and the public's—than I do now." Instead, she sent Stedman a copy of *Dead to the World,* a five-act drama originally translated from French by her father and "entirely done over by me. . . . Now it is greatly improved and more dramatic." Ward, Vezin, and Raymond all liked it, she said, and she wanted Stedman to read it and pass it along to Bayard Taylor and William Winter. Winter "wanted me to let him know when he could be of service," she explained, and "now is the time."[23] Set in Paris during the Restoration after Napoleon I, the sensational melodrama describes the vindication of the mother and lover of a nobleman and the reunion of mother and son. The convoluted plot nearly defies brief synopsis. Gaspar Godard, a sergeant in the French army during the Napoleonic Wars, and his pregnant wife, Lucette, are separated during a battle, and Lucette is presumed dead for the next twenty years. Meanwhile, promoted to general but blinded by an explosion in the field, Godard marries an aristocrat who violates her vows. When Lucette finally arrives on the scene after years in a convent, Godard acknowledges that she was "the only woman I ever loved. She who bears my name, whom I have surrounded with luxury, respect, and gratitude . . . has ignobly betrayed me." The play ends as the false wife and stepmother overdoses on opium and dies, opening the way for Godard and Lucette to reconcile and recognize their son. Field was keen to place the script with a manager but failed; she eventually published it in 1891.

Most of the other plays she wrote during these months were formulaic one-acters, virtual dialogues, with two characters, a man and a woman, locked in a battle of the sexes. Field translated from French a one-act farce of mistaken identities entitled *Caught Napping* in January 1877, in which a widow and widower quarrel until they fall in love. (The best line, delivered by the widower: "If nature abhors a vacuum, how she must abhor me!")[24] It too failed to sell, though Field eventually published it in 1890. She also wrote another one-act comedy entitled *Two Quarrelsome Cousins* for Madge Robertson, who bought the copyright. The play dramatizes the spontaneous romance of two characters, one a widow and the other a bachelor misogynist. It too was never staged, though Field published three different versions of the play under three different titles between Christmas 1877 and 1892. It was her second published play, and it betrayed Field's own disappointment in love. In one version, the misogynist offers his "cousin" the same advice Trollope had given Field in 1862: "you ought to marry" because "a woman like you needs a protector to shield her from the world."[25] In the spring of 1877, she was reportedly scripting a new play for F. B. Chatterton of the Drury Lane Theatre.[26] It may be one of the fragments or unproduced plays that survive among Field's papers at the Boston Public Library (*The Wrong Flat, Oshkosh in London,* and *The Blind Side*) or that she later published *(A Family Jar).*

The greatest theatrical success of Field's career, however, came in the production of her one-act comedy *Extremes Meet.* The play was almost entirely original. As she recalled, she took "a French plot, altered it very much toward [the] end in order to make a good picture for the curtain to fall upon, changed scene from Vienna to London, and made new dialogue."[27] She debuted the play at St. James's Theatre in London on March 12, 1877, and it kept the stage there for eleven weeks. In it, the ingénue Maud seeks the help of the misogynist Captain Howard in breaking the match between her sister and his brother. (The best line, delivered by Howard: "They say that in heaven there is neither marrying nor giving in marriage. I suppose that's why it's heaven!")[28] In about thirty minutes of real time, they engage in a war of wits, negotiate a treaty of friendship, and finally become engaged. However slight, the play struck a chord among British audiences and theatrical critics. Field received by far the most favorable notices of her career; for example, in the *Examiner* ("Miss Field's acting is easy, graceful, and animated"), the *World* ("Miss Field plays with ease and grace"), the Paris *Figaro* ("Miss Field is as bright on the boards as she is on paper"), the *Dublin News Letter* ("Miss Field has an engaging manner, a sympathetic voice, and an easy and graceful carriage"), and the *Sporting and Dramatic News* ("Miss Field acts with infinite grace, point, and perfect naturalness"). To be sure, the critic for *Theatre* offered some constructive criticism, specifically that by "assuming simultaneously the functions of authorship and stage illustration she loses the double check which she would have had if she had made her debut in some one else's piece" or "had entrusted some other actress with the creation of her heroine."[29] But in general the play was received with accolades. "I've made a real success in play and acting," she reported.[30] Ward, Vezin, William S. Gilbert, Arthur Sullivan, and Marie Taglioni all congratulated her on her writing and acting.[31] "I probably never should never have attempted to write the comedietta which is so well received here nightly," she admitted, "had I not wanted a part in which to make a London debut." Nor had she expected it "to do half so much as it has done."[32]

Nor did Field's success in *Extremes Meet* escape the attention of American reviewers. According to the *New York Herald,* Field "achieved a marked success. The dialogue is polished and witty." The *New York Tribune* reported that she "was throughout good, and in some parts excellent."[33] Conway was similarly impressed: "If any London theater manager had the perspicacity to invest, so to speak, in Kate Field, that lady would declare dividends," he wrote in the *Cincinnati Commercial.* "Whenever and wherever she gets an opportunity to make an appearance on the stage she is certain to prove herself possessed of a new variety of ability."[34] She continued to revise the play during its run. "I've improved on it very much," she insisted in mid-May 1877, and Vezin "says I do it as well as it can be done." Still, she had grown bored with it over the months. "I'm sick to death of the thing," she admitted. "Now I want something bigger." "I've had more than enough of my comedietta," she wrote her friend Laurence Hutton a week later. "I want a heavier gun to fire off."[35] By the end of the year, *Extremes Meet* had been issued in both London and New York—the third of her plays to be published—and Field was unanimously elected to membership in the Dramatic Authors' Society of England.[36] She had hoped to open in another play at St. James's in the winter of 1877, but the free-love advocate Victoria Woodhull had rented the theater, "disgracing my country and my sex," and "so I shall let it alone until she has departed and the place well fumigated."[37] Field never again performed in a scripted play. She had proved to her own satisfaction that the New York critics were wrong, and she never again permitted one of them to publish a word, favorable or not, about her acting.

Still, Field found plenty of other heavy guns to fire off in the press. She interviewed Sir Julius Benedict, a distinguished musician, composer, and maestro, for *Scribner's.* She attended a reception in honor of former President Grant hosted by the U.S. ambassador to Great Britain, Edwards Pierrepont, on June 5 and cabled a report about it to the *New York Herald.* Among the guests were the once and future prime minister William Gladstone, Robert Browning, Lord Houghton, the novelist William Black, Arthur Sullivan, Julia Ward Howe, T. H. Huxley, Moncure Conway, and Smalley (who also mentioned Field's presence at the reception in his report to the *Tribune).*[38] She returned to Pierrepont's home a month later for the Fourth of July celebration, where she chatted with Grant, "more talkative than usual," and saw "six hundred of our country people."[39] She interviewed Heinrich Schliemann, the reputed discoverer of the ruins of Homeric Troy, for the July 1877 issue of *Belgravia* and the article propelled that number of the magazine through three printings.[40] It was even copied in the *New York Tribune*. Field later joked that Schliemann was a difficult "catch." She had to meet him as early as six in the morning, and on one occasion she "didn't go to bed at all. I received him in a ball-dress, and *he* came in evening suit! Both of us had been at parties until five!"[41] Field later urged John Hay to appoint Schliemann to a diplomatic office, ideally U.S. ambassador to Greece. In September she began writing squibs for the *Whitehall Review* and in November occasional unsigned editorials and book and theatrical reviews for the *London Examiner*. She vacationed that fall with the painter Hennessy and his wife in Trouville and Le Havre on the coast of France and wrote up the events in two long articles for the *Herald*. "I wear as little as the law allows," she wrote Stedman. "I bathe in the sea and have an appetite that would do credit to a boa-constrictor. The amount of bread and milk I consume is appalling. Cows run when they see me approach and bakers gaze upon me as a special Providence."[42] "Five weeks of sea bathing and 'bread and cream' have done wonders for her, made her over 'new,' and her friends say she is 'fat,'" as her bête noire "Jennie June" Croly reported.[43] In Paris for five weeks toward the end of her holiday, Field attended the theater or a dinner every night. Ristori hosted a party in her honor; Governor Samuel J. Tilden of New York and Louis Blanc dined with her; and Victor Hugo received her and gave her an inscribed copy of his most recent book. The French dressmaker Charles Worth, the inventor of the fashion show, escorted Field around his shop on the Rue de la Paix and "feasted" her at his villa at Suresne—he called her "une femme adorable"—while she took notes of their conversations.[44] She also bought five evening dresses from Worth at an average cost of $500.[45] Back in London in November, she lectured on Dickens in both St. George's Hall and Sadler's Wells Theatre to enthusiastic crowds and favorable reviews by the London *Spectator* ("interesting, brilliant, and eloquent"), *World* ("manner and delivery are excellent"), *Daily News* ("a marked success"), *Telegraph* ("perfect self-expression"), and *Globe* ("sparkling wit and humor").[46]

Perhaps most importantly, Field in February 1877 began to contribute a weekly column entitled "Intercepted Letters" to the London magazine *Truth* that soon evolved into a picaresque epistolary roman à clef in sixty-four parts featuring four American tourists afoot in Europe: Puss, the author of the letters to her friend Ella in New York; Puss's brother Bob; her cousin Tom; and their Aunt Fanny. "I've made a hit" with the installments, Field wrote Stedman in May. "The clubs are talking about them which is a good sign and the editor says he wants me to be his mainstay."[47] The form was ideally suited to her chatty disquisitions on such topics as the races at Ascot, cricket at St. John's Wood, shooting contests at Wimbledon, and an afternoon with P. T. Barnum. Like Field, Puss crossed the English Channel to France in late September, and she vacationed at the same manor on the seacoast as Field, Le Manoir de Pennedepie. Puss was also promised by her host that she did not need to dress—"at least, no more than was required by law."[48] Puss, like Field, returned to London in November shortly before the British fleet entered the Dardanelles, a confrontation that briefly threatened war with Russia. She also attended an opening at the Grosvenor Gallery, where she saw George Eliot, Lewes, Browning, and George Grossmith, who had recently performed in the role of Sir Joseph Porter in Gilbert and Sullivan's *H.M.S. Pinafore.* If the Gallery had "fallen to the ground at that moment," Puss quipped, "England would have lost her greatest novelist, her greatest painters, several able statesman, renowned musicians, clever men of all professions, and numbers of charming women"[49]—Kate Field among them. She was in the prime of her career, a woman with many talents and a sterling reputation. "It seems to knock people down," she remarked without bluster, "that a writer can do anything but write."[50]

She was recruited by Alexander Graham Bell in November 1877 to promote the telephone in Great Britain—a job she performed so well she soon (if briefly) became rich. Bell arrived in England in August 1877 to found a British phone company and to sell stock in it. He was introduced to Field in early November by mutual friends—including the Rhode Island entrepreneur W. H. Reynolds, who had purchased controlling interest in the

English patent on the telephone—and Field agreed to lead the British advertising campaign.

She immediately touted the invention in her column in the *Whitehall Review* for November 10. "There *is* something new under the sun, and I've seen it," she bragged.

> I have talked through the telephone, have been heard an eighth of a mile distant, and have received perfectly distinct answers by the same means of communication. Mr. Bell has only recently brought his invention from the United States, where it is being put to practical use. . . . This is the crowning achievement of the electro-magnetic telegraph, and is destined to bring about as great a revolution in the economy of life as did the introduction of steam. A fortune awaits Mr. Bell and the public-spirited Americans who have invested capital in their eighth wonder of the world.[51]

She later described the experience in more detail:

> I sat at a desk, at the top of which was an electric bell. On both sides of the desk, depending from iron arms, was a small pear-shaped wooden instrument, bearing a strong family resemblance to the stethoscope. The small end of each instrument was connected with a telegraphic wire. I was in the presence of the Telephone. "Is this all?" I asked. "All!" exclaimed the superintendent. "Isn't it enough, provided the object be attained? Isn't simplicity a charm in inventions as well as in people? Would you feel happier if the Telephone were the size of a steam-engine? Before you say another word, touch that electric bell, put one telephone to your ear and the other to your mouth." Feeling quite crushed at being so sat upon, I obeyed orders, and straightway I heard an unknown voice exclaim,—
> "All right; what do you want?"
> "Who are you?" I asked.
> "I'm every inch a man, and by your voice I know that my questioner is a lady."

Field was persuaded on the spot of the practicality of the telephone. "I foresee the day when . . . every house will be connected," she avowed. She expected that "opera and theatre will shortly be turned on like gas and water," and "every household will be taxed according to the amount of Patti, Irving, *Olivia, Diplomacy,* Toole, or *Our Boys* consumed." She even predicted the advent of the picture-phone: Combine the telephone and the electroscope "and two persons, hundreds of miles apart," will not only speak to each other but "they will actually *see* each other!" As she wrote Laurence Hutton, "My last craze is the *Telephone.* That *is* wonderful! And there's no end to its utility. I'm making these people understand it and the Government has already taken it up."[52] The British Government had, in fact, contracted to adopt Bell's telephone as part of the Post-Office Department.

Less than a week after reporting her first trial with the telephone, Field scored a journalistic coup by placing a three-thousand-word history of Bell's invention in the London *Times.* "Although Mr. Bell has been but a few months in England," she reported, "his invention has already commanded the attention it deserves. There has been telephonic communication between this island and Jersey" and some businesses had installed the device. She mailed a clipping of the article to Stedman a few days later. As she noted, "It has excited very great attention, called forth warm praise from the editor, and Bell, inventor of the telephone, says it is the best article that has ever been written on the subject. It inspired a leader in *The Times* soon after and has been of great advantage to the telephone in which there is a great fortune." In addition to writing for the *Times,* Field contributed unsigned articles—in effect, press releases—about the telephone to such leading English newspapers as the London *Telegraph* and *Daily News* and the *Manchester Guardian.* She mailed unsolicited articles to *Saunders's News Letter* in Dublin and the *East Anglican Daily Times.* By January 7, 1878, according to her diary, she had submitted a total of twenty-one articles on the telephone to British papers, and she continued to write and send them (e.g., to the *Newcastle Chronicle*) as late as January 15.[53]

When Queen Victoria requested a demonstration of the new invention, Bell and his staff hastily organized a "royal séance" on the Isle of Wight. They arranged to telephone a program of songs and other entertainment featuring Field and lasting about half an hour from Osborne Cottage, the home of Sir Thomas Biddulph, the queen's private secretary, to the Queen's council room at Osborne House on the evening of January

14. "Placing a telephone between the top opening and lid of the upright piano," she later explained, "Miss Kate Field played her own accompaniment and sang 'Kathleen Mavourneen' into the telephone. The Queen listened with delight, expressed her thanks telephonically . . . , and the applause that followed was heard by Miss Field through the telephone." Never a shrinking violet, Field subtly expressed her sympathy for the Irish Republican cause by performing a popular Irish folk song for the queen. She then sang Shakespeare's "Cuckoo Song" from *Love's Labour Lost* and "Comin' Thro' the Rye" and declaimed the epilogue to *As You Like It,* "all of which were heard distinctly." Two days later, the queen asked to buy the two telephones still installed at court and, as Field observed, "it may come to pass that Her Majesty in the Isle of Wight will converse with Lord Beaconsfield in London, thus sparing the aged Premier the necessity of a day's journey."[54] As Biddulph soon wrote Bell, "I hope you are aware how much gratified and surprised the Queen was at the exhibition of the Telephone here on Monday evening. Her Majesty desires me to express her thanks to you and the ladies and gentlemen who were associated with you on the occasion." Bell wrote Field to thank her in turn.[55]

Field also hosted on January 16 what must be one of the earliest press conferences in journalism history. She noted in her diary that she planned "to invite the Press to a Matinée Téléphonique and get one general chorus of gratuitous advertising before the opening of Parliament." The event, held at the Bell offices in London, was a "great success," according to her diary entry for that day. She invited the press as well as prominent artists, authors, actors, musicians, and scientists. "Today town all alive with the Telephone news furnished by me," she added in her diary. "Quite two hundred persons were present, including the American Minister [John] Welch, Sir Julius Benedict, Hermann Vezin, Genèvieve Ward, [editor of the *Philadelphia Press*] Colonel [John W.] Forney, [George] du Maurier, and William Black. All delighted with Telephone."[56] In an unsigned report on the event she wrote for the *New York Herald,* Field supplied the names of more of the attendees: Dilke, Conway, Arthur Sullivan, Louise Chandler Moulton, artist John Millais, historian J. A. Froude, and the actors W. H. and Madge Kendal. She noted under the cover of anonymity that "Miss Kate Field, who has charge of the artistic and literary department of the *Telephone*, received the assembly." She also added self-servingly that, though Bell had been in England since August, "it was not until the 16th of November that the *Times* published an elaborate essay on the telephone and its applications. This article, which Professor Bell declares is the best that has ever been written on the subject, excited great attention."[57]

The success of the so-called matinée téléphonique prompted Field to host a series of "telephone receptions" at the Bell offices on Cannon Street in the winter and spring of 1878. As the London correspondent of the *Hartford Courant* reported, "all classes come to stay five minutes to see the wonderful invention, and stay three hours to see each other. . . . Telephone receptions, inaugurated by Miss Kate Field, are one of the 'taking' things of the season. The unconventional and pleasant way in which it is done, and the newness of it attracts all who are bidden to the 'Telephone Séance,' as it is called." Field again carefully selected the invitees. Among those who attended a reception in early March, for example, were Anthony Trollope, publisher John Blackwood, Lord Macduff, Lord and Lady Henniker, and several Members of Parliament;[58] and on March 11, as she wrote Stedman, "Prince Louis Napoleon, Duchess of Westminster, & a large party of swells" including Lily Langtry, J. L. Toole, and Hamilton Aidé "lunched at the Telephone rooms," where they had "a grand time singing & experiment-ing." Toole was persuaded to speak into the device "a little French from a certain popular comedy" he had written.[59] The last of these receptions, in early April, was a private affair for George Eliot. Field had invited the novelist to the matinée téléphonique on January 16, though she failed to attend. "Only once did I succeed in luring her away from The Priory," Field later reminisced, "and that was to see the telephone about which she was very curious. Yes, she would come with Mr. Lewes, provided no one else was present. So one afternoon George Eliot visited the office of Bell's Tele-phone in the city and for an hour tested its capacity—'It is very wonderful, very useful,' she said—'What marvelous inventions you Americans have!' It was the last time I ever saw her."[60]

In February 1878, Field also published a sixty-seven-page pamphlet to advertise Bell's telephone. A collection of newspaper articles, mostly her own, a copy of Sir Thomas Biddulph's letter of thanks from the queen on the dedication page, and a transcript of Bell's address before the Society of Arts on November 28, 1877, *The History of Bell's Telephone* priced at six-pence sold over a thousand copies. Much as Walt Whitman anonymously reviewed the first edition of *Leaves of Grass,* moreover, Field puffed her own book at least twice in unsigned reviews. "Miss Kate Field's edition of 'Professor Bell's Telephone,' giving the history of the invention, ought to be read by every non-scientific person, simply for the information it conveys in an easy and readable form," she declared in the *Whitehall Review.*[61] Or as she wrote in the *New York Herald*—despite the fact there was no U.S. edition of the volume—Kate Field "has edited a little book on the Telephone, called 'Bell's Telephone,' which has all the bright, and clever, and truthful things that have been said about the Telephone, including her own articles. . . . It is a most readable and interesting little book."[62] Field also took the invention on the road, "exhibiting it and lecturing about it" in several cities.[63] In the end, Field's publicity campaign paid off in spades. In March 1878, half of the British rights to the telephone were "purchased by very rich Englishmen, the other half remaining in American hands," as Field reported from London. She was paid for her efforts with stock in the company. As she wrote William Winter in June 1878,

> One of my faits accompli is the Telephone. From November until March I had it on the brain. To me fell the entire literary and social department. I started with a long article in *The Times* (as you've seen in my little book) which excited great interest and gradually pervaded the entire press of this country. Of course all this meant lucre. I never did more profitable work. I was glad of it too in other respects as it brought my executive faculties into play, and won me the respect of many leading men, to say nothing of the esteem of *The Times*' editor.

She was convinced the "business if properly managed will be very lucrative," and by her own estimate her shares were worth approximately forty thousand dollars.[64]

"All good Americans before they die visit Stratford-on-Avon," Field once averred. "Belonging to this race," she made the trip in March 1878 "and saw the Shakespearean Memorial, a really admirable pile of buildings comprising theatre, library, and picture gallery" still under construction. Before she left the village, she was asked by the mayor, Charles Flower, to assist the local committee in raising money to complete the project, especially from her fellow Americans. She had earned a reputation as a successful publicist for promoting the telephone. "While thinking over the matter," she later explained,

> I had a dream which may not have been all a dream. I dreamed that my ancestor, Nathan Field, the dramatist and friend of Shakespeare, came to me saying, "Do it for *my* sake. Your country people revere my old manager's name. You almost believe that you invented Shakespeare. We owe to you the preservation of his birthplace, for not until that greatest showman on earth, P. T. Barnum, was about to pack up the crumbling house and carry it to America did we awake to a sense of its value. The light that falls upon Shakespeare's grave peers through an American window. Just before leaving England, Joseph Jefferson, your comedian, took his infant child to Stratford, that it might be baptized with the water of sweet-flowing Avon. The letter in your hand asks for a bit of ivy from Shakespeare's birthplace, that the graduating class of Yale University may plant it on the green of their Alma Mater. Do it—but not now. Your country is poor, and charity begins at home. But something can be done now; the echo of which will be heard in New York and San Francisco. English actors will gladly serve their master's cause."[65]

Field wrote a few letters to friends to solicit contributions, but they "did not materially enlarge the subscription fund."[66]

Rarely at a loss for ideas, however, she organized a charity performance of a light comedy at the Gaiety Theatre in London on the afternoon of May 22 to benefit the Shakespeare Memorial. Field and Vezin played the leads. In reviewing the play, the *Theatre* noted that "[t]he piece itself is one of those bright *levers du rideau* with which every frequenter of Parisian theatres is familiar." After the play, Field delivered a brief appeal for funds. "I think it is a disgrace that Stratford should be without a place in which from time to time the poet's plays may be represented by great artists as Wagner produces operas at Bayreuth," she concluded her speech. "When

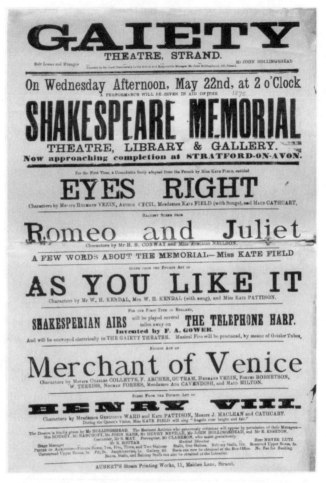

9. Playbill for Shakespeare Memorial benefit, 22 May 1878.
Courtesy of Boston Public Library.

the spire of Shakespeare's church greets the tower of Shakespeare's theatre the actor's art will have received its just recognition."[67]

Field planned another treat for the hundreds of people in attendance that afternoon. She figured "that the introduction of the Telephone harp in one or more *ent'actes,* especially if the harp were played in Shakespeare's house at Stratford, would add greatly to the interest of the occasion," as she had explained to one of Bell's managers. To ensure the success of the event, she was forced to "attend to everything before as well as behind the curtain," so she became "advertiser, manager, ticket-seller, actor, singer, author, speechmaker all in one." She had applied to the post office for a line between the theatre and Stratford-upon-Avon, a distance of a hundred and thirty miles, but the postal officials "refused me, coolly saying they intended to oppose the Telephone as long as possible . . . and moreover they knew music could *not* be conveyed such a distance," she complained. She then "applied to the Great Western Railway for one of their wires, and with a courtesy unknown to the Post Office, our request was granted. But still we needed a wire from Paddington station to the Gaiety Theatre. This favor the Great Western asked of the P.O. and the officials dared not refuse." The organ music transmitted over the wire that afternoon was tinny—"I've heard much better music at less distance," Field allowed—but she was delighted that the "bigwigs" in the post office were "awfully disconcerted at hearing music 130 miles away!"[68] She conceded that technical problems had plagued the event—"an invention at the Gaiety end of wire, used for the first time," had malfunctioned and was only "put in order at the last moment. The airs down on the bill were played at Stratford but not until the Fisher's hornpipe had been reached did *we* hear anything." As a result, the press had largely "ignored or ridiculed" the music "because as music it was absurd. What did they expect?"[69] For example, Smalley panned the "attempt to execute musical airs on a telephone harp." The music, he said, sounded as though it were "played by an orchestra composed of a toy trumpet and a penny whistle."[70] "I don't envy Smalley his gall or his reputation over here," Field carped in response.[71] On the other hand, the London correspondents of the *New York Times* and the *New York Herald* thought the music was "distinctly heard" and was "distinctly audible."[72] In all, the benefit raised $2,250 of the $40,000 required to complete the Memorial, and Field received congratulatory letters from Gladstone and Edward Pigott, the Examiner of Plays. Pigott wrote her that if she had been "one of the original 12 apostles you would have taken the bread out of the mouths of all the parsons and lawyers that have followed them, for you would have converted the whole world right off the reel."[73]

On June 27, in the interval between projects, Field left London for the continent for rest and recuperation with the Hennessys. "I can't tell you how tired I am of this town," she admitted to Stedman. "I've worked

10. Kate Field's *profile perdu* in Paris, 1878.
Courtesy of Boston Public Library.

hard since the middle of October."[74] The Paris Exposition had opened in May, but the "beginnings of World's Fairs are rarely worth seeing," she insisted. "It is always better to plunge into the middle of things. Then all the rough edges are smoothed, and the vast buildings are properly clothed."[75] Even on vacation, however, Field continued to work. She met the young American painter Frank Millet, who was an art juror, and their friendship soon "ripened," as she put it.[76] From late June until late July, while lodging in "a quiet hotel near the Grand Opera," she contributed three unsigned reports about the Exposition to the *New York Tribune* and a trio of "intercepted letters" about it to *Truth*. Her *Tribune* dispatches were flat, devoted to the Swiss school system, American visitors to the fair, and the advantages of free trade. But the installments of her novel in *Truth* were as lively as ever, with a satire of the ugly American "Professor Talkee Talkee, LL.D., A.S.S." and an anecdote about a Yorkshireman who tried to hail a cab in the Rue Scribe by shouting "cochon" (pig) instead of "cocher." She also reported that she had posed for an exposition photographer with her "right ear and the back of the head to the camera for a *profile perdu.*"[77]

While in Paris, Field planned an escape to Switzerland with her old friend Mme Ristori. They railed to the southern Alpine resort of St. Moritz, over six thousand feet above sea level in the Upper Engadine, in late July and remained there over a month.[78] "We've left the equator" in London and Paris "and climbed the North Pole," she bragged in *Truth.* "I've discovered the existence of a previously unknown gland." Or as she put it later, St. Moritz enjoys "nine months winter and three months cold weather" a year.[79] According to Lilian Whiting, these weeks with Ristori in the Swiss Alps "were always treasured by Kate as among her richest experiences." In late August she railed to Paris, and in September to Normandy, where she visited Hennessy, who painted her in Greek costume.[80] In early November she returned to Paris and began to submit excerpts from her journal to the *Continental Gazette,*[81] the first (though by no means the last) time she dipped into her diary for material to publish. In late January 1879, she finally crossed from Calais to Dover and, with the Hennessys and other Americans, rented a furnished house in Portland Place, London, and shared expenses.[82]

Meanwhile, Field continued to raise money for the Shakespeare Memorial. Between late 1878 and early 1879, she received another $2,500 in donations from such friends as Vezin, Barnum, Longfellow, Conway, Schliemann, Hutton, Stanley, the elder Henry James, Samuel French, W. J. Florence, Henry Irving, and George W. Childs.[83] Not everyone compiled with her request for money, however. Anthony Trollope protested that he did not care "two pence for the Shakespeare Memorial or Mr. Flower. If there be any one who does not want more memorials than have been already given, it is Shakespeare! Mr. Flower is a worthy old gent,—who wants to go down to posterity hanging on to some distant rag of the hindermost garment of the bard of Avon; but I don't want or care to assist his views."[84] In recognition of her hard work on behalf of the Memorial—"Stratford

11. Kate Field in toga. Courtesy of Boston Public
Library.

holds me in affectionate regard," as she noted[85]—Field was invited to perform at the opening night of the theater on April 23, 1879, the 315th anniversary of Shakespeare's birth. In fact, she recited the "Dedicatory Ode"
by Westland Marston at the beginning of the evening, so Kate Field was
literally the first person to appear on the stage of the first permanent
Shakespeare theater in Stratford-upon-Avon. She wore an evening dress of
blue and white *moiré antique,* trimmed with lace, with gold ornaments and
blue feathers in her hair. As she stepped onto the stage "she was received
with a hearty round of applause," according to the *New York Times,* and she
declaimed the poem "with grace and spirit," according to the *New York
Tribune.*[86] After a performance of *Much Ado About Nothing,* the first night's

play, Field was again called onto the stage to sing "God Save the Queen."[87] Two evenings later, Sir Julius Benedict conducted a concert of music with lyrics by Shakespeare and Field sang "I Know a Bank" from *A Midsummer Night's Dream*, "Where the Bee Sucks" from *The Tempest*, and "Should He Upbraid" from *The Two Gentlemen of Verona*. As the *New York Times* reported, "She sang the difficult music with precision, and her enunciation was in every way admirable."[88]

She had nothing more to prove. She planned her return, if not in triumph at least in dignity, to star in a one-woman variety show entitled *Eyes and Ears in London,* a precursor of vaudeville in the history of American musical theater. Field had scripted "an entertainment of an entirely novel description," a "serio-comic musical monologue. It will embrace sketches of all phases of London society, rich and poor, East and West, dinners public and private, parties, opera, music-hall, theatre, Rotten Row, cabbies, police courts, House of Commons, a suicide off London Bridge, &c. Every sketch will be illustrated by a song, humorous or otherwise, some written expressly for me," as she wrote from Great Malvern, near Worcestershire, in August. Her friend George Grossmith, of Gilbert and Sullivan fame, had composed the music to her libretto, and Field even hoped Arthur Sullivan would contribute a song.[89] Before her departure, in fact, she submitted biographical sketches of Gilbert and Sullivan to *Scribner's,* cementing her friendships with them. (Privately, however, she thought Gilbert "a quarrelsome whoppist" and Sullivan "a selfish snob.")[90] She was paid a mere ten dollars a page for these articles, or a total of only $120.[91] On the advice of her doctor, she went to a water-cure in June to build her strength and "didn't write a letter for two months."[92] After an absence of over four years, Field finally sailed on the SS *Britannic* from Liverpool for New York on November 27 and arrived on December 6 to rehearse the comeback she had plotted for months.[93]

8

New York Redux

FIELD RENEWED HER FRIENDSHIP with Elihu Vedder soon after she returned to the United States. She took an apartment in the Victoria Hotel on Fifth Avenue in New York. Coincidentally, Vedder was in the city preparing to mount an exhibition of his paintings, and he accompanied Field to a dinner in honor of the editor George William Curtis one evening in January 1880. Afterwards, he wrote his wife that "Kate puts on many airs, but she ought not to stick out her feet followed by her little legs quite so far." Field brought Aunt Corda to the opening of the exhibition in February. For the past three years, Cordelia Sanford had been confined to the Butler Hospital, a mental asylum in Providence. Field visited her there upon her return from England and told Vedder that her aunt suffered fits of insanity "in which she tried to take her own life or that of any person who might be conveniently near." When he saw her at the exhibition, however, Vedder thought she was "fat and gross looking but not at all the complete wreck they had prepared me to see." In fact, Aunt Corda "was delighted to see me, bought the picture I had worked on like a demon." Still fascinated by the occult, Field also took Vedder to a séance by the "mind reader" Stuart Cumberland when he came to New York.[1]

Meanwhile, she was rehearsing her so-called "musical monologue" with the pianist Adolph Glose. "Kate Field brings back with her from London a somewhat novel entertainment—neither a lecture, nor a dramatic monologue, nor concert—but a little of all three,"[2] the *New York Tribune* announced in its January 16 edition. Two months before Field performed *Eyes and Ears in London* on any stage, the *Springfield Republican* printed a tentative program.[3] The two-hour show, interrupted by an intermission, opened with Field's arrival in London fog and rain in a balloon and her declaration that "the British empire is the one on which the sun never sets and rarely rises." She then sang "The Lovely Umbrella," which assigned a type of umbrella to each class of society. She next described the Underground and the overground omnibus and recounted the "sins of that perennial wretch, the cabman." After imaginary visits to the Zoological Gardens and Madame Tussaud's wax museum, she parodied a speech after a dinner hosted by the London Streets Potato Canning Company. At a supposed reception with the Lord Mayor, Field illustrated the English ignorance of America. A "distinguished Member of Parliament" asked her where she was born. "You are not a Southerner, I know." How? "Because the Southerners *all* have black eyes and black hair." She replied that she was a native of Missouri. "Missouri? What State is that in?" asked the MP. Field answered that Missouri *is* a state. "Oh, yes, yes," returned the MP. "I was thinking of *Mississippi*." In "Silent Song," Field burlesqued an amateur singer, Mme Sotto-Voce, who believes she has a voice especially adapted for the drawing-room but in fact has no voice at all—the audience hears only the piano. In some versions of her musical monologue—the program was flexible and she added and omitted several songs over time—Field also sang a piece entitled "Don't," the lyrics of which she wrote and later published.[4] It is virtually the only part of the script that survives.

> O, how I wish you wouldn't, Bob—
>   You're such an awful tease;
> Now, don't you know all women like
>   The men who try to please?
> Do take your hands from off my book;
>   Don't tread upon the cat!
> Will you, sir, let my curls alone?
>   What next will you be at?
> Don't! Don't! Don't!
>
> Because I was a little goose,
>   And said "Yes," as you plead,
> You need not think I'm sure to go
>   Where'er I may be led.

I've been engaged before, friend Bob,
    To Hal, and Tom, and Bill,
And if you don't behave I'll turn
    You off—indeed I will!
Don't! Don't! Don't!

Don't touch me! When I liked you best,
    'Twas on your manly knees;
Get down again, sir; 'tis a pose
    That with you most agrees.
What! Dare refuse, unless, forsooth,
    I pay you with a kiss?
O, Bob, you naughty, naughty man—
    And has it come to this!
Don't! Don't! Don't!

Near the close of the show, Field parodied *Carmen* by singing an entire Italian opera in only five minutes, a piece especially written for her by Grossmith, which consisted of a recitative by the prima donna, a serenade by the tenor, a duet between the two, and a grand chorus, all represented by Field and a chair on stage. In fact, the production required no stage props except for three umbrellas for her first song, two chairs, and a reading-desk.

Field tried out *Eyes and Ears in London* in the provinces—Utica on January 21, Stamford on February 2, Bridgeport, Norwalk, and Danbury, Connecticut, in early March— before debuting in Boston on March 10 and New York on April 9. Resplendent in her formal dresses by Worth, she performed it regularly over the next year throughout New England and in venues as far south as Baltimore and Washington, D.C., and it became something of a smash hit. The Boston reviewers were particularly impressed. The *Post* opined that the musical monologue possessed "a piquant humor about it which is irresistible," the *Boston Journal* declared it was one of the "most brilliant and sparkling [shows] that has been introduced in Boston for a long time," and no less complimentary were the *Advertiser* ("a variety show, but one which would not profane a church vestry"), the *Traveller* ("just what one might expect from a brilliant woman"), the *Transcript* ("an unequivocal success"), and the *Globe* ("bright, clever, original, thoroughly entertaining").[5]

12. Kate Field, ca. 1880. Courtesy of Library of Congress
Prints and Photographs Division, LC-USZ62-46351.

Field performed to a standing-room matinee audience at Horticultural Hall in Boston on March 13. Nora Perry noted that "several encores testified to the pleasure of her listeners."[6] James T. Field wrote her two weeks later that he would "not soon forget" her "delightful evening."[7] On the anniversary of Shakespeare's birth in late April, she performed her monologue at a benefit for the Stratford Memorial at Chickering Hall in New York.[8] Field was greeted, too, by enthusiastic audiences and favorable reviews at the Baltimore Academy of Music on April 27 ("bright and characteristic"), at Lincoln Hall in Washington on April 30 ("a kind of entertainment never attempted before"), and at the Griswold Opera House in Troy, New York, on May 14 ("wonderfully comical").[9] The following year, she performed selections from her monologue at a benefit to raise money for a Poe memorial at Booth's Theatre in New York. Others on the program included Clara Morris, Alexander Salvini, John T. Raymond, and Steele Mackaye.[10]

Field's appearance in Providence in January 1881 was marred by the arrest the next day of a young Englishman named Marshall Lowe who was stalking her. Asked by the police why he was following Field, Lowe replied, "That is a private matter between she and I, about which I will say nothing." He insisted that they were longtime friends. Only once during his arrest did he refer by name to Field, whom he described as "a remarkable woman. . . . I guess she is about thirty-five years of age, is she not?" In fact, Field was forty-two.[11]

Field's refusal to marry, the assertion of her right *not* to marry or even to entertain a suitor, had made her (in)famous, at least among journalists. According to gossip "without the slightest foundation," she was secretly engaged or already married in the summer of 1870.[12] When she contributed regularly to the *New York Tribune*, she was rumored to be engaged to Whitelaw Reid. She insisted a year or two later that "the man who has held her hand in his more than two or three seconds does not live"—to which a columnist for the *Brooklyn Eagle* quipped, "Who would have thought it could be so lethal?"[13] In the summer of 1876 she squelched a rumor that she was returning from England to marry an American critic. "I should like to know who the fellow is," she joked with a reporter, "but there is one reason why the pretty story can't possibly be true—for how can I marry what does not exist in America?"[14] The next year, she publicly denied another rumor that she had moved to England because she had suffered a disappointment in love. "I came here because I wanted to come, not because I was driven," she told an interviewer. "As to the gallantry of the American man, the best friends I have in the world are American men, and if I have not married one it is because I love too many of them."[15] She admitted to a years-long flirtation with the dashing newspaper editor William Henry Hurlbert, "a very handsome, fascinating, gifted, accomplished, naughty fellow" who enjoyed a reputation as "a lady killer." Field wanted to prove "there was one lady at least who could be bomb-proof against his charm."[16] She also admitted to Stedman in 1876 that she had twice received proposals of marriage "which I gratefully declined. One [from Albert Baldwin] would have made me awfully rich," but "I love other things better. Probably there never lived a more romantic woman than I." Similarly, she later explained to the poet C. W. Stoddard that, while she was "a woman without a purse," she "might have had the purse but the price was too high. It cost self-respect." Or as she once reiterated to her Aunt Corda, "I believe in love. I don't believe in being tied to a man whom I cease to love. Therefore the less said to me about marriage the better." Nor did Field believe it possible to reconcile a career and marriage. "I need a clear head to accomplish the work I must do in this world," she told Lilian Whiting, "and nothing so unfits a sensitive nature for mental exertion as emotional intensities."[17] Nothing remotely resembling a love letter from her pen survives. She almost certainly remained celibate her entire life.

In truth, between mid-1880 and mid-1883 Field wrote virtually nothing for publication and rarely performed on stage. While singing in Boston in the spring of 1881, she was troubled by the same bronchial disease she had suffered in Florence twenty years before.[18] More to the point, her time during these years was largely devoted to her plan to revolutionize the marketing of women's haute couture. Emboldened by the success of her campaigns on behalf of the Shakespeare Memorial Theatre and Bell's telephone—and with her small fortune in stock in the telephone company—Field launched a quixotic enterprise in February 1880. It would prove to be the worst blunder of her life. Modeled on an operation established in London in

1877, the Co-operative Dress Association (aka the Ladies' Dress Association and the Women's Dress Association) aimed to import, manufacture, and sell women's and children's dress goods and millinery at wholesale prices, pay dividends to investors, and share profits with employees. Field had once purchased a designer dress for only $30 at the London cooperative and she was struck by its business methods. She planned to replicate the store in New York and she was characteristically confident it would prosper. In late February she claimed in a letter to the *New York Tribune* that "the founders of the Dress Association are astounded at the favor with which their scheme is received."[19] By early April 1880 she was trolling for investors with brochures for bait. "You will see by the enclosed," she wrote the painter Lizzie Boott, "that we are incorporated, organized and have begun business in the way of stock-taking."[20] She wrote John Hay, at the time undersecretary of state, to ask how she might "stir up the Washington women and press about Ladies' Dress Association."[21] The company sold out its initial stock offering of 10,000 shares at $25 per share within weeks, with subscribers in every state and territory in the Union. The list of investors reads like a Who's Who of prominent Americans, among them Mark Twain; James and Annie Fields; Julia Ward Howe; Holland; Stedman; Howells; Osgood; Murat Halstead; Charles Dudley Warner, editor of the *Hartford Courant;* Moses Beach, editor of the *New York Sun;* F.A.P. Barnard, the president of Columbia University; the lawyer David Dudley Field, one of her distant cousins; the author Jessie Benton Frémont; the former political boss Thurlow Weed; the actors Edwin Booth, Genèvieve Ward, and Lawrence Barrett; the Broadway impresario Lester Wallack; the Civil War general William Tecumseh Sherman; three U.S. senators; two U.S. representatives; the governor of Rhode Island; and a former governor of New York.[22] In June both *Harper's Weekly* and the *New York Tribune* reported that the Association "promises to be a great success."[23] The joke made the rounds that Field had moved "to amend the resolution of the dress-reformers. To the injunction 'Let us be appropriately clad,' she would add: 'Let us also continue to be pretty.'"[24]

But the project was dogged by controversy and mismanagement from the beginning. Some subscribers failed to pay for their stock, a shortfall of about $23,000 even before the Association opened its doors.[25] A bigger problem was that Field proved to be an inept businesswoman. At the first meeting of potential investors at the Victoria Hotel in late March, she announced that she had selected a board of directors composed of her friends, including Howe, and that the shareholders would have no voice in the direction of the company during its first year. To deflect criticism, she insisted that "the association will be managed by business men on business principles" and the "organization of the association is entirely in the hands of able lawyers."[26] (A wag replied, "Bad for Kate Field. She says that her co-operative enterprise is in the hands of able lawyers, which is a very forward state indeed.")[27] The brouhaha was an omen of things to come.

In a moment of madness or genius, Field and the other directors decided to hire the founder of the London dress association, Anthony Pulbrook, to manage their business. Even before leaving England in November 1879, Field had called upon Pulbrook, who signaled his willingness to come to the United States. He told her "that if I saw a promise of sufficient support," he would "have no objection later on to proceed to America and organize a similar institution to the one I organized in England and give the American ladies the benefit of all the experience I had gained from the English venture."[28] Trouble was, Pulbrook's demands were exorbitant. He offered in March 1880 to organize the New York association for a salary of $10,000 plus $1,000 paid in advance and 1 percent of gross sales every year the company paid dividends. These terms "were impossible," Field groused in May. Unfortunately, she soon offered Pulbrook similar if not better terms. She embarked for England on June 12 in the *Spain* and within a month she had wooed Pulbrook away from the London Ladies' Dress Association by promising him an annual salary of $15,000.[29]

While in Europe to hire Pulbrook, Field took the opportunity to improve the occasion. She dined on Independence Day at the Westminster Hotel in London with James Russell Lowell, the U.S. ambassador to the Court of St. James; the actors Christine Nilsson, Helena Modjeska, and Lawrence Barrett; the industrialist Cyrus Field; William Winter; the Irish politician and novelist Justin McCarthy, the impresario Carl Rosa; Moncure Conway; and George Grossmith.[30] She frequented the London theater, of course—Geneviève Ward in *Forget Me Not,* McKee Rankin in Joaquin Miller's *The Danites,* and her friend James T. Raymond in *The Gilded Age.* In a dig at Mark Twain, however, she noted that while Raymond's "acting has taken immensely" it is "unfortunate that he should not have a play better suited to English taste."[31] She interviewed Charles Bradlaugh, whom she had not seen for several years, in mid-July.[32] She also crossed the Channel to Paris and Baden-Baden, and on a whim and in company with a man—identity unknown—she took a train nine hours through Karlsruhe, Stuttgart, and Munich to Oberammergau to see the Passion Play there. It was a disappointment, particularly given the blatant "spirit of speculation" in the village, the transformation of "a religious performance into a circus." She was also critical of the amateur performers ("Judas made great efforts to act, but, after all, he was only fussy") and the length of the play, eighteen acts in eight hours ("The art of condensation is less known in Germany than among more nervous nations").[33] She returned to England and sailed from Liverpool aboard the *Adriatic* on October 12, arriving back in New York on October 23.[34]

At the time the hiring of Pulbrook seemed a coup for the New York association. During the months of recriminations that ensued and amid the charges of secret dealings, Field maintained that the offer to Pulbrook had been approved in advance by the board of directors. "Early in June I gave notice to the directors of our Association that I should sail at once for England," she explained, "and suggested that Mr. Pulbrook be invited to co-operate with us. The suggestion was accepted." In "securing Mr. Pulbrook's valuable aid, I believe I have done the right thing for the Dress Association." Pulbrook at first agreed to begin work in New York in August, though "important business" detained him in England until early January 1881. As a result, the association "cut down . . . every dollar of expense" until Pulbrook "and the proper time for advertising should arrive."[35]

Perhaps predictably, given the brevity of the courtship and the overly generous conditions of his contract, Pulbrook's employment was short-lived and ended in a messy divorce. He resigned after barely four months on the job, alleging that Field had refused to surrender to him the authority required to manage the business. In late April, over Pulbrook's objections the board of directors elected her—"a lady," he complained, "who had had no experience whatever in the dry goods business"—as president of the association.[36] On her part, Field wrote a friend, "I'm tired out and wish we were all in Heaven where Dress Ass'ns will be in vain."[37] To make matters worse, she sued Pulbrook on May 13 in an effort to recover about $2,500 of the roughly $6,000 he had so far received in salary, which she claimed was owed to her personally in a side-deal they had made, and she procured an attachment in the New York Supreme Court against his luggage, effectively preventing him, if only temporarily, from returning to England.[38] The New York press reveled in the controversy. The *New York Graphic* claimed that Field owned preferred stock in the association if it failed, and that in founding it she was motivated more by greed than altruism.[39] In an interview with the *New York Times*, she was asked to explain her reasons for the suit, and she tried to downplay its significance by refusing to say "a single word about the matter till it comes up in court." She reiterated it was "a private affair and is none of the public's concern," though she added that she was "utterly disgusted with human nature, and if I ever undertake again to interest myself in the affairs of anybody but myself, why I hope I shall have my head chopped right off."[40] Two weeks later, she dropped the suit when Pulbrook's lawyer threatened her with a countersuit for detaining his client in the United States.[41] After a short-lived proxy battle—Field referred contemptuously to "the few idiots who gave him" their stockholder votes—Pulbrook and his lawyer finally "capitulated unconditionally" and withdrew "all opposition to the Association."[42]

Meanwhile, Field and the directors tried to put the best face possible on the fiasco. On May 22, they hired John Wales of the dry goods company Spalding, Wales & Company of Boston and a "merchant of high standing and unimpeachable integrity" as general manager.[43] They signed a three-year lease on a six-story building with sixty thousand square feet of space on West 23rd Street for twenty thousand dollars a year, moved into it in August, and began to buy inventory and hire employees. They planned a grand opening for business on October 3. Field worked during these weeks, she said, "like a dog from ten in the morning until ten at night in the interest of the Association, from which I receive no salary, and which has cost me in time and professional loss $25,000.[44] As she confided to Stedman, "if I keep on much longer in the dry goods business, my brains will be so muddled that I shall be utterly incapable of rising above an advertisement."[45] She declined an invitation to lecture in New Mexico, though it was "most tempting and would mean shekels," because she could not "desert the ship at this juncture when we are nearing land."[46] She was determined to conduct the business according to the most progressive principles: the association building featured such amenities as seats for sales clerks, two safety elevators, and a lunchroom, circulating library, and reading and reception rooms on the fifth floor. The seamstresses employed by the association bought their meals at cost in the cafeteria.

Despite the best of intentions, if not the best-laid plans, the business went to smash in little over a year. It never paid dividends to its investors nor shared profits with its employees. Fields claimed later that "Wales killed it the first six months."[47] Certainly there were signs the business was failing by April 1882. Wales had been fired for incompetence and running the business into debt.[48] At the first and only stockholders' meeting, on April 11, Field stationed a private detective at the front door of the Union League Theatre with orders "to keep out reporters."[49] Though the association boasted some five thousand stockholders, half of them in New York, only eighty or ninety of them attended the meeting. They were mostly friends loyal to Field and they elected a slate of directors she had proposed. Some of the dissidents grumbled that the goods were overpriced, with dresses designed by Worth, Pigat, and Heutenaar costing upwards of $300 and men's tailored suits costing as much as $200.[50] In retrospect, too, the association was clearly undercapitalized, with too many shareholders, too low a value per share, and too thin a margin for error. In late May, Field explained to Jeanette Gilder her inability to place a company ad in the *Critic:* "we've cut down again and shall hereafter confine ourselves to a few dailies and certain weeklies with a large circulation."[51]

Field tried to compensate for the slashed advertising budget by contributing a series of articles on fashion between January and April 1882 to *Our Continent,* a Philadelphia weekly edited by Albion Tourgée, best known today as author of the novels *A Fool's Errand* and *Bricks Without Straw* and for defending Homer Plessy before the U.S. Supreme Court in 1897. Field essayed such topics as "Gloves," "American Taste in Dress," and "American Dress Goods." In one column, for example, she hailed the "rational gown" or "divided skirt" invented by Lady Habberton and imported for sale by the Dress Association.[52] While these essays were widely copied and may have

13. Ad for Co-operative Dress Association, *New York Graphic*, 29 July 1882, 192.

proved her authority on matters of fashion, they did not reverse the fortunes of the association. Far from steering the company on a fiscally prudent course, in fact, Field seemed to fiddle while Rome burned. She lived in regal style at the Victoria Hotel, and she routinely received visitors in her fifth-floor association office adorned with a portrait of her by Frank Millet. First exhibited at the National Academy of Design in New York in the spring of 1881, the painting—now lost—represented her seated on a divan piled high with yellow satin cushions in one of her Worth dresses, a black silk evening gown, décolleté, sleeveless, and bordered in red. As the art critic of the *Brooklyn Eagle* remarked, Field "is looking out at us with a half meditative expression on her face, her head resting upon her hand, the elbow of the slender arm resting on the back of the divan, and the other arm disposed gracefully upon her lap."[53] Despite the red ink splashed across the company ledger, moreover, Field continued to vacation in Europe, ostensibly to supervise the association buyers and to select goods for import. She sailed for Europe aboard the *City of Berlin* on June 18, 1882, her fifth transatlantic crossing in less than three years—despite the signs the business was failing. She conceded that most of her three months abroad would be "devoted to some spa [specifically near Mt. Doré in central France], where I shall toy with warm mineral water and aspire to an appetite," though she also promised to "keep my eyes open, and when I see anything adapted to the C.D.A. it will be bought."[54] She frequented London and Paris theaters, heard Patti in a new French opera, saw Ellen Terry in *Romeo and Juliet*, Modjeska in *Odette*, the Kendals in *The Squire*, and the divine Sarah Bernhardt in *Camille*.[55] She wrote Stedman the next month from London that the buyers in Paris were "under my supervision and the result will be very fine next Autumn. I shall send over a complete collection of *Persian Curios* and if the Art Museum wants them, they'd better speak quickly."[56]

But sales in the fall were dismal. "The bad trade of this autumn prevented our regaining lost ground—no reserved cash settled the matter," she admitted afterwards.[57] The company was forced to lay off some employees and reduce the wages of others. "We expected a good Christmas season which would have made things right," Field allowed. "It did not come and the debts contracted by John Wales were too heavy to carry."[58] The association shut its doors permanently the day after Christmas 1882.

With listed assets of $239,000 and liabilities of $129,000,[59] the company might have seemed solvent but for the fact that, apart from its $30,000 in cash, its inventory and fixtures could be liquidated for little more than a small fraction on the dollar. As soon as the news of the bankruptcy became public, Albert Baldwin wrote Field to offer his help. "Should the closing of the C.D.A. embarrass you financially," her former suitor pleaded, "I beg that you will allow me to do all that a sincere and devoted friend ought to. If you will permit me to be of service to you, as occasion demands, I shall take it as a great favor."[60] In the wake of the business failure, Field was not above finger-pointing. She blamed the closure on the fickle spending habits of the stockholders (whom she had recruited); on the incompetence of Wales (whom she had hired); on the mismanagement of the European buyers (whose work, she had repeatedly insisted, she supervised); and on the word *co-operative* in the company name (which she had selected). The fact remains, too, that in the last months of the association, even as some employees were furloughed and the wages of others cut, she began to draw a salary "as a means of getting back some of the money" she had earlier "advanced to try and save it." Isaac Bailey, a former director of the association and Field's friend since 1869 when he contributed money to buy the John Brown farm, laid the blame for the bankruptcy squarely on Field, "the accomplished but altogether impractical lady who was chosen President of the organization," for interfering with Wales' management. The *Brooklyn Eagle* editorialized that Field may have been "unfortunate in the selection of her employees" but "the stockholders were most assuredly unfortunate in the selection of the president." Field long suffered from the fallout from the failure; for instance, that she had proved "that women are not inferior to men. They can engineer a financial disaster with equal cleverness and dispatch."[61]

In the end, the failure of the association irreparably damaged her reputation. While the bankruptcy of Field's Dress Association in 1882 may seem similar on the surface to the bankruptcy of Mark Twain's publishing company a dozen years later, there is a fundamental difference: whereas Twain repaid his creditors in full and emerged from his financial embarrassment more beloved than before, Field chose to wear the mantle of victim. When her old friend Stedman confronted her about the failure of the business and his own substantial loss, she protested he had never "consulted me as the wisdom of selling your shares." At least she could not be accused of insider trading. She had loaned the association $15,000 of her own money, the "last $2500" since she had returned from Europe in late September—would she have done so "had I known it would fail"? In addition, she had lost her entire $3,500 stock investment. "If I told you nothing about the condition of C.D.A. when failure became inevitable," she remonstrated, "I did my duty, which was silence. As an officer I should have been guilty of grossly unbusinesslike conduct to have breathed impending failure to a soul." Besides, she was "not permitted" to intervene in the affairs of "the merchandise dep't where all the harm was done."[62] Or as she brazenly informed another of her former investors, "Dear Madam, your stock is utterly worthless. You have probably lost $25.00—I have lost $3500.00 in stock and $15000.00 in money loaned. The Association was managed by men and killed by them."[63] She elsewhere complained to the assistant editor of the *Century* that she had "been cruelly slandered in the Press and I am terribly hurt in consequence," that she had lost her entire investment of nearly twenty thousand dollars and two years of her life in the collapse of the enterprise. Never did she admit her own responsibility for the disaster; instead, she merely figured she had been too "trusting to the capacity of others."[64]

The happiest moment in the troubled history of the Dress Association no doubt occurred the day Oscar Wilde came to lunch. When Wilde cleared customs in New York on January 3, 1882, he carried with him a letter of introduction to Field from Hermann Vezin, their mutual friend. As Vezin wrote to Field, "I have given Oscar Wilde a letter to you. You will, I hope, like him very much. He is *very* clever, one of the most entertaining men I ever met, & as you know is the high priest of aestheticism here. . . . I am sure you will be glad to be of use to him."[65] Wilde presented his letter of introduction to Field three days after his arrival.[66] She invited him to a "bohemian lunch" at the Dress Association on January 11, and Wilde not only accepted but urged her to invite some of her artist friends. Over the next couple of days, she asked Stedman, Vedder, Millet, and Clara Morris to join the party. "Wilde is clever and wants to meet artists only," she wrote Stedman.[67] Meanwhile, too, Wilde's and Field's paths often crossed over the next few days. On January 8 they met at a reception at the Croly home on East 38th Street. Among the other guests: Morris, Alexander Salvini, and Henry Watterson.[68] Two evenings later, Field attended Wilde's address "The English Renaissance" at Chickering Hall, and immediately after the lecture she saw him again at a reception at the Fifth Avenue mansion of the casino owner John Mack and his wife. Others in attendance: the reform Democratic politician Robert B. Roosevelt, uncle of Theodore; the Crolys; and Louisa May Alcott.[69]

The following afternoon at two, Wilde arrived at the offices of the Dress Association sporting a white ivory walking stick and attired in a dark-green Prince Albert coat with a dark-green handkerchief in his pocket and a dark-green cravat knotted at his neck. The guests lunched in Field's private office, which had been decorated for the occasion. "On the walls hung panels of Japanese embroidery," the *New York World* reported. "The napkins used at lunch were of Japanese paper, white and very heavy, almost like cloth. After lunch everyone wrote his or her name on Japanese fans."[70] About five P.M. Wilde left the Association offices to dress for yet another reception that evening.[71] Over the next few days the luncheon attracted a good deal of attention in the local press. The *New York Graphic* took the opportunity to satirize both Wilde's sexuality and Field's commercialism. The foppish Wilde was "measured for his petticoats" at the luncheon, according to the *Graphic,* and he was also "the recipient of a pair of gilt edged corsets, made expressly for him by the Co-operative Dress Association. During the official measurements the shareholders of the Association" assumed "poses of æsthetic adoration."[72] On her part, Field later described the luncheon more matter-of-factly in interviews with reporters. "I was sitting at a little gathering, chatting with Oscar Wilde," she explained, when the æsthete suddenly declared, "Ah, you Americans never travel in your own country. You go abroad and do England and the Continent, but you never see anything of your own country." Field replied, as she remembered, "that when we next met he should not have that to say to me."[73]

They next met, however, only five days later at a reception for Wilde at the home of the publisher Robert Stewart Davis in Philadelphia. The guest of honor at one point "joined the ladies" in the third floor library, where he chatted with Field and Louise Chandler Moulton.[74] No doubt Field had grown fond of the so-called "apostle of æstheticism," and she soon rallied to his defense against the harsh attacks of the newspapers. On January 27, the day before Wilde arrived in Boston, she sent a letter to the editor of the *Boston Journal* in the form of a parable. In a cover note, she explained that she was disgusted by the uproar over Wilde's lecture tour.[75] "Once upon a time," the parable opened, "there was a young man who was sent to a great university. Being clever and studious he bore off the honors of a 'double first.'" Had he "frequented a barber, cultivated his muscle, taken to horses and other ennobling dissipations society would have accepted him as a nineteenth century man." Instead, he "wandered from academic groves to the regions of Piccadilly, shook his locks in the face of a short-haired fraternity, and apostrophized sunflowers and lilies instead of betting money on the Derby." He was declared "an idiot," but he discovered in this caricature a rich opportunity "and embraced it. This young man waked up one morning to find himself notorious, which today is the same as being famous." He decided to go to America and lecture. "Did the young man request the entire American press to make him the subject of leaders and interviews—to chronicle his movements as those of few lions ever had been chronicled? Did he implore love-sick maidens to shower him with appeals for his autograph, and suggest that men and women to whom he was not accredited should deluge him with invitations to dinners and receptions? By no means." So which was the fool—"Press, Public, or 'Double First'?"[76] Field went so far in one of her essays in *Our Continent* as to defend Wilde's preference for knee-breeches in lieu of trousers.[77]

Even as the buttons were coming off the Dress Association, Field found time to complete her long-delayed critical study of Charles Fechter for Osgood's American Actor Series in the summer of 1882. Based largely on her two articles on Fechter in the *Atlantic Monthly* in 1870 and her reviews of his acting over the years in the *New York Tribune, New York Evening Mail,* and *Boston Herald,* the 205-page book also incorporated biographical material given her by Fechter before his death and memoirs of the actor by Wilkie Collins, Hermann Vezin, and Edmund Yates, the editor of the London *World.* It might better have been entitled "Pen Photographs of Charles Fechter's

Acting," given its attention to the style of his performances. Though a bit of a pastiche, Field's *Charles Fechter* was generally well received by critics when it appeared in September 1882 as, for example, in the *New York Times* ("interesting and vivacious") and *Boston Globe* ("tenderly and faithfully" written).[78] Field was so encouraged that she began to research a similar book on Adelaide Ristori.[79] But then a bombshell. In an unsigned review in the *Nation* in November, Brander Matthews, an influential drama critic and a decade later the first professor of dramatic literature at Columbia University, excoriated the book. It was "decidedly the poorest of the six volumes" in Osgood's series. Rather than a close study of Fechter's career, it was "a journalistic extemporization and really has very slight claims to be considered as literature." In particular, according to Matthews, Field "absurdly" overrated Fechter's importance to the Parisian stage.[80] Thirty-five years later, however, Matthews in his autobiography tried to redress his criticisms. Field "misconceived" Fechter's position in France, to be sure, but in reviewing her book he "had dwelt on this defect, probably to show off my private knowledge of Parisian stage history." He learned later from a mutual friend that "my review wounded her grievously" and "she wondered who could have been guilty of it." Soon after its publication, both Matthews and Field

> dined with the Stedmans and I took in Kate Field to dinner. We had never met before; and as we were both interested in the theater our talk turned upon the stage. And, so our common friend informed me later, she suddenly jumped to the conclusion that I must be the writer of the review which had hurt her feelings so keenly. But by no change of her cordiality toward me was I led then to suspect this discovery at the dinner-table. Her manner remained serene, perhaps more obviously so than mine, since I was inwardly conscious of the anonymity of my review.

Only in his autobiography did Matthews finally concede that Field's *Fechter* "was a pretty good book" after all,[81] and he and Laurence Hutton commissioned her to contribute a sketch of Fechter to their coedited *Actors and Actresses of Great Britain and the United States* in 1886.

After the failure of the Dress Association, Field kept the promise she had made to Wilde to tour the West. "I became so ashamed of sailing east year after year," she explained, "I made up my mind to learn as much of my own country as I knew of Europe."[82] She made plans to visit friends in Arizona and, like Theodore Roosevelt and Owen Wister, to try the strenuous "west cure" for her health. In July 1883, after a brief visit to the Sanfords in Newport,[83] Field crossed the Mississippi River for the first time in her forty-four years and headed for the American outback. She never again sailed to Europe.

9

Zion

"I WOULDN'T LIVE IN THE WEST for all the wealth of the Indies," Field had announced from southwestern Ohio in February 1871. "It would be splendid misery. There is much to admire—and certainly I am treated with bounteous hospitality; people in five minutes treat me as though I were a bosom friend,—but there is too much spitting and *rawness* and too little culture to please me."[1] She eventually repented her snobbery. She considered traveling west of the Mississippi as early as April 1874, when Helen Hunt Jackson advised her about the price of train fare to Colorado.[2] Four years later, she reiterated her desire to visit the state: "I've never yet found a summer resort where it didn't rain everlastingly—Newport, Rhode Island, excepted—and there is but one more experiment left for me to try—Colorado. There we are assured that we can stake our last penny on six months of uninterrupted blue sky, no heat, no cold, and no mosquitoes."[3]

Eighteen months after lunching with Wilde, Field honored her pledge to "go West." Leaving New York, she paused overnight in Chicago, where she was personally escorted by George Pullman, the railroad car industrialist, around his company town south of the city. She addressed the employees from the stage of the town theater before continuing her journey, "feeling that Mr. Pullman deserved well of his countrymen."[4] On July 19, 1883, she arrived in Denver and registered at the Windsor Hotel with a half-dozen trunks and plans to linger in the region for at least a month. Much to the amusement of Eugene Field (no relation), the managing editor of the *Denver Tribune*, she had even brought a canvas sitz bath hundreds of miles lest she fail to find a porcelain tub in the "wild and woolly west."[5] Still, he pronounced her "one of the most brilliant and popular of all the noted women of America." On her part, Field explained that only "the other day I crossed the Mississippi for the first time. In the East they have a habit of running over to Europe, and year after year I have been going with the crowd. This year I resolved to do something different, so I packed up my things and started; and here I am." She hoped to find an apartment "where I can have a piano and a parlor in which to receive my friends, which is impossible given the crowded condition of the hotel." She wanted not only "to see the city, but to know the people. I want to be with them and thoroughly understand them." Even the rival *Denver Times* agreed that "Denver is lucky" that such a celebrity planned to "stay with us a long while," and the *Denver Republican* declared that Field "will probably write a book on Colorado and its people, especially its people." No one "could better grasp the true spirit of Western character, and handle it with a tact which would give it its originality and spontaneity without the trashy hyperbole with which most writers have embellished it."[6]

Over the next several weeks Field traveled throughout the state, camping out near the Needles and inspecting the San Juan silver mines.[7] She contributed a "very spicy article" on mental telepathy "inspired by the air of Colorado" to the *Denver Tribune* for July 29,[8] and she performed her musical monologue at a benefit for the First Congregational Church two evenings later. Eugene Field applauded the entertainment as "one of the best ever given in the city." She held the attention of her audience for nearly two hours. Similarly, the *Denver Republican* averred that Field had

> delighted the most cultivated audience that was ever assembled in Denver. . . . No other woman could have given the very cleverly compounded *potpourri* of fine satire, with now and then a shade of vaudeville in it, in a church and before the audience which was there last night, without offending somebody's taste. Not that there is anything in her monologue that would profane the most sanctified place, but had any other woman than Kate Field given a burlesque of Italian opera in a church and used the preacher's chair for a mock balcony, it is not at all likely that some finical person would have been more or less shocked. Happily Miss Field did not shock anybody.

Would that have been the case. She was excoriated in the *Denver Times,* the same paper that had welcomed her to town hardly a week before. The reviewer condemned the "folly" and "vulgarity" of her presentation and particularly the décoletté style of her dress, "the effect of which is heightened by a display of diamonds that is simply barbaric. Her face is much 'made-up,' and her hair is dressed and 'banged' after the style of a very unæsthetic milk-maid." Then the coup d'etat: "She is old and scrawny." Fortunately, a more seasoned editor intervened and apologized the next day.[9] (For the record, Field added twelve pounds to her five-foot, three-inch frame during the first three months of her western trip.[10] The months of work and worry over the Dress Association fiasco had taken their toll.)

Undeterred, Field delivered her Dickens lecture at the same church on August 1 to unqualified praise in the local press. She was Dickens' "most sympathetic and intelligent interpreter" *(Rocky Mountain News)*, his "champion" *(Denver Republican)*, and a "brilliant" and "gifted young lady" *(Denver Tribune)*. Even the *Denver Times* conceded that "whatever criticism may be indulged regarding Miss Field's London monologue, her lecture on Dickens is certainly a most enjoyable presentation."[11]

She learned two days later that her uncle Milton Sanford had died suddenly in Newport. She considered returning east to attend his funeral and comfort her Aunt Corda, but Cordelia Sanford's private nurse Alla Newton encouraged her to stay away. Not that Field was too brokenhearted over his death: "My uncle was the worst sort of Democrat."[12] Instead, on August 5 she railed south to Manitou Springs, where she registered at the Beebee Hotel.[13] She soon called on Helen Hunt Jackson at her home in Colorado Springs[14] and, on August 10, she delivered her Dickens lecture at the Opera House in the city. So great was the demand to see her that a special train was dispatched for the convenience of theatergoers from Manitou; and, as the Colorado Springs *Daily Gazette* reported the next day, "nearly everyone left the house thoroughly well satisfied" with her performance.[15]

Two weeks later, Field had the signal honor of christening a town on the Denver & Rio Grande railroad between the capital and Colorado Springs. According to the *Castle Rock Journal,* many "distinguished guests," including Field, were invited to the Loch Katrine resort on Saturday, August 25, for the purpose of selecting its new name.[16] Field suggested "Palmero" after General William J. Palmer, the founder of Colorado Springs and former president of the D&RG, because "no town along the entire system bore his name." As she recalled later, "I proceeded on a short campaign of education, the result of which was that when the vote was taken on the picnic grounds, 'Palmero' won by a large majority."[17] She was awarded a building lot in the town, though she was never given a deed or even told where the property was located.[18] By the time the new town plat was recorded in November 1883, the town had been rechristened Palmer Lake.

Field lived at the newly opened Antlers Hotel in Colorado Springs for the next six weeks.[19] On October 13, en route to Salt Lake City, she delivered her Dickens lecture in Grand Junction, at the confluence of the Grand and Gunnison rivers, and spent the next day touring the valley in company with George A. Crawford, the founder of the town. As a reporter for the *Grand Junction News* noted, "the day was superb and the play of light and shade upon the Grand Mesa made a picture that must impress any beholder."[20] She had hoped to stop in Grand Junction several days, but she learned "that suitable accommodations for a more extended stay" than a single day "could not be procured" nearer than "the Mecca of Mormonism." She hurried to Salt Lake City and registered at the Continental Hotel two days later, planning to pass no more than a week or two there before continuing to New Mexico and Arizona. She would not visit the desert Southwest for another eight years, however. Instead, Field spent the next eight months in Utah studying the habits and habitat of the Latter Day Saints. "I am regarded as more or less demented by eastern friends," she admitted.[21] But her research into Mormonism during these months inspired the greatest reform campaign of her career.

Field landed in Utah with no preconceptions about the Saints. Her father had satirized the Mormon communities in Missouri and Illinois nearly forty years before in the *St. Louis Reveille,* but his daughter never mentioned the religion in print before 1883. She insisted later that she knew "absolutely nothing about Mormonism" prior to arriving in Salt Lake City.[22] She delivered her Dickens lecture in the Congregational Church there on October 23 and performed her musical monologue at the Salt Lake Theatre on November 4.[23] Meanwhile, her curiosity about the local culture was piqued. "I could not help it," she explained. Nor did it take her long to form an opinion. As the *New York Graphic* reported in December 1883, "Kate Field is disgusted with Mormonism."[24]

While in Zion, Field contributed essays about Mormonism to several papers, particularly the *Boston Herald*. She was intrigued by the mysteries of Mormon society and, according to Lilian Whiting, "Every facility was accorded to her by Federal officials, military officers, leading Gentiles and apostates."[25] She interviewed a defrocked Mormon bishop and befriended both Eli Murray, the Gentile governor of Utah Territory, and Judge C. C. Goodwin, the editor of the *Salt Lake Tribune,* a local Gentile newspaper. Even some prominent Mormon women cooperated in her research, including Emmeline B. Wells, editor of the *Woman's Exponent,* and Romania B. Pratt, a prominent local physician. She was "treated kindly by the Mormons for about three months," she later recalled, "but when I began to write about them they dropped me." "No Mormon more faithfully attended services in tabernacles and ward meeting-houses than I," she insisted, as on January 13 when "I heard a Mormon elder tell his simple congregation that Gentiles were 'hell-hounds barking at their heels.'" The address "was filled with hatred toward the United States, and I went home marveling at the freedom with which Mormons preach treason and poison youthful minds with falsehoods." She traveled as far south as Sandy and as far north as Logan to tour as much of the new temple there "as Gentile eyes may gaze upon."[26] She also attended every session of the fifty-fourth conference of the Mormon church, held in Salt Lake City between April 4 and 6, 1884, and wrote a report about it that consumed an entire page of the *Boston Herald.* She was unimpressed by the "religious farce."[27] "You'd have thought that an agricultural fair or a circus had come to town," she joked. The morning of the first day, Apostle George Teasdale insisted from the pulpit on the thinnest of evidence that "there was more trouble in monogamous than in polygamic families." The first speaker on the second day of the conference was "Apostle Lorenzo Snow, possessed of little voice and no ideas." Of the thousands of Saints in the Tabernacle during the conference, Field observed, "the vast majority were cattle on two legs—obedient, subservient cattle, not to be blamed for being themselves."[28] Ironically, she later added, Heber C. Kimball, Brigham Young's first counselor, "called his twenty wives 'cows.' He ought to have been a judge of their mental caliber."[29] As Field wrote Stedman after living seven months in Zion, "If I'd known what a 'big job' Mormonism is, I never should have had the courage to touch it."[30]

She always expressed sympathy for the female victims of plural or "celestial" marriage, which she called a "peculiar institution" akin to slavery.[31] Far from enjoying lives of leisure, as the Mormon apologists claimed, the wives of polygamists "work like galley slaves and support the husband, the great lazy hulk, and he lives in clover."[32] Field's dispatches from Utah were filled with stories about the plight of the "misguided women who are but accessories to crime" and calls "to devise means whereby the leaders of this hierarchy shall be brought to judgment."[33] She contradicted the report of a federal commission that polygamy was dying out, a central premise in the recent anti-Mormon bill of Senator George F. Edmunds. But Field's largest guns were trained not on polygamy, "a mere incident in the wrong of Mormonism," but on the crime of treason.[34] As she wrote the Unitarian minister Andrew P. Peabody, the Mormon church was in reality "a vast business and political machine bent upon undermining our government."[35] Or as she said elsewhere, "Mormonism is to this republic what the Canada thistle is to agriculture," with its missionaries "the flying seed."[36] Sometimes she disparaged the LDS church with a medical metaphor, as a "plague" or disease in the body politic. In any case, the accusation that it was "organized treason" permeated every essay she wrote and every talk she delivered thereafter on "the Mormon monster." Nor was she ignored by the authorities. The *Ogden Standard Examiner,* a church-controlled paper, complained that she was "making a general nuisance of herself" with her persistent questions.[37]

On the other hand, on June 18, 1884, the day before Field left Utah for the East, Goodwin editorialized in the *Salt Lake Tribune* that apart from church officials Kate Field was probably the most informed person in the world on Mormonism "and its effects upon men, women, and governments. . . . If she proposes to lecture, she ought to be able to prepare a better lecture on Mormonism than she has ever yet delivered." This editorial was soon reprinted in the *Boston Globe.* Eighteen months later, Goodwin remembered that while in Zion his friend Field had "interviewed hundreds of Saints and sinners" and that "at her own expense she traveled north and south."[38] As a result of her painstaking research, Field became a recognized authority on Mormon theocracy and Utah politics. "Accident acquainted me with 'the true inwardness' of the Latter Day Saints' scheming," she once

explained, "and duty rather than inclination prompts me to tell the tale."[39]
On her part, too, Field to the end of her life praised Goodwin for his courage in trying to redeem "a great territory from church domination." He
"fought for liberty" for over twenty years "without fear and without favor."
He told her in Utah in 1883 that he "supposed there are 10,000 earnest,
honest people, men and women, who every day pray to Almighty God to
rid this country of me, and I suppose there are a hundred thousand who
wish I were dead."[40]

En route east in late June 1884, Field paused briefly in Colorado
Springs before proceeding to some of the old Mormon settlements in Missouri, Illinois, and Ohio to continue her investigations.[41] On July 9, for
example, Field was in Jefferson City, the Missouri state capital, to examine
"the records of the State department in regard to the Mormon war" in
1838 and other documents that "may throw light on the subject of Mormonism." In Richmond, Missouri, she interviewed A. W. Doniphan, "one
of the generals commanding the state forces in Daviess county during the
Mormon war," as well as David Whitmer, the last surviving witness to the
Book of Mormon. In Gower, Missouri, she visited David R. Atchison, another
general during the Mormon war; and in Independence she interviewed
both Joseph Smith, Jr., and Alexander Smith, sons of the Mormon prophet,
both of whom repudiated polygamy. The "Josephites" proved, to her mind,
that Mormonism need not embrace either heterodoxy or treason. She also
traveled to Nauvoo, Illinois, founded by Joseph Smith in 1839; to Carthage,
Illinois, where Smith was killed in 1849; to Painesville and Kirtland, Ohio,
and to Palmyra, New York, where Smith allegedly found the golden tablets
on which his religion was based.[42]

Back in Boston in mid-November, Field extolled her western experiences. "I am glad to be again in the East," she told an interviewer for the
Boston Herald, but "traveling intelligently and slowly over this country is
equal to a liberal education." She returned weighing fifteen pounds more
than when she left, was "much stronger and my muscle is creditable to my
sex."[43] She met the British novelist Edmund Gosse at the home of Louise Moulton in mid-December, and she soon returned to the same social
circles in which she had moved the year before,[44] but without the same
confident swagger. Bostonians may brag that they live in "the hub of the

universe and that the West can teach" them nothing, she admitted, but "it has taught me more than half a dozen trips to Europe."[45] (She conceded that she was "about half a Bostonian" herself—to which a New York wag replied, "So she has a better half, like the rest of us.")[46] She began a book about Mormon history—never published, if finished, and now lost—which at least two publishers rejected for want of a market. The American West was normally packaged for sale at the time to eastern male readers who enjoyed blood-and-thunder escapist fantasies. Who wanted to buy a book about the oppression of Mormon women or the treason of Mormon elders? In 1886, she even wrote Mark Twain in his office as director of the American Publishing Company of Hartford to solicit his interest in the book. "I'm told you have a very poor opinion of me because I have lectured against Mormonism," she began her letter. Apparently she had forgotten his comments about Mormons in *Roughing It* (for example, the *Book of Mormon* was "chloroform in print" and Mormon women were "slatternly" and "pathetically homely"). "You represent a big publishing house. I am writing a history of Mormonism which I think will be entertaining as well as enlightening. Such a book is fit only, it seems to me, to be sold by subscription. Does it appeal to you from a business point of view? I think I know what I am writing about."[47]

In his reply, Twain allowed how he too opposed Mormonism, much as he harbored strong reservations about Christian Science and other faiths that threatened to become state religions. But he would not endorse any abridgement of religious freedom. "Your notion and mine about polygamy is without doubt exactly the same," he explained,

> but you probably think we have some cause of quarrel with those people for putting it into the religion, whereas I think the opposite. Considering our complacent cant about this country of ours being the home of liberty of conscience, it seems to me that the attitude of our Congress and people toward the Mormon Church is matter for limitless laughter and derision. The Mormon religion *is* a religion: the negative vote of all of the rest of the globe could not break down that fact; and so I shall probably always go on thinking that the attitude of our Congress and nation toward it is merely good trivial stuff to make fun of. Am I a friend to the

Mormon religion? No. I would like to see it extirpated, but always by fair means, not these Congressional rascalities. If you can destroy it with a book,—by arguments and facts, not brute force,—you will do a good and wholesome work.

If his "business decks were clear," he added, he might be persuaded "to publish such a book," but "they are not clear now" and "it is hard to tell when they will be. They are piled up with contracts which two or three years—and possibly four—will be required to fulfil." Twain claimed that he had had to "pigeon-hole" indefinitely one of his own "finished and ready" books, on which he had "spent nearly ten thousand dollars," to "make room for other people's more important books."[48] The claim was a brush-off: Twain had no finished manuscript on hand, and he would not complete *A Connecticut Yankee in King Arthur's Court* for another two years. Still, Field bought the excuse. "That 'Mark Twain' should wait for anybody's book is absurd enough to print, but I won't betray your embarrassment of—riches," she replied. "When I left [Utah] I attempted to publish a book on the Mormons," Field later reminisced, but "my publishers would not accept it, as it was not a paying subject." She eventually realized that "[t]here is really no money in a book on Mormonism."[49]

She chose instead to publicize her quarrel with Mormonism by taking to the stump. "Thwarted in my original intention, there was nothing left but the platform," she explained. A single speech delivered in many towns, she realized, might shape "more public opinion than a dozen books could have inspired."[50] She summered in 1884 at the homes of friends in Glen Haven, New York, and South Norwalk, Connecticut, where she wrote and rehearsed a lecture.[51] The first version of her address on the Saints ran six hours, however, so she revised it into a series of three lectures—"The Mormon Monster," "Polygamy in Utah," and "Social and Political Crimes in Utah"—that she delivered dozens of times during the 1884–85 lecture season throughout New England and New York. She tried out "The Mormon Monster" in Newton Centre, Massachusetts, on October 22, and she delivered it again to a "crowded audience" in Worcester, Massachusetts, on November 10.[52] She spoke in Boston the evening of November 18 with James Osgood, E. P. Whipple, Phillips Brooks, T. B. Aldrich, Annie Fields,

Sarah Orne Jewett, and the governor of Massachusetts all in the hall.[53] "At Tremont Temple all the gray beards turned out and formed a curious background to the woman in a long-tailed gown," she joked.[54] The lecture struck a chord, however. The audience was enthralled, and the reporters were enthusiastic in their praise. The *Boston Traveller* declared it was "one of the most remarkable addresses of this age," and the *Boston Globe* predicted that her anti-Mormon crusade would prove to be "the great work of Miss Field's life."[55] By the end of December she was lecturing on Mormonism almost nightly in and around Boston in such towns as Woburn, Lowell, Pawtucket, Worcester, Providence, and Cambridge. In late winter and spring 1885 she spoke in Albany, Syracuse, Cambridgeport, Brooklyn, Philadelphia, and Washington. While in the nation's capital to lecture on February 26 and to attend the inaugural ball of Grover Cleveland on March 4, she "lived under the roof of a most kindly host," Hugh McCullough, the once and future secretary of the treasury,[56] and she lobbied congressmen, new cabinet members, and Justice Stephen Field of the U.S. Supreme Court (a distant relative) on the Mormon issue.[57] Her talk was hailed in the *Washington Republican* as "a brilliant and admirable discourse, bounding in good points and witty thrusts."[58]

In her lectures, as in her essays from Utah, Field objected less to the institution of polygamy, even as she depicted its "chamber of horrors," than to the tyranny of theocracy. "I treat of Mormonism as a political machine of organized treason," she explained. "Mormonism makes serfs of its followers" and "becomes organized treason" to the laws of the United States.[59] "Bad as polygamy is it is only a secondary evil. The great crime of Utah is treason. The laws of the Mormon Church require the members of that church to disregard the laws of the United States whenever they clash with the church laws. The history of Mormonism is a history of treason against the General Government."[60] The remedy? Field proposed the enactment of a national marriage law in lieu of special antipolygamy legislation, which had proved to be as unenforceable as civil rights laws in the South. She noted that "marriage is left to the sweet will of State legislation, whereby men and women are married in one State and very much the reverse in another."[61] The disenfranchisement of Mormons and the extirpation of polygamy, she contended, would hack at the roots of theocracy. "Deprive them of the ballot," she insisted, "and polygamy will die a natural death."[62] Certainly, she added, Utah should not be admitted to the Union so long as it was governed as a Mormon theocracy. Better yet, the federal authorities should disenfranchise everyone in Utah, both men and women, Mormon and Gentile, and govern the territory with a legislative commission of loyal citizens appointed by the president and confirmed by the Congress.

Field also contributed several articles on the "social and political crimes of Utah" to such papers as *Harper's Weekly* and the *North American Review*. Her essay "Mormon Blood Atonement" in the *NAR*, in fact, documented the alleged ritual practice of shedding human blood. It elicited an angry reply from Joseph A. West, a Mormon bishop. She was keen as well to publish a piece on Mormonism in the *New York Tribune*. She sent a manuscript to her friend Laurence Hutton and directed him to "offer it to Whitelaw Reid, *Tribune*, not mentioning any terms as my object is to get article printed and then to talk terms. It's a sensation to benefit the cause I want. . . . I hope the thing will get into *Trib* as it should start from the metropolis."[63] "It will be strange if *The Tribune* does reject an article the sole purpose of which is to call attention to suffering Southerners who at the risk of their lives have broken away from Mormonism," she added a week later. "It will teach me a lesson as to big newspaper desire to break up this iniquity." But reject the article, or at least this version of it, the *Tribune* did. Instead, her essay "Utah Politics and Morals," for which she was paid a mere thirty dollars, did not appear in the paper until September 1884, and in it she discussed not the "suffering Southerners" who were apostates from Mormonism but the reasons James G. Blaine, the Republican candidate for president in 1884, had denounced the Latter-day Saints. To her embarrassment, Field was soon compelled to deny that the article signaled her return to favor at the newspaper: "I don't write for *N.Y. Tribune*, saving very occasionally," as she wrote a friend.[64] In fact, "Utah Politics and Morals" was the last piece ever published in the paper by Field, who once upon a time had been one of its featured contributors.

She continued to crisscross the country with her anti-Mormon lectures for the next several months. She delivered them in such towns as Cleveland and Cincinnati, Ohio; Englewood, Oakland, and Chicago, Illinois; and Crawfordsville, Greencastle, and Evansville, Indiana. After visiting her aunt in Newport in early July 1885, she spoke on "The Social and Political Crimes of Utah" in Framingham, Massachusetts, on July 16,[65] before vacationing the next several weeks in Marblehead Point and Clifton Springs, New York. She was invited by Henry Ward Beecher, George William Curtis, and former secretary of state William M. Evarts to speak at Chickering Hall in New York on November 21, 1885, where she addressed "a large, intelligent, and attentive" audience and illustrated her talk with a stereopticon.[66] Under the auspices of the Grand Army of the Republic (G.A.R.), she lectured on Mormonism in the Upper Midwest every evening except Sundays during the first seven weeks of 1886,[67] toured New England in March, and delivered by her own count some forty-five lectures that summer and fall in Iowa, the Dakotas, Wisconsin, Minnesota, Illinois, and Michigan in communities with such names as Paw Paw, Weeping Water, Lone Mound, Coldwater, and Marshalltown.[68] She returned east, according to the *Iowa State Register*, "with a pocket full of shekels, good health," and a host of new friends.[69] While in Minneapolis in late August she ad-libbed a short speech at a public reception for General Lucius Fairchild, the former governor of Wisconsin and the new president of the G.A.R.;[70] and while in Michigan she met the Mormon dissident Ann Eliza Young, the nineteenth (more or less) wife of Brigham Young, who had become an outspoken critic of polygamy.[71] The *Salt Lake Tribune* even credited her with the adoption of an anti-Mormon plank in the platform of the Michigan State Republican party that year.[72] In late September, while returning east from her lecture tour, she spent an evening in Chicago with her friend Eugene Field, who gloated that they "discussed everything from literature down to Sir Charles Dilke and back again. A mighty smart woman is Kate!" She also told an interviewer while in the city that she had declined a job offer from Dilke. She preferred to remain in the United States.[73]

At the invitation of Grover Cleveland, while in Washington to attend a banquet of the Loyal Legion, an association of former Union army officers, Field went to the White House to discuss the Mormon question with the president on February 23, 1886. Cleveland "was good enough to waste some time upon me," she tactfully told an interviewer the next day, "and while it could have been of no particular advantage to him, it was a very great pleasure and satisfaction to me." She had supported Blaine in the election of 1884, fearing that the Democrats would be soft on Mormonism, but, she conceded, "in the social revolution that is to come who knows but Grover Cleveland may be the savior of his country?"[74] A day or two later, Field sent Cleveland a copy of this interview with a note that she was a "woman who can hold her tongue" along with "some Mormon scraps to be read by you at your leisure."[75] According to Catharine Cole, the Washington correspondent of the *New Orleans Picayune,* Field told her that she had "given the President a piece of her mind on the Utah question,"[76] though the details of their conversation remained confidential. At the very least, their meeting fueled speculation that Cleveland might select Field to be governor of Utah—a notion soberly endorsed by editors of both the *Salt Lake Tribune* and the *Philadelphia Press.* The idea was ridiculed in other circles. The *Brooklyn Eagle* joked that Cleveland hesitated to appoint Field because he favored "the employment of all peaceful expedients before resorting to extreme measures" and the *Utica Observer* cracked wise that Governor Field would certainly "solve the Mormon problem. After living in the same Territory with Kate a couple of years, every Mormon youth would become a confirmed bachelor."[77]

Her anti-Mormon campaign was, of course, rife with controversy. In particular, Field was accused of exploiting the Mormon problem in sensational lectures for entirely selfish reasons. The *San Francisco Alta California* claimed, for example, that she had earned thirty thousand dollars with "The Mormon Monster" and planned "to build a house in Washington with the money."[78] (In fact, Field was convinced that "the value of real estate" in the District was increasing and had merely invested in property at Rhode Island Avenue and 16th Street, between Dupont Circle and the White House in the northwest quadrant of Washington.)[79] Though Eugene Field facetiously described her in the *Chicago Daily News* as "the beautiful and accomplished young millionaire litterateur,"[80] she was certainly no longer wealthy. She had earned virtually nothing during the year she lived in Colorado and Utah, living on the remnants of the money she had earned as a publicist for the telephone. As early as September 1884, before delivering the first lecture on the topic, she stated matter-of-factly that "[i]f ever I get back the money I've spent on Mormonism I shall be lucky."[81] Three days before debuting with "Polygamy in Utah" in Boston, she explained to the *Boston Globe* that she would have preferred "to entertain the public with 'Eyes and Ears in London' than to horrify with Mormon polygamy and treason. It takes infinitely less vitality out of one to laugh and be merry than to wax indignant over human wrongs and the criminal negligence of our government."[82] Two years later, she continued to insist that "if money were my sole motive in lecturing, I should have avoided 'Mormonism' as punctiliously as I avoid rattlesnakes or any other poison. The subject is not attractive." She would "rejoice greatly" when she could "take up a more agreeable theme in which there will be infinitely more money."[83]

The criticisms of Field in the Mormon press were, moreover, invariably sexist or condescending or both. According to the *Ogden Standard Examiner,* Field was a "venerable maiden" who had been "successful in filling her own pockets out of the anti-Mormon agitation business." A "charming little virgin" or alternatively "Sir Kate Field," she profoundly misunderstood the Latter-day Saints: "What a pity it is that someone did not marry the charming little Kate years ago, so that she could have learned something about the mysteries of monogamy before she tackled polygamy and 'Mormonism.'" Joseph F. Smith, a member of the First Presidency of the LDS church, once referred to Field as a "vixen" who with her "rattling-stinging tongue" effectively opposed Utah statehood. As recently as 1971, a prominent Mormon historian speculated that Field was "probably a latent lesbian. If so, this would help account for her later revulsion against Mormon patriarchal society and polygamy."[84] In any case, Field feared in 1884 that she had become a target of Mormon vigilantism. "The Danites have sworn to kill me," she said. "I know they are dogging me all over the country." She claimed her life had been threatened before she left Salt Lake City in June 1884 and that someone had tried to sabotage her train in Kansas City while she was en route east a few weeks later.[85]

For better or worse, moreover, Field's anti-Mormon crusade skewed her politics for the rest of her life. To prevent Mormon "treason," she proposed test or loyalty oaths. From there it was but a small step to literacy tests for voters, both male and female—precisely the means by which the South would legally limit black voting until the 1960s. That is, Field was amenable to disenfranchising both Mormons and blacks—a point all the more glaring when in 1890 she suggested solving the "race problem" in the South by granting the franchise to white women in order to negate the votes of black men, exactly as the Saints had granted suffrage to Mormon women in order to cancel the votes of gentiles.[86] The poor and illiterate recruits to Mormonism sent to Zion by its foreign missionaries fostered her bias against immigrants. Though a self-described "radical" in her twenties, Field became in her forties a reactionary xenophobe who nevertheless believed her nativism enlightened and progressive.

Long resident in either Boston or New York, Field settled in Washington, D.C., as her base of operation during her anti-Mormon activities. "I am more and more convinced that Washington is destined to be the social, literary and artistic centre of this country, as well as the political," she declared.

> It is the only town which is beautifully and systematically laid out; whose streets are properly paved; where there are breathing places throughout the town, lungs as it were; where there is no commerce; where there is a certain repose necessary for society; and where the climate, if not absolutely perfect, is on the whole better all the year round than anywhere else in the United States. . . . Washington is becoming the Mecca for Americans of leisure and of wealth.

Between lecture tours in early 1886 and after moving into a D.C. hotel, she bought a chestnut thoroughbred named Tuck and became a familiar figure on horseback around the city. "I was in the saddle yesterday from 10 o'clock to 12," she told a reporter in February, "and in 15 minutes after leaving the Arlington House I was in the country, and a very beautiful country it is, too."[87] In April she returned to the capital from her lectures in New England and moved into an apartment at Welcker's Hotel on 15th Street with a parlor where she might hold court.[88] In May she attended the House Judiciary Committee hearings, where she heard, as she put it, "unique and interesting arguments for and against additional legislation in Utah." As usual, she weighed in on the proceedings, ridiculing the posturing of a pro-Mormon congressman on the committee.[89] At the invitation of three cabinet secretaries as well as a "hundred of the most prominent men now in Washington," she was invited to speak about the LDS and delivered her

14. Kate Field on horseback, ca. 1890. Courtesy of Boston Public Library.

anti-Mormon lecture at the local Congregational Church at 10th and G streets with John Hay in attendance. (Over the years, Field was invited to discuss the Latter-day Saints in many different denominational churches, for predictable reasons.) The *Washington Capital* declared the lecture "one of invincible logic, graphic presentation, and thrilling power." The "fire and eloquence of the orator" held the audience "in breathless silence, broken only by frequent applause."[90]

In the end, Field's relentless attacks on "the Mormon monster" carried the day, if only temporarily. In February 1887, the Congress passed legislation, the Edmunds-Tucker Act, which disenfranchised polygamists (and women, most of them Mormons), required plural wives to testify against their husbands, escheated Church property, abolished the Nauvoo Legion militia, and dissolved the Perpetual Emigrating Fund Company. The bill "led to the partial Americanization of portions of Utah," and "with all its faults I rejoiced in its passage and was glad to be a potent factor in its creation," Field allowed, at least publicly.[91] Privately, she groused that the law failed to require a loyalty oath by voters: "Perhaps half a loaf is better than no bread, but I'm disgusted."[92] Still, more than any other individual she was credited with rallying the forces that led to the law. "She has been equal to half a dozen newspapers, half a score of attorneys and a panorama," Goodwin editorialized in the *Salt Lake Tribune*. "She has done yeoman work in the lecture field, through the press and in interviews with men and women all over the country. She performed special work in Washington, and, we believe, it was due more to her than to any other one person that the legislation, which culminated in the Edmunds-Tucker bill, was put in motion in the House." The *New York Evening Post*, similarly, asserted that "to Miss Field's efforts, on the platform and with her pen, was due in no small degree the solution of the Mormon problem." The *Chicago Times-Herald* agreed that "to Kate Field more than to any man or to any other woman is due the extirpation of American polygamy."[93]

The passage of Edmunds-Tucker did not end Field's campaign against Mormonism, its "organized treason," or her opposition to Utah statehood. On the contrary, in February 1887, the same month the law was enacted, she left New York to carry the fight to the West. At the age of forty-eight, she was on the road for the next eighteen months, by far the longest lecture trip of her life.

10

Out West

FIELD SLOWLY WORKED HER WAY WESTWARD in February 1887, speaking on Mormonism in upstate New York and northern Ohio. At Plymouth Church in Indianapolis on the 24th, the young May Wright Sewall, future president of both the National and the International Congress of Women, attended Field's lecture. "No one who heard it," Sewall later wrote, "will ever forget that lucid exposure and relentless denunciation of the subtle private deterioration and subtle public dangers that lurk in polygamy."[1] During the next three weeks Field scurried around Kansas, lecturing in Kansas City on March 4, Topeka on the 7th, Lawrence on the 8th, Wichita on the 9th, Newton on the 10th, and Manhattan on the 11th. She spoke on Mormonism in Atchison on March 21, a day or two after investing $3,000 in local real estate, expecting the property to jump in value during the "boom" there in land prices.[2] She arrived in Omaha two days later, speaking on March 29, before pressing on to Colorado. Introduced by the local congressman G. G. Symes, who asserted that "had it not been for Miss Field the Edmunds-Tucker bill would never have become a law,"[3] she lectured on "the Mormon monster" at the First Baptist Church in Denver on April 12. The next day, she railed to Colorado Springs, registered at the Antlers, and in the evening of April 14 she repeated her lecture at the Opera House there. While at the Springs, Field also visited the grave of Helen Hunt Jackson, who had died in August 1885, on Cheyenne Mountain above the city. As she wrote Lilian Whiting, "I walked several rods in a foot of snow to get to the grave, but only a few steps beyond I found bare rock, where I sat in the sun for an hour, and thinking of the unique woman and generous heart that had passed many a day in the same place, I gazed upon the beautiful plain that stretches to the Missouri River."[4]

Field was given a heroine's welcome at the G.A.R. Hall when she arrived in Salt Lake City in late April for a month-long visit. Jennie Froiseth, president of the local chapter of the Women's Relief Corps of the G.A.R., declared that "there is no woman in America whom I admire and esteem more than I do Miss Field" before presenting her with a diamond-encrusted gold badge of honor. A week later Field was invited to speak by a hundred and thirty Mormon apostates and Gentiles, including C. C. Goodwin and Eli Murray, whereupon she rented the Walker Opera House in Salt Lake City and lectured on May 17. She was introduced to an overflow crowd by Murray, and wearing the G.A.R. badge around her neck she delivered a longer version of "The Mormon Monster"—"I shall take nothing from it but shall add to it"—than the one she had declaimed dozens of times over the past two-plus years in the East and that had been dismissed by the Mormon hierarchy as a tissue of lies and distortions. She even touched on the sensitive issues of the doctrine of blood atonement and the Mountain Meadows massacre. The next day, Goodwin in the *Salt Lake Tribune* reported that Field's voice had been "clear, her modulation perfect, her emphasis well-timed, her delivery unhesitating, and her words delightfully chosen."[5] She repeated the lecture without the change of a word in Ogden on May 23. "I delivered the tissue of falsehoods in the city of the enemy," she told the *New York Herald*, "and had the satisfaction of having it universally endorsed by the Gentiles and apostate Mormons, and being treated with profound silence by the Mormons themselves. It was all the proof I wanted that I had told the truth." "I bearded the lion in his den," she later declared. "I gave that lecture verbatim and received the endorsement of a crowded assembly of gentiles and apostates. With the greatest good will for the Mormon people, I said nothing that was not historically true, and had no object but their emancipation."[6] Audiences in the West, she believed, were "more alive to the political meaning of Mormonism" than those in the East. In New England she was sometimes "asked 'who is Joseph Smith' and 'whether Brigham Young is still alive.' We needn't talk about English ignorance of this country when the Atlantic coast knows so little about the Far West."[7]

15. Kate Field with medal, 1890. *Sun and Shade* 5 (May 1893): plate 65.

A month later, Field surfaced in Oregon with plans to sail to Alaska. She had hoped to visit the Far Northwest as early as the summer of 1885, but instead she had extended her lecture tour of the Midwest. "I started for Alaska," she wrote Whiting, "but at the rate of speed with which I was approaching it, I probably would have reached it near the close of the twentieth century."[8] She was more successful in the summer of 1887. She delivered her Dickens lecture in Portland on July 1, and after paying the $90 fare she embarked for the Great Land aboard the sidewheeler *Ancon* from Port Townsend, Washington, four days later. "The journey promises well," she wrote the *Juneau Alaska Free Press* on July 5,[9] and in fact the trip had recently become popular with genteel travelers. The Pacific Steamship Company conducted twice-monthly excursions from Portland and Port Townsend to Alaska during the tourist season between July and September, and more than 25,000 passengers sailed to Glacier Bay and back on its vessels between 1884 and 1890.[10] The *Ancon*, captained by James Carroll, navigated the Tongass Narrows and stopped in Wrangell and Killisnoo en route north. The ship anchored at Juneau early in the morning of July 12, and some local citizens called on Field at seven A.M. with a request "that I lecture while the steamer lay at the dock." Soon the local brass band, "consisting of four home-brewed musicians," serenaded her.[11] Juneau at the time was a bustling mining town with nine general stores, three hotels and a lodging house, nine saloons, two breweries, two drugstores, two cigar factories, a pair of hardware stores, a photo studio, a confectionery, a laundry, a millinery shop, three schools, churches, a hospital, a weekly newspaper, as well as a barber shop and a dance hall that doubled as an opera house. It boasted a population of about 1,250 divided almost equally between whites and natives.[12] Field delivered her Dickens lecture at the dance hall later that morning to an audience of several hundred miners and a dozen women. She was, as the *Portland Oregonian* reported later that month, the first person ever to deliver a formal lecture in Alaska,[13] and she claimed afterwards that she "never had a more attentive audience." In payment, she was given a vote of thanks, a Haidas Indian carved goat-horn spoon, a bottle of virgin gold, a subscription to the local newspaper, and a dinner at the best hotel in town. Then she was ferried three miles to Douglas Island, where she rejoined the other passengers aboard the *Ancon*. The ship sailed seventy-five miles northwest to Muir glacier—the "most beautiful" glacier she saw, "which is over 300 feet high"—at the north point of Glacier Bay, where the ship reversed course, stopping at the territorial capital of Sitka, Port Tongass, and Vancouver Island before returning to Port Townsend in late July.[14] As she wrote Whiting, "It rained twelve days out of seventeen; and we had fog two more! I wore out a pair of arctics on shore and went about in a riding-habit and a seal-skin. The habit did away with petticoats, and in it I defied mud and ascended the Muir glacier. Alaska is very interesting to me, and I shall probably go to work on a lecture at once."[15] The *Free Press* predicted that she "will undoubtedly write a very interesting book of her travels in Alaska."[16] Meanwhile, Field spoke in Port Townsend on July 26, in Tacoma on July 28 and 30, and in Seattle on August 2.

She sailed for San Francisco aboard the *George W. Elder* in late August 1887 to write up her Alaskan experiences in comfort there during the fall and winter. Shortly after her arrival, she was interviewed in her rooms at the Occidental Hotel by the *San Francisco Chronicle*. "Alaska is a deeply interesting country," she explained, "and it has been shamefully treated by the United States Government. The United States acquired the country twenty years ago, and up to 1876 it was under military rule. Then that was withdrawn, and for ten years there was no government whatever, and even now the Probate Court and the United States Commissioners can hardly be called that."[17] Rather than educating the native peoples of Alaska, the government in Washington had virtually ignored them. As a result, "they have become utterly demoralized by contact with the whites. This is particularly the case with the women. The Government is responsible for this demoralization." Field also showed the reporter some of the items she had bought in Alaska: a Chilkat blanket, polished wood, jewelry, rattles, a stone knife, a ladle in the shape of an eagle, woven mats and baskets, and a wooden effigy of a dancing Eskimo woman. Though the *Boston Post* claimed later that this figure was "of such rarity that not even the National Museum [i.e., the Smithsonian Institution] possesses one like it,"[18] the piece was likely unimportant. Field was not an informed or expert collector and genuine relics had already been replaced by curios in the souvenir market.

Field was interviewed a second time by the *San Francisco Chronicle* a month later, soon after touring Mission San Jose, the vineyards of Napa Valley, and the Mariposa Big Trees[19] and just before she was scheduled to perform her musical monologue at Union Square Hall. She explained that "in the lecture I am now writing" on Alaska, she paid scant attention to its scenery. She devoted the equivalent of only half a column of newsprint to the topic "and in that space I include the glaciers. If I dilated on the scenery I should put people to sleep."[20] Instead she described the moderate climate, the abundant resources, the promising future of the vast territory; and she reproached Congress for its continuing indifference to the region. In fact, her lecture "Despised Alaska" originated as a 177-page manuscript that survives among Field's papers in the Boston Public Library. "In preparing a lecture I can't help writing the equivalent of a book," as she explained to her friend Laurence Hutton. From the mass of manuscript "I cull what will hold a public for an hour and a half."[21] Though the manuscript remains unpublished in its entirety, Field mined it like a stone quarry for future articles and essays. Little in it, in fact, has not reached print.

"People have strange ideas about Alaska; all born of ignorance, the mother of most mistakes," she began. She sought to dispel the "myth of the icebox," the notion that Alaska was merely an Arctic wasteland. Ironically, she had been asked by "a man in Dakota who wore a Buffalo fur for a shirt, 'What fiend possesses you to go to that cold climate?'" She observed that the thirty thousand natives and several thousand whites in Alaska coexist "comfortably," and she praised the "wonderful and unique scenery" of the "almost fairy region." Whereas in Switzerland "a glacier is a vast bed of dirty air-holed ice that fastens itself like a huge porous plaster to the side of an Alp," in Alaska "a glacier is a grand torrent that seems to have been suddenly frozen when about to plunge into the sea." She compared the Muir glacier, "which marks the extreme northerly point of pleasure travel," to "Niagara Falls frozen stiff." Field also described fish canneries at Killisnoo and Tongass Island, the rich gold mines and mills in Juneau, and the coal fields along the east bank of the Chilkat River. Like Thoreau, she scorned the influence of white "civilization" on the native cultures. The "Indian village at Juneau" is "very squalid," she noted, because "the white man has been there with his corrupting lucre. Unfortunately for the Indian, so-called civilization inevitably begins at the wrong end." She also quoted "a neat, intelligent British Columbia Indian" in Wrangell who told her that "before white men came, the natives often lived to extreme old age." Field "unceremoniously invaded every native house in Wrangell and Sitka" where she "was always greeted with a smile" and she in turn addressed the inhabitants in elementary Chinook. Though untrained in ethnology, Field recounted some native folktales in her lecture. An advocate of cremation, she described "the spot where natives burn all their dead, except the '*shahmans*' or medicine men," on a hilltop near Sitka. As usual, she also condemned the government for its indifference: "A veritable dog in the manger, Congress will do nothing for Alaska nor is Alaska permitted to do anything for herself."[22]

By December 1887, in addition to a draft of her lecture, Field had completed several articles on Alaska for magazine publication. These essays were based on both the diary she kept on the voyage and various sources she consulted, among them some of the classics of Alaskan writing, including Frederick Whymper's *Travel and Adventure in the Territory of Alaska* (1869), George H. Dall's *Alaska and Its Resources* (1870), John Muir's *Cruise of the U.S. Revenue-Steamer Corwin* (1883), Eliza Ruhamah Scidmore's *Alaska: Its Southern Coast and the Sitkan Archipelago* (1885), and George Davidson's *Resources of and Developments in Alaska* (1888). Field had also interviewed many natives, among them John Kadishan and "Old Betty" Zeetle of Wrangell. She outlined in these pieces a remarkably progressive agenda consistent with her convictions, her sympathy with the plight of the indigenous peoples of Alaska, and her goal to rally popular support for "despised Alaska." Though long a defender of minority rights, particularly those of black Americans, Field had never before defended the rights of native Americans or native Alaskans. In each of these essays, however, she took a page from her friend Helen Hunt Jackson's *A Century of Dishonor*, a documentary record of the federal government's repeated betrayal of Indian rights and violation of Indian treaties. Field's Alaska writings offer a series of snapshots of the Great Land between the First Organic Act of 1884 and the Klondike gold rush of 1897–98.

Field's travelogue "A Trip to Southeastern Alaska" followed the route of the *Ancon* and appeared in *Harper's Weekly* accompanied by ten pen-and-ink drawings of sites she had visited the previous July. She reminisced about her steamer journey in a familiar genre and with skills she had refined in her best-selling European travel books. She described Muir glacier, so named by the captain of the *Ancon* in 1883, in exquisite detail:

> Imagine a glacier three miles wide and three hundred feet high at its mouth . . . in front of which your steamer anchors; picture a background of mountains fifteen thousand feet high [Mounts Barnard, Abbe, Bertha, La Perouse, Marchainville to the west], all snow-clad, and then imagine a gorgeous sun lighting up the ice crystals with rainbow coloring. The face

of the glacier takes on the hue of aqua-marine, the hue of every bit of floating ice, big and little, that surrounds the steamer and makes navigation serious. This dazzling serpent moves at the rate of sixty-four feet a day, tumbling headlong into the sea, and as it falls, the ear is startled by submarine thunder, the echoes of which resound far and near.

Field sampled native cuisine on the voyage—she thought Alaska cranberries "the best in the world," though she abstained from fresh salmon after inspecting the canneries ("knowing what I know . . . I am willing that other people should eat them"). She thrilled, or so she claimed, "at the sight of United States troops drilling on Alaskan green" at Sitka, a "stupendous force" of thirteen marines, including Lieutenant George T. Emmons, assigned to "one small gunboat," the USS *Pinta*—the entire posting of "the United States Navy in Alaska waters!" Sherwood has fairly described the *Pinta*, built in 1864 and finally retired in 1908, as "a fourth-rate man-of-war with small armament." Yet the navy presumed to rule the Alaskan Panhandle with this old tub.[23] On her part, Field noted, tongue in cheek, that "it was edifying" to behold the marines protecting the dilapidated dock where passengers and freight were landed—and yet Congressmen William S. Holman of Indiana and Samuel J. Randall of Pennsylvania, members of the House Appropriations Committee, had defeated an expenditure of $20,000 "to make this wharf of Alaska's capital safe." While she was in Sitka, Field purchased a totem of some kind, "a marvelous black image of some impossible demon," for thirty dollars from the family that owned it, but "the sale of that black demon created a revolution in the village" and "the terrified family begged it back." She also visited the mission school attended by fifty boys and fifty-three girls, virtually all of them native children. "More good natured people I never saw," she averred. Yet she also recognized the vulnerability of the native population to diseases unknown to them before their "association with the whites," particularly consumption or tuberculosis.[24] Field encouraged the missions and the military to teach basic hygiene to the natives.

In a second, more contentious article, "Our Ignorance of Alaska," published in the *North American Review,* she chronicled "how Congress has neglected a great country."[25] She challenged the calumnies perpetuated by

Henry W. Elliott, who had once suggested that apart from the activities of the Alaska Commercial Company the economic worth of the region was slight;[26] she sided with George Dall, the so-called "dean" of Alaska experts, in his debates with Elliott over the economic promise of the territory; and she railed against the perfidy of the federal government much as she had done in campaigning against polygamy and Utah statehood. The Civil War general Irvin McDowell, "never visiting Alaska and therefore unbiased by personal knowledge," had proposed that the ostensibly worthless territory, like Mark Twain's Mexican plug, either be sold or, if a purchaser could not be found, that it be given away. Fortunately, Field added, "Alaska was not given away. It has only been thrown away. . . . Ten years of no government and military occupation brought to Sitka and the Alexander Archipelago rum and ruin—nothing more." Far from a wasteland, she observed, the land had bountiful resources, among them coal, timber, iron, copper, lead, sulfur, galena, graphite, marble, cinnabar, and, of course, gold. Oil had been discovered "on the mainland opposite Kodiak Island." As for the charge that agriculture in so northern a clime was impractical, Field mentioned the huge turnips and potatoes she had seen and the "butter made for me by the Scotch housekeeper of Wrangell mission," proving "that cows were a success in that region." Alaska bid fair to become "one of the richest fisheries in the world," too, with seventy-five species of food fish swarming in its waters, particularly salmon, cod, halibut, and herring; and abundant sea animals such as whale, walrus, sea-otters, fur-seals, and hair-seals. To be sure, Field warned that "the sea-otter has almost disappeared" and "the seal will be exterminated if promiscuously slaughtered"—an assertion of the environmental ethic she had learned from Thoreau. In reply to the cavilers who still believed that the territory was a drag on the U.S. economy, she estimated that Alaska "sends out yearly double the wealth brought in," more than any other territory except Dakota.

Trouble is, Field continued, Alaskans still suffered from the policy of benign neglect adopted in Washington. The civil government imposed on the territory was "ridiculous, anomalous, unjust, and fraudulent." The institutional infrastructure to encourage economic growth hardly existed. The Congress had approved mail service from San Francisco to Tahiti and the Fiji Islands, but not to the Aleutian Islands, and the cities of Sitka, Juneau,

Wrangell, and Killisnoo received only semimonthly mail service. No laws governed the sale, purchase, or mortgaging of private lands because the entire territory was still theoretically in the public domain. Before passage of the First Organic Act by Congress in May 1884, similarly, Alaska had no local judicial system, and even after the act, which imposed the Oregon criminal code on the Great Land, criminals were still sent to Portland for trial. Jury trials were not legal in Alaska because Oregon required jurors to be taxpayers and taxes were not levied in the Territory. "Verily, we are a most economical nation!" Field quipped. "We begrudge the establishment of a collector of customs at Sitka on account of a deficit in the revenue, and send criminals fifteen hundred miles in search of justice!" Even since the appointment of a territorial governor, district judge, district attorney, and federal marshals in 1884, the citizens of Unalaska "who need to avail themselves of the district court at Sitka [twelve hundred miles away] must go first to San Francisco" and return to Sitka, "journeying nearly 8,000 miles instead of 2,400!"[27] Field was no less an effective political pamphleteer than she was a popular travel writer.

Unfortunately, "A Trip to Southeastern Alaska" and "Our Ignorance of Alaska" were the only two essays Field composed in San Francisco in late 1887 to appear in the magazines for which they were written. She circulated the other manuscripts among the *Atlantic, Cosmopolitan, Century, Lippincott's, Forum,* and *Popular Science Monthly* to no avail, as if the national ignorance of Alaska were a self-fulfilling prophecy. In the winter of 1888 she also harbored the hope that Harper and Bros. might "consider my suggestion of a book on Alaska" because "if I can get up a book" she might recover the cost of her trip and research. But nothing came of this proposal either. In the end, her campaign on behalf of "despised Alaska" and the rights of its citizens was a financial failure. "Alaska has cost me $2200 and six months of time," she wrote Hutton. "So you see I'll never get back my money except I lecture on the subject."[28] Much as her Alaska essays earned little money and her proposal for an Alaska book died aborning, however, she delivered her Alaska lecture on only five known occasions.

In January 1888, before leaving northern California, Field rode through the Yosemite Valley on horseback, an excursion that left a deep but disagreeable impression. Though the distant scenery was beautiful, much of the land "was enclosed by hideous, cruel, barbed-wire fences," she complained, and "I couldn't walk. There were no foot-paths." Trees had been cut down "promiscuously," leaving "an army of ragged stumps that make portions of the Valley look like a brutal backwoods clearing."[29] She soon added the preservation of the region to her list of pet projects. In late January she headed south to Santa Barbara, then in early February to San Diego. She arrived there on the steamer *Santa Rosa* in the early evening of February 7 and immediately ferried across the bay to Coronado Island, where she registered at the Hotel Josephine, a three-story, Eastlake-style building on Orange Avenue between 3rd and 4th Streets. A reporter for the *San Diego Bee* was waiting for her, though Field rebuffed his attempt at an interview. She had docked at half-past seven, she explained, and "it is now 9," so her "knowledge [of the area] is limited to the wharf and an omnibus." She begged for a chance to tour the city before she was asked to express an opinion of it, though like a civic booster she declared that she expected the city to prosper—it was "the manifest destiny of the Pacific Coast"—through tourism and investment. She planned to linger several weeks "in order to become acquainted with this marvelous State," particularly with its southern part. "I want to see San Diego thoroughly and shall be glad to be shown the way, as I come a perfect ignoramus." A reporter for the *San Diego Union* also pressed her for comment, and she finally acknowledged that San Francisco "needs to recognize in San Diego a rival." The progress of southern California, she thought, was "wonderful and very interesting, and I shall know more about it after I have seen your city by daylight."[30]

A day or two later she began to speak her mind. With a population of about 35,000, San Diego and Coronado Beach in the winter of 1888 boasted five daily newspapers (the *Bee, San Diegan, Union, Sun,* and the *Coronado Mercury*) and Field was repeatedly interviewed by each of them during her visit. She told the *Sun* on February 8 that she liked "the town, the climate, and the people," and she informed the *Union* the same day that she was "delighted with the climate here. The temperature is remarkably equable throughout the day and night."[31] As she wrote Whiting,

Coronado Beach is across the bay from San Diego and is well situated for view of ocean and mountain. The day is lovely, and as I look out upon mountain, sunshine, and the glitter of a placid sea, I wish you were here to enjoy its loveliness. An Eastern woman is playing Mendelssohn extremely well in the adjoining parlor. *Les extremes se touchent.* I know *you* would exclaim at the fine scenery, the delightful air, the glorious sun, delicious fruit, and the general *dolce far niente.*

Over and over again I wish you were here. It *is* so lovely and so lazy. I can't do anything—not even write a letter without an effort. The work I came here to do remains undone, and I am desperate in one sense while utterly indifferent in another.[32]

On February 9, Field toured the new and fashionable Hotel del Coronado on the southern shore of the island. It would not officially open its doors until February 14, but some guests had already registered. Field promised to transfer her lodgings there in a few days,[33] but she did not, probably because the rooms were too expensive. Besides, she was satisfied with her accommodations at the Hotel Josephine.

Field was regarded during her residence in San Diego not only as a professional travel writer but as something of a travel expert, and so she was expected both to comment on the attractions of the region and on how to enhance them. Privately, she allowed that she was more impressed with San Diego than with Santa Barbara. "The climate is drier and the nights and mornings are less cool," she wrote. "Coronado Beach will soon be very attractive. Send your friends to my hotel which is pretty clean and quiet."[34] Publicly, she warned against the threatened industrialization and commercialization of the island. It was "a beautiful little place—a regular little gem—and you might have here an ideal spot, but I don't like the notions of foundries and factories and oil refineries and machine shops coming here. Coronado is such a pretty, clean, restful spot that it should be kept entirely for fine residences, beautiful gardens, and lovely drives, and it is a mistake to contaminate its Heavenly breezes and Edenic sunshine with the smoke and dirt of iron works." Coronado should become "the abode of artists and scholars," she declared, like such bohemian enclaves in the East as Saratoga Springs and Greenwich Village.[35] As for San Diego, Field added, "I really think Old Town is the best place over there. The ruins of the old Mission are very attractive to me, and already I have visited there several times since

I came here, and I hope to go many times more." She criticized the myopic members of the San Diego city council, who had "well-nigh ruined" the route from downtown to Old Town by granting overlapping franchises to steam motorlines and railways and then proposing "to build a fine boulevard parallel with their tracks." Still, Field predicted "a great future for the city, and there is no reason why a great commercial center will not develop here in time." She also expected San Diego to become an agricultural center. Though the city at the time had to import "fruits and vegetables to supply the demand," Field observed that many local Chinese farmers were planting "vegetable gardens, and they will become rich in a short time at the business." She also recognized the strategic value of San Diego harbor, potentially the most important Pacific port south of San Francisco.

As for the vexing problem of potable water, Field offered a suggestion. To be sure, some people "can drink lime-water and be benefited thereby, but many more are seriously injured." In fact, she insisted, bad water may do "as much harm in its way as bad whisky." But the residents of the city "have the remedy in their own hands if they choose to use it." While the water channeled from the mountains may be

> freighted with lime, Heaven sends you rain, pure and soft and health-giving. Every house should have its cistern, and *if* every house *had* a cistern, nobody would be obliged to drink lime in solution. Were it known to travelers that soft water was provided at all hotels and boarding houses, many an invalid would gladly come to breathe your balmy air. . . . The dew or fog or whatever you please to call the moisture in the air on this coast is sufficient, if caught, to supply every family with soft water.

Field cited the example of J. B. Elliott, a former railroad official credited with planting the cypress and eucalyptus trees along the rail corridor from Leucadia to the ocean. Elliott lived half a mile from the beach and had never dug a well because "his cistern supplies all the water necessary for domestic purposes." His 2,400-square-foot roof captured a hundred and forty gallons of water every day, over 51,000 gallons per year "without counting the rainfall." Similarly, the Hotel Josephine supplied its guests with drinking water from a cistern. Though they "bathe in hard water,"

Field noted, "they drink rainwater twice filtered, and thus avoid laying the seed of ill-health."[36]

On February 16 she sailed on the steamer *Montserrat* for Ensenada in company with former Nevada congressman Thomas Fitch and his wife.[37] The region had recently been opened to immigration by the International Company of Mexico, a U.S.-Mexico consortium dominated by American businessmen. On board the ship she "met prominent railroad officials who had come east with their families; I met brilliant lawyers, shrewd capitalists and charming women, all bound for what the old Mission fathers christened more than a hundred years ago Tierra Perfecta."[38] Field registered at the new Hotel Iturbide with its magnificent view of the bay of Todos Santos. "Here I am on Mexican ground—only 65 miles south of San Diego and yet out of my own country!" as she wrote Hutton.[39] With a population of about fourteen hundred, Ensenada was "prettily situated," but the cuisine there was "not what it ought to be. Fancy living on salt water and having no fish!" Still, she met "unusually agreeable people" in the town, "some of whom I had either known or long heard of in New York society." On February 20, she was interviewed by telephone by the *San Diego Bee.* "I am agreeably disappointed" by Ensenada, she admitted. "I was told that I'd be disgusted in half an hour. I've been here four days and I'm not disgusted yet." The bay "is beautiful, and the finest bit of it, to my thinking, is Punta Banda," a prominence on the southern side, which she predicted would eventually become a popular resort for Mexican and American tourists. "The scenery is fine, and the estuary at this point forms a lake that will be capital for boating and fishing. Close beside this lake is a hot spring of great medicinal value, while back of it rise hills, most easy to climb, and from the top of which there is a beautiful view of the Pacific coast." The American hosteller Gabriel Erb planned to build a 600-room hotel in Punta Banda to rival the Hotel del Coronado as soon as a pier was completed. "The intended big hotel at Punta Banda," Field thought, "will undoubtedly be a capital resort for Mexicans and Americans."[40] On February 25 she again went to Punta Banda for a clambake and "tea squall" and to enjoy the "sun and mountain and sea and peaches in bloom!"[41]

While in Lower California, Field also toured the San Rafael valley. "One beautiful morning I sat in a buckboard behind two roadsters" bound for the valley twenty-six miles east of Ensenada, she reminisced. "Up mountain and down," she traveled until noon before eating lunch "on the ground in the pneumoniac month of February!" Field was impressed by the commercial potential of the valley, "twenty miles long north and south and ten miles wide" with a flowing river "and more than one marsh" indicating "how near water lives to the surface of the earth." With good reason, she thought a gold rush to the region was imminent. "Toward the north end of the valley sleeps the small town of Real del Castillo, meaning the mine of Castillo," she reported. A generation earlier gold had been discovered there, but the people had been too poor to mine the wealth, so "the fecund mountains of San Rafael have been left almost undisturbed. But the coyotes will not be masters of the situation much longer. The prospector is going in with his pick. Mining companies are already setting up claims." Field predicted that the coming gold rush to Lower California, "a boom that will surprise many people in California," would "do more toward opening up the country than all the advertising in the world" by ensuring the construction of railroads. San Diego would benefit, too, because "all the supplies, for the present at least, will have to be sent into the lower country from and through the city." Field conceded that "some San Diegans will be greatly disgusted to read so much praise of their next door neighbors," but "I believe in telling what to me is truth" and "I also believe that Southern California and the entire Pacific Coast will be benefited by additional emigrations."[42]

Though rich in minerals, the valley was even better suited to farming than to mining, she thought. While gazing across "the cañon, sheltered from winds and rich in foliage," she imagined "a not distant future when its fertile valley would be the home of the olive and the walnut, and its hills would be terraced with grape vines." Had the valley been located in San Diego County "instead of being seventy-six miles south of it in Mexican territory," she figured, "there would be much beating of drums and tooting of horns." In all, the San Rafael valley was "capital farming country, and will soon be inhabited by thrifty farmers, the only people who ought to think of going into that region—unless it be a few mechanics and carpenters."[43]

Field was so enthusiastic about the prospects for Lower California that, an unapologetic economic imperialist, she recommended that the United

States buy the peninsula from Mexico just as William Seward had bought Alaska from Russia in 1867. It belonged, she insisted, "to us by necessity."[44] The "comparatively unknown peninsula" might legally be owned by Mexico, but it was "more remote from [Mexico] than from the United States" and she expected that eventually the Mexican government, "seeing the absurdity of holding on to a peninsula she cannot reach overland except by going through our territory and which she will never develop," would sell it. Indeed, President Porfilio Díaz had "already sold eighteen million acres to the International Company of Mexico." That is, Field approved wholeheartedly the elaborate plan of colonization sponsored by the Company. It was, she said, "a magnificent enterprise." The promised internal improvements would require "time, money, and brains," but "I have faith." The Mexican government seemed no less determined than the American investors to make "the International Company's grand scheme a success. Let the piers be finished at Ensenada and Punta Banda and the railroad be built to Yuma and Lower California will cease to be an unknown country." Field was at pains to assure her friends that, unlike their impulsive countrymen to the east, "the Mexicans of Lower California are an amiable, peaceable people, from whom little trouble need be expected." The local peons were so docile, she added, that they could easily be trained to perform all forms of domestic labor: the "amiable Mexican and Indian women" can be "taught far more readily than can the common variety of emigrant that condescends to serve American citizens for a valuable consideration." George H. Sisson, a San Francisco engineer, vice president and general manager of the Company and reportedly "a remarkably clever man," certainly "has a great opportunity to distinguish himself." Field's only regret was that the central office of the Company was three thousand miles away in Hartford when it "ought to be in San Diego."[45]

Field returned to San Diego from Ensenada aboard the *Monserrat* early in the morning of March 1 in order to keep a lecture date. Among her fellow passengers was W. E. Webb, the land commissioner of the International Company, who was returning to his home in New York. Their arrival was delayed some twelve hours by stormy weather, which cemented Field's belief that a rail should be laid between the cities. "I have never experienced more misery in less time than during last night's gale," she allowed, "but the *Montserrat* behaved well, and barring seasickness I am none the worse for the journey, perhaps the better."[46] In retrospect, she did not recommend a tour of Lower California to anyone except visitors to San Diego, though she did envision "a future for this region." She urged her friend Hutton to wait three years, until railroads were built and hotels more comfortable, before booking a trip. Then "Lower California will be worth your seeing." The area "is more interesting than Southern California. The climate is better and the Mexicans and the Spanish language give it a novelty."[47]

As promised, Field delivered "The Mormon Monster" to a full house at the First Methodist Church on the evening of March 5. Attired in a garnet silk dress with a low-cut bodice, a long train, short sleeves, and a collar trimmed in white lace, pince-nez in hand, she spoke for an hour. As the *San Diego Sun* reported the next day, "No public speaker was ever greeted with a finer audience in San Diego than the one which gathered in the new Methodist church last evening to listen to Miss Kate Field's lecture." She praised Dickens before a large gathering of the Unity Club at the Unitarian Church of San Diego a few days later.[48] Over the next couple of weeks she visited the American Ostrich Company breeding farm on Coronado Island,[49] she rode around the island with the manager of the Hotel Josephine in his buggy, and on the evening of March 22 she delivered her Dickens lecture to another large audience—the "wealth, beauty, fashion, and intellect of San Diego, young and old"—at the Methodist Church. Stylishly dressed in "a white silk skirt *en train* and a crimson satin waist faced with old gold lace," Field reminisced for about an hour and a half, her address punctuated with "frequent applause and expressions of pleasure."[50]

Two days later, as her visit was drawing to a close, she was again asked her impressions of San Diego by a local reporter and her answers were by turns caustic and cautious. "I have seen very little that is uncomplimentary," she began, but she quickly added that "you have given yourselves and have received from others more treacle than is good for you. Your digestion is out of order in consequence." She also warned against the adventurers who would prey "upon the unwary and extract the very gold from their teeth if police do not stand by with cocked revolvers." San Francisco had resorted to vigilantism to maintain order in the 1850s, she reminded the readers, but San Diego "will have no need of such committees if your best citizens go to the polls and elect honest, intelligent men to office. It will be a great pity if so promising a seaport falls into unscrupulous hands." Nor should San Diegans brag that their city is "no worse than New York. It ought to be better. New York is the nation's metropolis. It daily receives the scum of Europe and has much to contend against. San Diego is beginning its career, has no such infliction and can readily dispose of its lawless element." Field also cautioned against too-rapid growth. Too many developments had been planned "for the good of the town," and some real estate brokers "have resorted to lying in order to put money in their purses." Among the "deadheads" she mentioned privately were Douglas Gunn, a future mayor of San Diego, and Theodore Van Dyke, a civic booster. But such ruses were unnecessary. "San Diego has an excellent harbor, a fine climate, and good scenery. With such a blessed trinity it is your own fault if you do not steadily advance."

As for "your present drawbacks"? After solving its sewerage problems, the city planners might lay out wide boulevards and select sites for parks. "Of course, you should have an opera house" too. If all "respectable citizens" supported "high license" or the sale of beer, wines, and light spirits, "you'll do more good to your town than prohibitionists ever dreamed of." The reorganization of the Flume Company guaranteed "this valuable system of irrigation will be speedily completed, and then your pretty valley of El Cajou will have all the water it needs to blossom as the rose." More local transit lines would also benefit the tourist, "the dairyman, and market-gardener." In order better to integrate Coronado Beach with the city, Field also recommended "more frequent ferry-boats" across the bay "at more moderate fares." Then an amazing prediction: "The day may not be far distant when a bridge will span the bay."[51] The prophecy was not realized for another eighty years.

On March 28 Field packed her bags and left San Diego by northbound train. Ironically, her expectations for the region were disappointed by the end of the local boom in real estate, the economic recession of 1888–90, and the bankruptcy of the railroad projects she had hoped would speed immigration and increase trade. Gabriel Erb began construction on the Hotel Erb in the spring of 1887 but never completed it. "Some day Punta

Banda will be a famous watering place," Field still insisted, "but not until millions of dollars and thousands of people have found their way to this remote corner of North America." As she anticipated, mining companies developed the gold fields around El Alamo, sixty miles southeast of Ensenada, else the recession in the region would have been worse. But her faith in the International Company of Mexico and its clever manager turned out to be entirely unwarranted. Sisson was implicated in a filibustering scheme that helped to discredit the Company and he transferred all of its assets in mid-1888 to the Mexican Land and Colonization Company. Field was disgusted. The reborn enterprise, she complained, "can never be satisfactory to us, as it is English in the worst sense of the term."[52] The Díaz government eventually charged the company with fraud.

After leaving San Diego, Field lectured on Dickens in Riverside. While in the "thriving little town," she made her "first public declaration against Prohibition" to the dismay of the local Baptists.[53] She was forced by illness to cancel her lecture in San Bernardino,[54] then pushed north to Pasadena. She wrote from the Hotel Westminster in Los Angeles on March 31 that she enjoyed the view of the San Gabriel mountains and had dined with John and Jessie Frémont but that she thought most Los Angelos "uninteresting," with real estate virtually their only topic of conversation "and 'booms' the rage." She had speculated in property in the District of Columbia and in Kansas, but if she had invested instead in southern California, particularly in San Diego "with its beautiful harbor," she realized, "I'd be a howling squillionaire." Instead, she was "a pauper because I've been goose enough to invest in land for a 'rise,' and it won't rise!" At the Grand Opera House in Los Angeles on April 12, she was introduced by General Nelson A. Miles, famous for his prosecution of the Indian wars in the West, before delivering "The Mormon Monster," and two days later she took a ferry to Catalina Island to spend the weekend with friends. She was unimpressed by the experience. As she wrote Hutton on April 16, "I've just returned from an island in the Pacific where I've been starved to death nearly."[55]

She left Los Angeles by train on April 27 for the Bay area,[56] where she tarried for more than two months. "Surrounded by hills, protected from the sharp air of the ocean by beneficient Tamalpais," she lived in San Rafael, which "deserves to be called the Sanatorium of Central California," as she observed. "To her sun and evergreen slopes, her hospitality and beauty, I owe ten weeks of happiness and more than ten weeks of health."[57] "Never shall I forget the summer I passed at San Rafael's charming hotel and scoured Marin County so persistently as to be gazed upon with respect by even the oldest inhabitant," she later reminisced. "Never shall I forget those golden days in the saddle."[58] Field spent these weeks researching and writing one of her best travel essays, "North of the Golden Gate," commissioned for publication in an expensive tour guide, *Picturesque California and the Region West of the Rocky Mountains.* She tramped uphill and down throughout Marin and Sonoma counties, rode the narrow-gauge North Pacific Coast Railroad from Sausalito to Cazadero, explored adobe ruins and redwood forests, coastal bays and backwater rivers and picturesque valleys, and in early June visited the lighthouse at Point Reyes, all the while using San Rafael as her home base. "Very like Mentone in the south of France," she noted, "San Rafael has more days that the invalid can spend out of doors."[59]

Field finally returned east in early August as the buzz about her latest venture hit the papers. She had been hired by Charles A. Wetmore and the State Viticultural Commission of California to promote California wines, much as she had publicized Bell's telephone, and "to enforce the doctrine" by both spoken and written word "that true temperance work in this country consists in substituting pure, light and cheap wines for beer and whiskey."[60] As if bearding the Mormon priesthood in its den had not been risky enough, Kate Field had decided to go head to head with the Prohibitionists.

11

Washington

NEVER AN ADVOCATE OF PROHIBITION, Field recommended as early as May 1864 the consumption of domestic rather than foreign wines during the Civil War as a way to reduce the national debt.[1] In November 1867, she praised John A. Andrew, the Radical Republican governor of the Bay State, for protesting "in the strongest language" the "prohibitory liquor law" that had incited "more drunkenness than was ever before known in Massachusetts."[2] Not that she approved of drunkenness, merely that she sought a "palatable substitute for the liquid Satan now preying on poor humanity." She rebuked the self-righteous do-gooders in the so-called temperance movement who wasted "a vast deal of good intention, energy, and money" in a cause inevitably doomed to fail.[3] She was stunned when her lecture on "Woman in the Lyceum" was advertised once as a benefit for the local temperance society, and she instructed her agent to write a note "denying the soft impeachment."[4] The "average masculine stomach in this country craves liquor, and society must be revolutionized before a better state of things can exist," she declared in 1875, long before she became a target of the prohibitionists.[5] "In all my life I have had but one opinion about prohibition and have never faltered in believing it to be the greatest enemy to actual temperance," as she insisted as late as February 1894.[6]

As an employee of the California Viticultural Commission, Field agreed to preach "the gospel of the grape" in several eastern cities during the 1888–89 lecture season. Not that she was a recent or faint-hearted recruit to the cause of "true temperance." Her firsthand experience while traveling through Iowa, Kansas, and Alaska in 1886–87 had reinforced her opposition to the teetotalers. In September 1886, Field recalled, the mayor of an Iowa town "assured me the [local liquor] laws were despotic" and routinely violated. Druggists regularly sold liquor for "medicinal" use. Field's lecture agent found a saloon where liquor was "sold not only to adults but to very little children, and drummers assured me that just as much liquor as ever was sold in Iowa. Every drug store in Iowa is a genteel groggery." At the "best drug store" in one town she "ordered half a pint of pure California brandy. I was assured I would have the very best. After the clerk had put on a large lying label, and secured my seventy-five cents, which was at the rate of $3 a bottle, I signed a certificate and the clerk gave me the brandy."[7] Trouble is, Field by her own admission signed the name "Sarah Jones" to the prescription, and as a result Mary T. Lathrop of the Women's Christian Temperance Union (WCTU) contended that she should have been arrested: "If there was any violation of law in that drug store, it was by the woman in front of the counter. To get that brandy she signed a fictitious name, and thus committed perjury."[8]

While touring Kansas in March 1888, similarly, Field had purchased "poor whiskey" in Atchison and spotted several private bars and drugstores selling liquor in Wichita. "I've recently been through Prohibition Kansas," she wrote Laurence Hutton, "and got so angry as to stir up the bile as effectually as though I've been to sea."[9] She also objected to the "stringent prohibitory liquor law—on paper" that forbade every resident of Alaska from drinking "one drop of wine or liquor unless he lies, smuggles, or defies the law!" Field recalled that during her visit to Juneau in July 1887 she "saw abundant evidences of whiskey" on the street. She counted no fewer than twenty-nine saloons in a village of slightly more than a thousand inhabitants. In fact, "the courthouse was next door but one to the 'Silver Bow Saloon,' a significant fact to which I drew an official's attention." Such blatant evasion of the law, according to Field, proved that prohibition was as impractical in Alaska as it was in most other places. Lest she seem to attribute the vice of alcoholism mostly to the natives, who had fermented such intoxicants as quass and hoochinoo from berries for generations, she averred that the white Alaskan population "of miners, traders, hunters and sailors can no more be made to drink water than can a dog attacked by hydrophobia." The only way to "advance the cause of true temperance"

in Alaska, she concluded, "is to permit the importation of wines and liquors, making them a source of revenue to the country; pass stringent
laws against adulteration; enforce so high a license as to greatly reduce the
number of saloons and improve their quality; and punish with heavy fines
and imprisonment all who sell intoxicants to minors, confirmed drunk-
ards or persons palpably under the influence of liquor."[10]

Field long lobbied for "high license" rather than prohibition; that is,
she believed the consumption of wines, beer, and light spirits the most
practical solution to the liquor problem. "My experience with the wine
drinking people in France and Italy has been that they are as frugal, industrious, and abstemious as any people on earth," she stressed. "For this reason grape culture should be encouraged, and there is no doubt that with
proper management, wine making will become one of the most valuable
and important industries of California. The substitution of wine drinking
for the wholesale guzzling of doctored whisky and brandy will be an important step toward the solution of the vexed temperance question."[11]

In brief, Field was eminently qualified by both talent and conviction
to defend the California vintners against the insinuations of the anti-
liquor crowd. "I have been reading about and investigating the temperance
question" for years, she observed in July 1889, and her interest in the issue
had been piqued by her "weird experiences in prohibition states." While in
California she had "learned the value of California wines" and had been
recruited by the members of the State Viticultural Commission "to assist
them in their work." "Napa valley is one vast vineyard, where some of the
best wines are made," she asserted, and during her visit there in September
1887 "I embraced what I call the gospel of the grape, believing with all my
soul that the road to temperance is not by prohibition, but by the substitution of light, pure, native wines" for hard liquor. She had consulted "some
of the best intellects in the country" before agreeing to speak in the East
on behalf of "true temperance." Put another way, "The State of California
considers my advocacy of Temperance so valuable to her great industry as
to pass a resolution to pay my incidental expenses" wherever she spoke.[12]
Field's critics charged that, in fact, she had been hired on a $3,000 annual
retainer, which meant that each of her lectures cost the state of California
several hundred dollars.[13]

In any case, during the months Field worked for the Viticultural Commission she discharged her duties with aplomb. In late December 1888, she urged the committee planning Grover Cleveland's second inaugural ceremonies to serve only California wines at the festivities.[14] She hosted dinners for such influential figures as Hugh McCullough, Stephen Field, Senator James McMillan of Michigan, and Representatives Robert Hitt of Illinois and William Walter Phelps of New Jersey that featured varieties of California wines, especially claret.[15] She also literally sold wines to her friends, offering Jeanette Gilder, for example, "good, sound claret for $2.40 a dozen quart bottles" and port for "only $1.75 a gallon."[16] Even her friends at the *Salt Lake Tribune* regretted her willingness to indulge her taste for intoxicants: "For some time she has been in New York," the *Tribune* soberly reported on December 30, 1888, "not only drinking wine conspicuously herself, but inducing others to do so."[17] She lectured on "The Intemperance of Prohibition" at the Grand Army Hall in Washington on March 22, 1889, and at Tremont Temple in Boston on April 12. The WCTU activists Lathrop, J. Ellen Foster, and Mary H. Hunt distributed prohibitionist tracts in the lobby before Field's lecture in Boston and shouted their disagreements with her from the audience during it.[18] Foster later excoriated Field: "It is to me a shocking thing that any American woman should use the press or the platform to uphold the sale of wine. Miss Field's views on the prohibition position seems to me to be wholly erroneous." On her part, Field charged that "The W.C.T.U's are as great a pest as phylloxera" or the lice that infect grapevines.[19] On June 17, 1889, much to the consternation of the orthodox, Field spoke at Pittsburgh city hall against the prohibition amendment to the state constitution on the ballot the next day in Pennsylvania, which failed overwhelmingly. In response, the National Council of Women passed a resolution that Field was "a disgrace to womanhood" and by her anti-prohibition campaign was "dragging women down to prostitution."[20] A month later Field was again compelled to reply to the accusation that she had been bought by the winemakers. "My association with the Viticultural Commission has had no more to do with forming my opinion on the question of prohibitory liquor laws than have the rising and setting of the sun. My opposition to prohibition is based on experience in prohibition states," she insisted, and "my conscience has never been for sale." Field pointedly asked why Foster, Frances E. Willard, and Mary Livermore were permitted to earn a livelihood by lecturing in favor of prohibition yet "it is an absolutely heinous offence for me to accept any remuneration whatever for arguing against prohibition, which I firmly believe to be the worst form of intemperance."[21] Even when she spoke on the "harmless" topic of "Despised Alaska" at the Methodist Church in Plattsburg, New York, in November 1889, she was hectored by the jackals: "The W.C.T.U. leaders drove about in carriages all day long urging people not to go hear me."[22] In the end, she insisted, "My association with the Vitacultural Commission cost me far more than the small fee I accepted for months of earnest study on a vital topic to the nation."[23]

Field quit her job with the Viticultural Commission after only one year when she tired of the abuse and the "campaign of personal defamation" mounted by her enemies. One newspaper had headlined its attack on her "Kate Field's Rum Work." The *New York Tribune* rallied to her defense, editorializing that "there was neither sense nor decency in making her the object of vituperation. Her arguments were open to rebuttal"— but no one cared to address her arguments, only to attack her character.[24] After her resignation, however, Field responded in kind to her critics in the way she knew best—in cold print. "I have been held up as a disgrace to my sex for being the only woman who has dared to oppose the amazing methods of prohibitionists," she averred.[25] She published an indignant broadside against "women politicians" that singled out the WCTU for special censure. The "fanatics" who paraded under the temperance banner, Field wrote, "mistake hysterical sentimentality for morality" and their "knowledge of the English language is as limited as their knowledge of human nature. Temperance does not mean total abstinence." The members of this group "have no right to call themselves either temperate or Christian." The sumptuary laws they bully legislators into passing "are opposed to personal liberty" and zealots "have no more right to destroy" property in barrooms "than they have to burn a house."[26] The essays won her few friends.

Field was often criticized, too, for refusing to join the campaign for universal suffrage. As early as 1871, Elizabeth Cady Stanton grumbled that Field did not think "enough of our movement to make a speech on

our platform" and "it ill becomes" her to doubt "the wisdom of Susan
B. Anthony or myself in welcoming anyone to our ranks who is ready
to share our labors."[27] Field was especially critical of Anthony later for
entering an "unholy alliance" with the Populist Party in Kansas merely
because its platform favored women's suffrage. "I may be very stupid,"
she granted, "but I still think that converts to women suffrage must be
obtained by appeals to reason, and that it is a mistake to ally a reasonable
cause to the unreasonableness of a party made up of every man's discon-
tent." Some women "will be frightened out" of the ranks of the suffragists
"if they think they must march with the grand army of cranks."[28] More
to the point, Field argued, only women qualified to vote should demand
the vote. "I have never felt it my mission to advocate suffrage for women,
for the reason that I don't believe in universal suffrage for anybody," she
explained. Suffrage should be "a privilege, not a right, granted only" to
men and women regardless of race or color who qualify by "education,
intelligence, virtue, and a small property holding." In addition, Field believed that some women did not want suffrage. If they "are not sufficiently
enlightened on the subject," she argued, why should they be given the
vote?[29] Little wonder that Field was rarely mentioned in the *Woman's Journal,* the organ of the American Woman Suffrage Association and the
leading suffrage paper in the country. The so-called "maternal feminists"
of the period disapproved of her.

Field long cherished the dream of editing her own magazine. As early as
1875, she wrote Stedman that if she owned a paper she would "ring" the
celebration of the Centennial the next year.[30] As it happened, one of the
last of Field's many careers was that of public intellectual and editor/pub-
lisher of the weekly paper *Kate Field's Washington,* first issued on January
1, 1890. As Whiting allowed, "There had been nothing in Kate's entire
life which had so concentrated her interest, and stimulated every gift and
grace of her nature, as this enterprise of founding and conducting a national review of her own. She thought of it by day and dreamed of it by
night."[31] Field widely publicized her editorial credo even before beginning
to issue the magazine:

I believe in Washington as the hub of a great nation.

I believe that a capital of a Republic of 60,000,000 of human beings is the locality for a review knowing no sectional prejudices and loving truth better than party.

I believe that [quoting Wendell Phillips] "men and women are eternally equal and eternally different"; hence I believe there is a fair field in Washington for a national weekly edited by a woman.

I believe in home industries; in a reduced tariff; in civil service reform; in extending our commerce; in American shipping; in strengthening our army and navy; in temperance which does not mean enforcing total abstinence on one's neighbor; in personal liberty.

I believe in literature, art, science, music, and the drama as handmaids of civilization. . . . I believe in a religion of deeds.[32]

She expressed no radical agenda in this credo. On the contrary, she was obliged constantly during the life of her weekly to defend her patriotism, her ameliorism, her middlebrow conservatism. As she promised a friend an entire year before the first issue appeared, "It will be politically independent, aim for the best society all over the country and warmly support the new states and struggling territories. It will oppose all sumptuary laws and therefore will oppose prohibition, but will treat of so many subjects as not to come under the category of an organ for any specialty. It will be *my* organ, and what I conscientiously believe of course the paper will advocate." She invested what remained of her telephone stock in the project and, echoing St. Paul's admonition in his first letter to the Corinthians, she announced that "it will avoid vituperation and endeavor to be *temperate* in all things."[33]

Field rented an apartment on the sixth floor of the new Shoreham Hotel in Washington, home of Vice President Levi P. Morton, where she hosted a salon every Sunday evening. Among her neighbors in the building were ten members of Congress, including Speaker of the House Thomas B. Reed. She installed a concert-grand piano, several easy chairs, and a red mahogany desk that had belonged to her mother. Next to her study was a den "packed with curios from the seven parts of the world," including objects of Alaskan art, several paintings by Vedder, her portrait by Millet, the framed and mounted autograph letter by Alexander Pope that Landor

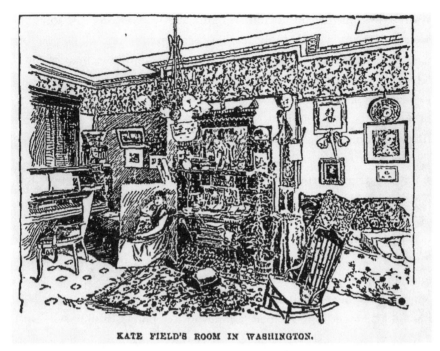

KATE FIELD'S ROOM IN WASHINGTON.

16. Field's apartment in the Shoreham Hotel, Washington, D.C. *Boston Globe,* 4 June 1893, 28. Note the sketch of Frank Millet's portrait of Field (since lost), center-left.

had given her in Florence thirty years before, and the letter she had received from Dickens in January 1868.[34] From her rooms she enjoyed views of the Washington Monument, the Capitol, the White House, the Treasury Building, Georgetown, Arlington, and the Potomac. She hired two young Vassar College graduates to assist her with the paper, Caroline Lingle and Ella Leonard, who had earlier run a country newspaper in New Jersey. She also hired Francis Leupp, a former reporter for the *New York Evening Post,* as her managing editor, and leased offices for them in the Corcoran Building a block from the White House.[35] Her staff, Field proudly reported, was "filled with regularly educated journalists, who have had years of experience."[36] Though the rumor circulated that *Kate Field's Washington* was edited by a man, it was soon squelched. Field ordered fifty thousand copies of the prospectus for promotional purposes, hoping to attract subscribers from across the country,[37] and she threw herself into the social whirl of

Washington. She became a familiar figure at White House receptions. She socialized mostly with Republicans, among them Senators Leland Stanford of California, Justin Smith Morrill of Vermont, John Sherman of Ohio, George Hearst of California, and Secretary of State Walter Gresham. Eminently "clubbable," she also frequented meetings of the American Academy of the Dramatic Arts and the New York Press Club, the same organization that had ostracized her during Dickens' visit a quarter-century before.

Each sixteen-page issue of *Kate Field's Washington* contained a fairly standard array of articles. Field always led the issue with three or four pages of editorials, political commentary, excerpts from her travel journals, or the script of a play. Over the months she also printed previously unpublished letters by Robert Browning, John Ruskin, Wilkie Collins, and Mark Twain, as well as her reminiscences of such figures as Landor, Dickens, Tennyson, George Eliot, and Charles Dilke. By 1893 she was literally emptying her files in search of material to fill the pages of the paper. Next was a department Field entitled "Grapevine Telephone," an interview with a newsmaker ostensibly conducted by telephone, inspired by her promotional work for Bell in 1878 and her telephone interview with the *San Diego Bee* while in Ensenada in February 1887. Among those featured over the years were Theodore Roosevelt, Charles Francis Adams, Albert Bierstadt, Gifford Pinchot, and the single-taxer Tom Johnson. A department entitled "The Players" reviewed plays and concerts; published interviews with such actors, producers, and playwrights as Bronson Howard, Edwin Booth, Henry Irving, and Dion Boucicault; and printed articles by Clyde Fitch and Daniel Frohman. Most issues included a few poems and a final page or two of advertisements and book notices. Among the books Field reviewed over the months were Mark Twain's *Pudd'nhead Wilson*, W. D. Howells' *A Hazard of New Fortunes*, and George du Maurier's *Trilby*. Her notice of Tolstoy's *The Kruetzer Sonata* in the issue of 11 June 1890 was cited in advertisements defending the novel from allegations of obscenity.[38] She lauded Childe Hassam's watercolors and the kinetoscope invented by Thomas Edison. *Kate Field's Washington* also published thirty early poems, essays, and tales by Charlotte Perkins Stetson Gilman, the most prominent intellectual in the American women's movement at the turn of the twentieth century.[39] Indeed, Field's example as editor and publisher may have inspired Gilman to establish her own paper, *The Forerunner,* in 1909. Other contributors included Hutton, Grace Ellery Channing, Clara Barton, Robert Ingersoll, Eliza Calvert Hall, the poets Charles Warren Stoddard and Harriet Monroe, the eccentric millionaire Gaylord Wilshire, the printer and lithographer Louis Prang, and Albert Bigelow Paine, later Mark Twain's official biographer and literary executor. Gilman was paid ten dollars for one of her pieces,[40] though the more typical payment was five dollars per column. Hutton received a complimentary year's subscription for his first contribution.[41] In truth, Field usually wrote much of the material in each issue, especially during the first couple of years, sometimes using such pseudonyms as "Everpoint" and "Straws" (pen names her father had used a half-century earlier) or "Olla," short for "Ollapodrida." She even covered the heavyweight title fight at Madison Square Garden between Gentleman Jim Corbett and John L. Sullivan on September 7, 1892, for her paper.[42]

From the first, the critical miscellany was a lightning rod for controversy. Anthony publicly alleged that Field's weekly was sponsored by liquor interests, specifically California brewers and vintners, and certainly the magazine contained advertising each week for such firms as Inglenook, the George Wiedemann Brewing Company, To-Kalon Wine Company, Pleasant Valley Wine Company, and Urbana Wine Company. Stoddard later conceded that the magazine had been "backed by friendly financiers,"[43] but Field disputed the implication that her editorial policy was dictated by them. As she replied to Anthony in February 1890, less than six weeks after issuing her first number,

> I heard that you had stated publicly that my paper was subsidized by liquor-dealers. I did not believe the story and have taken the first opportunity I ever had to pay you respect by giving you the place of honor in my issue of Feb. 12th. I did this half on your account, and half on account of the suffragists and prohibitionists who because I don't entirely agree with [them], either slander me basely or let me severely alone. I can return good for evil and give anyone who is honest a fair hearing in my paper. I don't expect to get the least credit for a decent act.[44]

Because Field also boosted Washington as the "hub of a great nation" and touted its potential for investors, local real estate developers also advertised in her magazine. In addition, she formed a limited partnership to publish the weekly, selling 240 shares in the company for $100 apiece, meanwhile retaining 260 shares and a controlling interest in the paper.[45] As Field wrote Hutton in September 1890, "I'm always fighting for the stage & ought to be backed by rich actors but, so far, they have not materialized even as subscribers." Or as she wrote Hugh McCullough in April 1891, she wished to sell stock in her company to residents of Washington "as I am 'booming' this lovely town and increasing the value of their property."[46] However egregious such apparent conflicts of interest, Field stoutly maintained that her weekly was independent of either party or faction—and there is no evidence that she ever quashed an article or changed a word in the magazine to suit an advertiser or a stockholder.

From all indications, *Kate Field's Washington* survived on its sale of advertising and stock because it enjoyed only modest income from subscribers and newsstand purchases. Little over a month after it commenced publication, Field wrote Anne Botta that the "Paper is doing very well but I want it to do better. I want the earth." A week or so later she told an interviewer that "[w]e are paying expenses . . . and we are only seven weeks old." She claimed in May that the weekly already had six hundred subscribers,[47] but the paper probably never attracted more than a couple of thousand at the height of its popularity. In order to attract more readers and increase advertising revenue, Field halved the price of the paper at the end of 1890 from four dollars a year and ten cents a copy to two dollars a year and five cents a copy. To help make ends meet, Field also continued to lecture occasionally for no less than a hundred dollars per date: in Virginia and North Carolina in the spring of 1890, Ohio in November and December 1890. (She delivered her Dickens address on November 30 before 1,600 inmates of the Ohio State Penitentiary in Columbus and, as the *Chicago Tribune* quipped, "not a man left the room while she was talking.")[48] Her total income from her investments and lectures was estimated at $15,000 a year.[49]

Whatever its paid circulation, *Kate Field's Washington* exercised an influence on American politics far out of proportion to the number of its subscribers. Among those who read it were President Grover Cleveland; Vice President Morton; Reed, the Speaker of the House; John C. and Jessie Benton Frémont; Charles W. Chesnutt; Charles Dudley Warner and George

William Curtis of *Harper's;* Richard Watson Gilder, editor of *Century;* Jeanette Gilder, editor of *Critic;* Mary Mapes Dodge, editor of *St. Nicholas;* and the Civil War general William Tecumseh Sherman.[50] Ambrose Bierce occasionally cited it in his weekly column in the *San Francisco Examiner;* William James mentioned it in his correspondence; and the novelist Gertrude Atherton remembered in her autobiography that it made "something of a sensation" and that she "read it with interest," too.[51] It became so quotable that some of Field's articles were syndicated for advance publication in newspapers across the country, and its articles were widely copied from Maine to Alaska and in England. Field bragged that "my Washington . . . is more quoted than any paper in the country."[52] Or as she told an interviewer in September 1891, "I am highly gratified at the way in which the baby has been received by both press and public. . . . I want the reading public to look upon this new review as a friend that will always have the courage to tell the truth, and will aim to do so without being stupid."[53]

Nevertheless, a few country editors with a wry sense of humor insisted upon attributing the paragraphs they copied from the paper to "Kate Field's Wash."[54]

During the life of the paper Field rallied support in it for several progressive if sometimes unpopular causes. She championed civil service reform, a key plank in the mugwump platform; indicted lynch law; and argued for international intervention in the Congo Free State to stop the genocide there. As early as 1864, influenced by the teachings of Wendell Phillips, she had defended the rights of freed slaves in the South.[55] In her weekly, she went even further in indicting racism and sympathizing with the victims of social oppression. "White citizens," she opined, have "allowed their poor brethren to live like pigs in alleys where tenements should not be tolerated."[56] In the fall of 1890, Field referred to W. E. B. Du Bois as the "best orator on Commencement Day" at Harvard the previous June, one of the first references to him in any national publication, and Du Bois later included this detail in his autobiography.[57] In early 1895, after joining the mourners of Frederick Douglass at the Methodist Episcopal Church on M Street, she hailed his legacy.[58] In all, as Field insisted in September 1891, her *Washington* took "what I believe to be the right side on every subject, regardless of politics."[59]

In historical hindsight, however, she was not always on the side of the angels. For example, Field opposed bimettalism or the "Great American Flapdoodle" of free silver, a populist project designed to boost the economy in the West; applauded the execution of the Haymarket Square anarchists in Illinois; combated the admission of New Mexico to the Union on the grounds that many of its residents spoke only Spanish; and advocated restrictive immigration laws at the height of the nativist movement. She hoped a cholera scare in Europe in 1892 would halt the approval of new visa applications.[60] She opposed the campaign to mount the Statue of Liberty on Bedloe's Island off the New York shore because, as she argued, "there does not seem any reason why one of the loveliest spots in a picturesque harbor should be spoiled" to welcome immigrants to the country.[61] She even went to Ellis Island, what she called a "powder magazine" in the shadow of the statue, to collect material for an article critical of the "foreign scum" America welcomed to its shores.[62] Not that she was opposed to all immigration per se so much as she was opposed to permitting new immigrants to vote. She warned in 1891 that "vigilance committees" would soon demand "that suffrage be restricted to native Americans and such foreign-born citizens as have lived here twenty-one years." "Prostitution of the ballot box and criminal looseness of naturalization laws," she alleged, "are bacilli more harmful than all the Asiatic cholera that could be imported with all the immigrants of Europe and Asia." And she turned a blind eye to anti-Semitism in both the United States and Germany; in fact, she asserted that wherever Russian Jews have immigrated "they have laid the seeds of disease" even as she maintained that "Germany has no anti-Semitic feelings."[63]

She was more astute in some of her other campaigns, as in the case of international copyright. As early as 1841, Joe Field had argued for stronger copyright protections for authors, and his daughter could do no less. She published in *Kate Field's Washington* contributions by Stedman, Brander Matthews, Oliver Wendell Holmes, W. D. Howells, and James Russell Lowell in support of international copyright, and she solicited a testimonial from Mark Twain. In "A Nation of Pirates," in her *Washington* for May 14, 1890, she observed that men and women of letters are "poorly paid compared to their peers in painting, sculpture, law, medicine or trade." But she also cited one exception to this rule: "Mark Twain is a humorist, and humor sells in literature as burlesque sells on the stage." Inexplicably, Field enclosed a copy of this essay with her request to Twain to send her a paragraph for her paper endorsing the adoption of a stronger copyright law. "Will you read enclosed and send me a word of denunciation for a column of authors that is to be in my next number?" she asked. "If you send, please let it be immediately. You understand my reference to humor is not *against* humor. People buy it and you are the exception to rule."[64] Not surprisingly, Twain ignored her request. No paragraph from his pen ever appeared in *Kate Field's Washington*. Still, Field claimed some of the credit for the copyright bill passed by Congress in 1891. She attended a dinner at Sherry's in April 1891 to commemorate the eighth anniversary of the founding of the American Author's Copyright League and to celebrate the new law in company with E. C. Stedman, G. W. Curtis, Brander Matthews, Representative Henry Cabot Lodge of Massachusetts, the publisher Charles Scribner, President Seth Low of Columbia University, the painter F. D. Millet, Ripley Hitchcock of Harper and Bros., the novelist George W. Cable, the sculptor Augustus St. Gaudens, and George Parsons Lathrop, son-in-law of Nathaniel Hawthorne and the founder of the League.[65]

Field's progressive politics were also apparent in her editorials about the American West, specifically the creation of Yosemite National Park. As Field wrote Mary Mapes Dodge early in the life of her paper, "I'm out gunning for Yosemite and am making converts."[66] In February 1890, she published in her *Washington* an open appeal to Leland Stanford "to rescue God's noblest work from the hands of vandals"—that is, to help preserve the Yosemite under the stewardship of the national government. "Every section [of California] commands attention," she wrote, "but above all looms Yosemite Valley, unique in character and grandeur, awe-full in solemnity. It is Nature at prayer. Human beings who remain unmoved in the presence of such scenery should walk on four legs and browse on tin cans." She urged Stanford to introduce a bill in Congress "for the preservation of Yosemite Valley," contending that if it were "controlled by competent officers of the United States, no such condition of nature and man as now disgraces it could endure." Robert Underwood Johnson, a champion of expanding the national park system, wrote her that her open letter to

Stanford was "*admirable* and will prove effective,"[67] and indeed two days after it appeared the *New York Times* commended Field's "vigorous protest" against the "neglect of the Yosemite. . . . Of the neglect there can be no doubt. All tourists have nearly the same story of discomfort and extortion to tell, though they do not tell it so vividly as Miss Field." The *Boston Herald* also editorialized that Field "is clearly right in calling upon Senator Stanford, as a California capitalist, to take means to aid in protecting the valley."[68] Yosemite National Park was finally established, at least partly through her efforts, in October 1890, and Field again did not hesitate to take at least partial credit for the legislation. *Kate Field's Washington* "deserves a great deal more than thanks from California" for lobbying on behalf of the park, she remarked, "but blessed are they who expect nothing, for they will not be disappointed." Or as she noted in her retrospective of her first year as editor of the weekly, "Remember that Congress has given to the world a National Yosemite Park two million acres in size, and do not forget the source of its inspiration."[69]

She also lobbied in her *Washington* and before Congress to eliminate all import duties on works of art. She testified before the House Ways and Means Committee, chaired by William McKinley of Ohio, on March 27, 1890.[70] She wore her best Worth dress, and one of the members of the committee told her afterward that the gown secured the passage of that bill. "When you've got something to do before men you had better wear French gowns," she later remarked—to the consternation of many of the women who heard her say it.[71] She also labored behind the scenes to convince "the most distinguished members" of the committee of the justice of her proposal.[72] In any event, her testimony persuaded Congressman Roger Mills of Texas "of the untenable nature of his former position," and the next day Field received a telegram from the Art League in New York "congratulating and thanking her for her eloquent and convincing address before the committee." Her testimony was also commended in several newspapers, including the *Philadelphia Ledger, Hartford Times, Boston Courier, Boston Post, Boston Advertiser, Boston Herald, New York Tribune, New York Herald,* and *New York Commercial Advertiser*.[73] The *Boston Traveller* editorialized that "in Miss Kate Field America has a speaker worthy to be called an orator, and her peculiar brilliancy and power were never more effectively displayed than

17. Kate Field in dress by Worth. Courtesy of Boston Public Library.

on this occasion."[74] As Stedman later wrote her, "If *Kate Field's Washington* were not (as it is) the brightest weekly that comes to us, your success in reducing the art duties would have been its sufficient excuse for being."[75] The McKinley bill passed the House, and McKinley personally assured Field that the committee members would stand "by their guns,"[76] but a compromise in the conference committee reduced the duty from 30 percent to 15 percent rather than eliminating it entirely.

So, characteristically, Field decided to take her campaign directly to the people, or at least to the art connoisseurs of the nation. She lectured on "Free Art" before art clubs in Missouri, Minnesota, Iowa, Nebraska, Colorado, Wyoming, and Utah in October and early November 1891. She argued, in a nutshell, that art imports were untaxed prior to the Civil War; that the duty on imported art had generated almost no revenue for the federal government after the Civil War; and so the tariff simply penalized museums and art collectors for no good reason. After an absence of over four years, she arrived in Denver on November 8, 1891, and accepted an invitation to stay at the home of former congressman G. G. Symes and his wife. She was impressed during her visit by the growth of the city. "I am amazed at the number and size of the new buildings; I was particularly struck with the Equitable building and the Brown and Métropole hotels. I should not be surprised if when the Brown hotel was finished it would be, as its projectors intend, the finest in the United States." The Broadway Theater, located in the Métropole, seemed to her "far superior to any theater in New York."[77] The day after her arrival, she sat for a pair of interviews with the *Denver Times* and *Republican*. She tactfully expressed no opinion on the issue of free silver ("I am not going to commit myself on a subject of which I know so little"). She denounced the recent Woodruff manifesto, which suspended (but did not end) the practice of plural marriage in Mormon teachings, as "an unmitigated hypocrisy and a fraud. It was issued because the Mormons were afraid that they would be disfranchised" or forced to take a loyalty oath. (Elsewhere, she joked that she had "heard President Woodruff many times and I never knew him to be guilty of an idea.") When asked if she was a suffragist, Field offered her standard response: "Theoretically I can see no reason why a woman should not be allowed to vote, but as a matter of fact I am opposed to woman suffrage at present. . . . When women go into politics they allow their emotions to run away with their reason. Take the Women's Christian Temperance Union. The moment it would get into politics it would pass laws as to what we should drink, and next as to what we shall wear."[78]

On November 11 she addressed the Denver Art League at the Post Office Annex to plead her case for free art. During her speech, she announced that Congressmen Sereno E. Payne of New York and John Henry Gear of Iowa had pledged their support to the bill to add foreign art to the "free list." At the end of her speech, the members of the League adopted a resolution requesting that the congressmen from Colorado support the elimination of the art tariff.[79] At the close of the meeting, former governor

Alva Adams spoke briefly and invited Field to visit his home in Pueblo, and she accepted the invitation with alacrity. First, however, she was compelled to respond to a critic who intimated that she was in the pay of "Eastern picture dealers" to campaign against the art tariff. She replied in the *Rocky Mountain News* that the allegation was beneath contempt and nothing more than "the ravings of an unbalanced mind."[80]

En route to Pueblo on November 16, Field was persuaded by the Reverend R. J. Mellen to speak on the subject of free art in the pavilion of the Antlers Hotel in Colorado Springs under the auspices of the local Unitarian society. As in Denver, the large audience, including the railroad executive and arts patron Louis R. Ehrich and the banker W. S. Jackson, adopted a resolution in favor of the repeal of import duties on objets d'art.[81] Field also marveled at the civic progress of the Springs. "What began as a pleasant village is rapidly developing into a town as unique in the culture of its inhabitants as in its scenery and climate," she noted. "Villa after villa appears where in 1887 there lay the virgin mesa. For miles Cascade Avenue is lined with the homes of wise men and women of the east who find here the health they lost at sea-level."[82]

She was even more intrigued by Pueblo, a burgeoning industrial town she had never before visited. As the guest of Adams, she received a grand tour of the iron and steel mills, the new Opera House Block, the Mineral Palace with its "gorgeously Egyptian" architecture and "no less than twenty-five domes." She dubbed the town "the Pittsburgh of the West" and confessed she was a convert to its future. "Within a dozen years a trading post of adobes and flannel shirts has been transformed into a community of thirty thousand souls eager for the best of everything, determined to conquer every difficulty in their path," she wrote. "Whatever is conceived is executed, and whatever is executed is an example for others to follow." While in town she also visited the offices of the *Pueblo Chieftain*, whose editors gossiped the next day that she "talks as well as she writes and is one of those bright, brainy women whom every journalist desires to meet and who when she departs leaves behind her the hope that she will soon come again."[83]

She left Colorado in late November and stopped in St. Louis to deliver her free art lecture before the local Artists' Guild. The *St. Louis Post-Dispatch* quoted Field to the effect that the tariff on foreign art was a "malignant stupidity," then added, "We shudder to think what Kate would say about the tariff tax on the poor man's necessaries."[84] On December 9, Field spoke before the Chicago Society of Artists, which also adopted a resolution in favor of her free art proposal signed by, among others, the sculptor Lorado Taft; the poet Harriet Monroe; and John Vanderpoel, a painter and teacher at the Art Institute of Chicago. The *Chicago Tribune* agreed with the spirit of the resolution: "The tax upon art is the most serious obstacle that stands in the way of art progress in America."[85] On December 14 she urged some two hundred members of the Society for the Promotion of Physical Culture—unbeknownst to her, the dress reform branch of the Women's Club of Chicago—to write letters and send delegations to their congressmen, but "when you go, don't go in dress reform gowns." Some of the assembled women "took exception to her remarks,"[86] and Field retreated to her home in Washington for the holidays.

On January 6, 1892, during a brief caesura in her political work, she caught a special train for San Francisco to attend the convention of the International League of Press Clubs.[87] In all, about a hundred delegates representing about twenty press clubs made the trip. In Chicago on January 7, they went over the World's Fair grounds at Jackson Park, visited the press room of the *Chicago Herald,* and attended a performance of Oliver Goldsmith's *She Stoops to Conquer* at the Opera House. At the Chicago Press Club, several of the excursionists, including Field, Mrs. Frank Leslie, and Oscar Wilde's brother Willy, spoke informally.[88] In St. Louis on January 8, the delegates toured the Merchants' Exchange.[89] The next day the group reached Denver, where Field registered at the Métropole. "The taste displayed in the appointments of this hotel is admirable," she wrote in her diary. "Here am I, seated in a beautifully furnished apartment, with bathroom attached, writing by electric light after a delightful hot bath which makes me feel akin to godly." The following evening she attended a performance of the comedy *A Texas Steer* at Tabor's Grand Opera House. "I need no conversion to the attractions of the West. Denver is an old friend," she added.[90] The delegates to the convention left Denver at midnight, arrived at the Royal Gorge early in the morning of January 10, and climbed 10,500 feet "to visit Leadville for ten minutes! I shall not vilify this extraordinary town by admitting that ten minutes suffice for inspection." Her impressions of the town were too fleeting. "I shall wait until Fate permits me to stop longer" before forming an opinion of the place, as she jotted in her journal. The travelers arrived after dark that night in Glenwood Springs. The bathhouse there, Field wrote, "excited universal admiration. Seven thousand feet above sea level, Glenwood Springs has a future as a health resort. Its mineral waters only need to be well known to be well patronized."[91] The delegates paused en route for two days in Salt Lake City, where Field was stunned to discover "sixty miles of electric railway," "seventeen miles of sidewalk," and "one street paved with asphalt."[92] They reached Placer County, California, on January 13, where she "touched and tasted" a variety of nuts and fruits at an agricultural fair.[93]

Field crossed from Oakland to San Francisco the next day and, after registering at the Baldwin Hotel, she spent a week at the conference in the city. "We are entertained to death and I am called upon for speeches just as though I were a Presidential candidate," she bragged.[94] On the stage of the Powell Street theater, she spoke on "the burning question of immigration," particularly on the injustice of "excluding the Chinese" while "opening our arms to the scum of Europe," when "they know less of republican institutions and their responsibilities than the Father of Lies knows of truth."[95] In fact, she considered Chinatown in San Francisco her "favorite resort" and the Chinese "an interesting, highly intelligent, industrious, patient, long-suffering, and *clean* people."[96] While in the city, Field also was asked to christen the warship *Monterrey* in the presence of President Harrison, and she compiled, though she insisted on using a bottle of California champagne rather than a bottle of French wine.[97] She also met Charlotte Perkins Gilman at a reception for the delegates hosted by the Pacific Coast Women's Press Association.[98] After the conference ended, she took the southern route through Arizona and New Mexico to Denver,[99] where she attended the banquet of the Greystone Club at the Métropole on February 9. "Three hundred Democrats sat down to as good a dinner as New York can furnish," she observed in the manner of a civic booster. "Today Denver's hotels rank with the best. Tomorrow the finest hotel on this continent will be found in the town which began with a miner's shanty in 1859."[100]

Back in Washington a few days later, she returned to the campaign to eliminate the tax on foreign art. She suggested in her weekly that Caroline Harrison, the wife of President Benjamin Harrison, join the fight by hosting a reception for American artists at the White House—and the first lady agreed. Thomas F. Waggaman, the director of the Corcoran Gallery, and Phoebe Hearst, wife of Senator George Hearst and mother of William Randolph Hearst, also "offered hospitality to the group." With a budget of $5,000 she raised from private donors,[101] Field organized an art congress or national loan exhibition of several hundred American paintings, including works by John Singer Sargent, Vedder, John La Farge, Millet, Albert Bierstadt, George Inness, and Eastman Johnson, mounted in the chapel of the Smithsonian Institution between May 18 and 27.[102] Admission was free and some 20,000 people attended. "Most of them were poor people, too," Field reported. "They were so anxious to see as much as possible of the exhibit that they wrote letters to me to have the time extended and to have the exhibit open on Sunday."[103] The Congress evolved into the National Academy of Art with such sponsors as Field, Whitelaw Reid, James J. Hill, and George Pullman.[104] As good as her word, Caroline Harrison hosted a reception at the White House on May 15, and Field testified again on behalf of free art before the House Ways and Means Committee on May 18. When Congress finally corrects "this discreditable piece of legislation," the *New York Times* editorialized, "justice requires that the greatest share of the credit shall be given to Miss Kate Field, who has worked with great energy and devotion and with excellent judgment for this result."[105] Congress finally and unconditionally revoked the tax on foreign art in September 1894, and the French government awarded Field with an Academic Palm or *Palmes académique* for her service to art and literature.[106] "One of the foremost women in America," she was congratulated by the *New York Evening Post* "upon the great honor," and the *Boston Herald* remarked that the French government had recognized "the power of woman in general and of women editors in particular."[107]

Field also agitated in her *Washington* for justice to Alaska and its citizens. She printed in the first issues of the paper the three Alaska essays she had written in San Francisco in late 1887 but had been unable to place for publication. In "Rum in Alaska," she ridiculed Prohibition and the naïve do-gooders in the WCTU.[108] In "Education in Alaska," published in two parts in her *Washington* in April–May 1890, Field examined "the right and wrong way to educate the Natives." Though raised a Catholic, Field had renounced the church while in Florence thirty years before and she roundly criticized every stripe of religious fanaticism, zealotry, and sectarianism she encountered. She appealed for missionary efforts to improve literacy and hygiene among the native children rather than to evangelize or convert them. She believed that hospitals were "absolutely indispensable if the natives in and about white settlements are to be saved"—her final phrase refers to physical, not spiritual, salvation. In a deft turn of phrase she compared the territory to an un(der)appreciated stepsister or charwoman: "Alaska is the Cinderella of the human family. Neglected by both Russia and the United States, she is today worse off as to education—and even morals—than when under the rule of the Czar."[109] And how to uplift a despised and overworked stepsister? Field's answer was well intentioned but unsurprising. She called for an extension of the conventional model of Indian schooling to Alaska. No white children, she elsewhere reported, "approached the perfection" of the discipline of the students at the Carlisle Indian School.[110] Finally, she serialized her semischolarly "Native Races of Alaska," a miscellany of legends, folklore, and anecdotes derived from her reading about the Inuits or Eskimos, the Athabascans or Yukon Indians, the Aleuts, and the Tlingit, in nine parts in her *Washington* between July and October 1890. Though untrained in ethnology, Field bragged to Hutton that her discussion of the native tribes was thorough and comprehensive: "nowhere will you find such a condensation of the whole Territory."[111]

In addition, Field argued that Alaska should be represented at the Columbian Exposition in Chicago in 1893. The various national pavilions would feature many indigenous peoples and their handiwork and so, she argued, "our native races must be given the prominence they deserve, not only for the sake of novelty, but for the sake of history and ethnology." (Of course, "novelty" and entertainment along the Midway Plaisance would supersede the stated ethnological purposes of such human exhibits at the Fair.) She also considered the Exposition a sterling opportunity to ballyhoo "the great land upon the purchase of which, at a cent an acre, William

H. Seward rests his claims to immortality."[112] She was prophetic: President Benjamin Harrison appointed two Alaskan commissioners to the Fair and they organized a modest exhibit in the Government Building in Chicago. Field, who had covered the Paris Exhibition in 1877, was no less eager to visit the so-called White City, and in May 1893 she headed west from Washington to attend the most important World's Fair in history.

12

Chicago and Beyond

"I HAVE JOURNEYED 1,000 MILES as fast as an exposition flyer could bring me to see with my own eyes the fulfillment of prophecy," Field reported in her first article, published May 31, 1893, as the World's Fair correspondent for the *Chicago Herald*.[1] The irony was not lost on her: she was an out-of-town reporter covering the Fair for a local newspaper. Designed to mark the four-hundredth anniversary of Columbus's voyage to the New World (albeit a year late), the Fair opened on May 1 and attracted several million visitors before it closed its gates on October 30. W. D. Howells, Henry Adams, and Theodore Dreiser, among others, were impressed by the grandeur of the exposition and wrote about it at length; and the building designs of Daniel Burnham, Frederick Law Olmsted, and Louis Sullivan inspired the City Beautiful movement and influenced the beaux-arts style of architecture for the next generation or more. Field arrived in Chicago in late May and addressed the Congress of the Press Women of the World in the Hall of Washington in the evening of the 26th. She spoke on the topic "A Woman's Paper versus a Paper for Woman" and as she opened her speech—delivered without notes—she both literally and figuratively removed her gloves. "It is just as well to discuss this question without gloves," she declared. "Journalists have a hard time of it—I mean the honest ones. Woman journalists have perhaps no easier time of it, but they always make a fuss about it." While she had hired two Vassar graduates to assist on her *Washington,* the paper was not pitched to appeal only to women readers: "Our review is for all classes—a woman's paper, while not in any special manner a paper for women." Indeed, Field concluded, "There is no need of a paper for women, but a paper for men and women."[2]

Noticing Susan B. Anthony in the crowd, Field invited her to the platform and declared that in future she would support women's suffrage, albeit with the same reservations she had always expressed. "I never believed in woman's suffrage," she said. "I never opposed it, but occupied neutral ground, because I did not believe in universal suffrage." But, Field added, "I have always advocated, and always shall advocate, although I never expect to get it, a restricted suffrage founded on education and character regardless of sex." Still, "from this time forth" she would "advocate woman's suffrage" because she "was tired of being classed with criminals, idiots and children," and she wished to protest "taxation without representation."[3] Anthony welcomed her to the fold, and Lucy Stone soon wrote to congratulate her "and the suffrage cause on your frankly avowed accession to it,"[4] little knowing that in fact almost nothing had changed. Field would attend a couple of suffragist rallies back in New York, but she was never active in the movement.

A week later, on June 2, Field addressed a standing-room-only audience in the assembly room of the Woman's Building, one of twelve major structures at the Fair. In retrospect, the assignment of a separate building to women, which amounted to de facto gender segregation, hardly represented a dramatic advance on the sexual status quo. But Field was more sanguine. She believed the Columbian Exposition heralded "the dawn of a new era for woman. For the first time in the history of the world women have been officially recognized in a world's exposition. You have this wonderful Woman's Building, designed by a woman" in Italian Renaissance style, "managed by women, and filled with the work of women." That women "could do any of these things" doubtless "was a revelation to thousands." On several other issues Field spoke "as a working woman for and in behalf of the working people." On immigration, for example, Field "failed to see the virtue of opening our arms to the scum of Europe and of closing them to the Chinese"[5] as the Chinese Exclusionary Act required. (Rarely possessed by the hobgoblin of a "foolish consistency," Field once argued that working-class immigrants in Pittsburgh should be denied the vote and elsewhere that the Indians and Chinese in California should be granted the vote.) Field also protested the closure of the fairgrounds on Sunday afternoons because the policy effectively prevented many working-class families from attending the Exposition, and she made a case for lower railroad fares to Chicago so that farm families might "take advantage of them and visit the greatest fair that man had ever made."[6] "Farmers and their wives need the Fair more than any other class," she avowed. "If the newly arrived-immigrant at Ellis Island can be given a sleeper across the continent for next to nothing, surely American citizens should be given equal accommodation for more money and less distance."[7]

She reiterated these points in speeches, her dispatches to *Kate Field's Washington,* and the dozen syndicated columns she contributed to the *Chicago Herald* between May 31 and June 22. From the pulpit of St. Paul's Universalist Church on Sunday evening, June 4, she confessed that she did "not belong to the elect, to the saints, but to the great army of sinners." Nevertheless, she criticized Congress for voting to close the Fair on the Sabbath. Not only was there no "text in the Bible" that supported the "Sabbatarians" from "a Christian point of view," Field asserted, she believed the Sunday closing law "unconstitutional" and "nothing less than insanity." Field was outraged that all fairgoers were admitted for nothing on some "free days." Whereas "men and women who had leisure any day in the week were admitted without cost," the working class, "hungry and thirsty for the beauty and instruction of the fair, were excluded" on Sunday, virtually the only day they could attend.[8] She went so far as to suggest that the White City, so-called for its electric illumination at night, was a holy shrine where people might worship. "I stand with reverence and thank God for its 'frozen music,'" she said, invoking Mme de Staël's definition of architecture. "The buildings are a symphony in white, singing such a sermon as I never heard before. Let it be open every Sunday and the admission on that day for the people be only 25 cents."[9] The "dream city" was, from Field's perspective, a divine revelation, an augur of the millennium, a foreshadow of the New Jerusalem. "From my point of view it is the solemn duty of everyone whose eyes have seen this glory of the coming of the Lord," she declared, "to labor unceasingly toward bringing our people within reach of the beneficent spectacle." She wanted "every man, woman and child in the United States to come and praise God for the divine revelations of Jackson Park."[10] There was more to see and hear, she said, "than an ordinary brain can digest in a thousand years."[11]

The same opportunities the leisure-class Chicagoans enjoyed, Field insisted, should also be available to the country folks who wanted to come to the Exposition but could not afford the expense because the railroads and hotels gouged tourists. Some ten million people lived within a two-hundred-mile radius of Chicago, and Field thought as many of them as possible deserved "a chance to obtain a liberal education by making a journey round the world at Jackson Park." She lobbied for excursion trains to Chicago. "It is a sin to humanity that twenty trains a day are not carrying to and from Jackson Park 20,000 strangers a day," she protested. Moreover, Field discovered that she could live in Chicago, where she roomed at the Lexington Hotel on Michigan Avenue, more cheaply than in New York if she shopped carefully: "I could arrange to pass the summer near Jackson Park for less money than I ever spent in the same length of time anywhere in this country." By the end of June, Field's views had prevailed: the courts had abolished Sunday closings, the railroad companies had reduced fares to Chicago—and the fairgoers had been provided with more transportation on the grounds of the White City.[12] On June 19, at the dedication of the California Building, Field again declared that "we should all unite in a mighty hallelujah to God and man for this, the greatest spectacle the universe has ever seen."[13]

Field even defended the exotic dancing of Little Egypt on the Midway Plaisance against the carping of the Philistines. What was the difference, she asked, between the "high kicking and leg parades of our farce comedies and burlesques and the contortions of the houris in the Midway"? Oriental dances feature "abdominal gyrations" that are "marvelous as gymnastics and impossible to women who have ever worn corsets." The "control of abdominal muscles" exhibited "by the dancing girls in Chicago-Cairo would, if possessed by American women, be the salvation of the race. Invalidism would be impossible, short breath would be impossible, and children would be born healthy." While the "peep show" otherwise might deserve to be ignored, the "vulgar men and women who have set up a howl against this performance would do well to look around the American ball room and dinner table and discover like food for prurient fancy. I am sick of Comstockian morality,"[14] Field added, a dig at the repressive sexual standards of the postal inspector Anthony Comstock. Never a prude, Field even believed "the human form divine" might be studied "from a religious point of view."[15]

Given the commercial opportunities open to her at the Columbian Exposition, Field also capitalized on her celebrity and traded on her name. "Until the close of the Fair Chicago will be the centre of the United States," she wrote Phoebe Hearst, and "the only place at present where brains can be turned into money."[16] She signed a contract to contribute to the *Chicago Herald* for six months, but the paper "broke the contract" by "giving the plea of poverty." She lost that guaranteed income after barely a month and "am hanging on by the eyelids. How long I can endure the strain I don't know. . . . I feel like a hunted animal driven into a corner."[17] She obviously needed money to keep her *Washington* afloat, and so she sold product endorsements. She dashed off a short pamphlet entitled *The Drama of Glass,* which was little more than an advertising brochure for the Libby Glass Company of Toledo, which had paid for the "exclusive right to manufacture glass at the Columbian Exposition." Its glassworks on the Midway directly opposite the Woman's Building, not far from the world's first Ferris wheel, burned seventy-five barrels of Ohio oil each day and attracted (by Field's estimate) a total of two million visitors during the Fair. "It was more than a mere exhibit," she claimed; "it was a practical education in the art of glass making" by "a hundred skilled artisans."[18] Soon Field was endorsing such products as Pettijohn's California Breakfast Food ("the most delicate and toothsome preparation of wheat I have ever eaten") and Anheuser-Busch beer.[19]

Ironically, the Fair opened only two days before a panic in the eastern financial markets plunged the nation into the worst economic depression to that date in American history. At the height of the depression nearly 20 percent of the labor force was unemployed, and at the Labor Congress of the Columbian Exposition in the fall, held under the auspices of the Chicago Women's Club, Field offered a suggestion that was "received with enthusiastic applause" by the audience. She proposed a "national labor bureau, with branches in every industrial center, which should exercise a supervisory power over the distribution of labor." Despite hard times, she insisted, "there's work enough for everybody, if properly distributed," and "it is a crime that a national bureau such as I suggest does not now exist."[20]

According to Whiting, Field's "plan of relief" was approved "unreservedly" by Carroll D. Wright, the U.S. commissioner of labor. Simply put, Field argued for the creation of a Department of Labor within the Cabinet with authority to gather and issue statistics to assist the unemployed.[21] It was an idea whose time would not come for another twenty years. Field also attended a daylong labor rally at the Central Music Hall in Chicago on November 12. Organized by the British journalist William T. Stead, it featured a brief speech by Field and concluded with adoption of a proposal to form "a civic federation for public welfare."[22]

Field took on one other project related to the Columbian Exposition before its plaster buildings were leveled. A group of businessmen, hoping to make a fortune, had moved the engine house at the federal armory in Harper's Ferry where John Brown had defied federal soldiers in 1859 to Chicago for display at the Fair in 1893. Field praised the exhibit, but after the close of the Exposition the so-called "fort" was abandoned, "packed in a backyard," as Field put it, and "exposed to hoi polloi." The B&O railroad offered to return it to Harper's Ferry at no expense and a local resident there donated five acres where it could be relocated, but it remained for Field, who also served as a member of the White City Preservation Association, to raise the money for its restoration. "The fort must be rescued at once or the winter's stormy and perennial hoodlums will leave not a wrack behind," she wrote after the fair ended, and "it should go back to Harper's Ferry, where it is sorely missed as the one historic building of a town that teems with memories of our civil war." Among the subscribers to the fund were Daniel Burnham, the principal architect of the Fair ($25); future president William McKinley ($10); Roswell P. Flower, the governor of New York ($50); the journalist and activist Ida B. Wells; and several brewing companies. In 1895, thanks in large part to Field's efforts, the fort was rebuilt some three miles from Harper's Ferry on a bluff over the Shenandoah River,[23] and in 1960 it was acquired by the U.S. National Park Service and moved again to a site near its original location.

During the prolonged depression of the mid-1890s, Field became increasingly conservative, even reactionary, on a broad array of issues. She continued to berate the prohibitionists, argue for Irish home rule, and oppose Utah statehood in her *Washington*, but she also excoriated the "charlatan"

Jacob Coxey and the soldiers in Coxey's Army for marching on Washington in spring 1894 to demand relief from their economic distress. She worked to preserve the John Brown fort, yet she acquiesced to the disenfranchisement of African Americans and protested that "the Negro" was "doing very well and is quite able to take care of himself. His place is in the South, and there he will remain."[24] She blasted the federal government for the massacre at Wounded Knee in December 1890, but she also believed in the inevitable disappearance of the "vanishing American" before the advance of a "superior" civilization.[25] Despite her embrace in Chicago of the rights of the working class, she condemned the "dipsomaniac" Eugene V. Debs for leading the American Railways Association into a strike against the Pullman Company and her friend George Pullman in the summer of 1894. She wrote a new lecture, entitled "America for Americans," that demonized the invaders who ostensibly threatened to ruin the U.S. economy, "dwelling at length on foreign immigration and the loose naturalization laws of this country."[26] Like many other Americans, she worried that cheap foreign labor would depress the job market for the entire working class, and she delivered the lecture several times during the winter of 1894–95 in midwestern towns such as Chicago, Cairo, and Galesburg, Illinois; Madison, Wisconsin; and Des Moines, Iowa. Characteristically, she took a position somewhere in the mushy middle between a rock (the Catholic Church, which favored lax immigration laws) and a hard place (the nativist American Protective Association). She also urged all women, including university graduates, to learn how to cook. "Cooking is the alphabet of your happiness," she announced, and if unable to cook "in the name of common sense, of the man you propose to marry, of the friends who may visit you, of an innocent posterity, don't rest until you have learned the business of almost every woman's life, which is to keep house well and economically." Given the choice between "book-learning" and "a trade which would make me self-supporting I should select the trade," she insisted. Given the choice "between amateur proficiency in music and practical knowledge of housekeeping I should select the latter." Why would she want to explicate the poetry of Robert Browning "if the meat is overdone and the potatoes are watery?" Lest Field seem too fastidious, Charlotte Perkins Gilman endorsed these controversial sentiments in a weekly paper she was editing in San Francisco at the time.[27]

Field began to suffer from exhaustion in late 1894, and she gleaned more and more of the material for her *Washington* from newspapers, the *Congressional Record,* and private letters. After issuing nearly three hundred issues over a period of slightly over five years, after contributing as many as three thousand items to its pages, Field suspended publication of her weekly in April 1895. "My physician told me I must either give it up for the present or give my life, and of the two evils I chose the lesser," she joked. She had contracted malaria in Chicago in the summer of 1893, and Whiting remembered that "her health was seriously failing" the following summer.[28] As Field explained in the circular she sent her subscribers announcing the suspension, "An attack of grippe, added to excessive work, forces me to give myself an interval of rest from the unceasing care of journalism. Without health, life is a delusion, and, as I have had no vacation for over five years, nature rebels. Unfortunately, I cannot relegate my work to another, as personal journalism demands personal presence. Self-preservation being the first law of nature, I must postpone the next issue of the *Washington* for perhaps another year. In that time I hope by freedom of responsibility to be of more value to myself and others. Brains need to be fallow no less than soil." She went to great pains to reassure her subscribers and advertisers alike that not only did she expect to resume publication but that the weekly had not failed for financial reasons. As she explained the day after the suspension was announced,

> Nobody knows what I have gone through within the last five years—starting as I did, only six months before the Baring failure, and from that on facing a succession of panics induced by stupid legislation. . . . The *Washington* is in good shape now to stop publication for a while. It does not owe a dollar—has not a single debt. Such subscribers as have paid in advance will receive their money back. I have paid off my office people, and got places for them—none turned out to shift for themselves. I have retained one young woman, increasing her salary to make it an object for her to stay a while, until all the business with subscribers is settled. I am not sorry to have had the experience given me by the publication of the *Washington,* even if the suspension should not prove, as I expect, temporary. To me it has been a liberal education. To have founded it was one of the good inspirations of my life. It has served the truth without fear and

without favor. If its weekly appearance gave its readers as much satisfaction as it has given me, my goal has been reached. What is more, it has taught me the value of money. I never before knew the value of money, but I know it now, and am glad of it.[29]

As far west as Omaha, the columnist Ella W. Peattie lamented the suspension of the paper. "The loss of *Kate Field's Washington* will be felt," Peattie noted. "It was a sheet where one could always find crisp, well-written and unusual opinions." W. J. McGee of the Columbia Historical Society declared the weekly had been "one of the foremost American examples of personal journalism. . . . To the future historian of the national capital *Kate Field's Washington* will be a boon, and the history of the nation cannot be written fairly without recognition of the journal and the shaping of public affairs through its influence." According to Rounseville Wildman, editor of the *Overland Monthly*, "*Kate Field's Washington* was not a failure. It was a gigantic success." The "practical reforms" it endorsed "make it rank high among the great journals of the past. The International Copyright Law, the reduction of the tariff on works of art, the admission of the new States of the Northwest, the civilization of Alaska, the preservation of John Brown's home, and the cause of true womanhood, true Americanism, and true temperance, all owe Kate Field much, more than the world will tax itself to remember."[30] Or as Field mused a month after she suspended publication, "The paper has been a great success and can be more so in better times and with better business management."[31] Only a year later did she guardedly admit that the weekly had failed financially, even if it carried no debt and was solvent at the end. "After losing $75,000" on the venture, she told an interviewer, "I turned the key in the door and left. I may start again, but it will be when I have $100,000 capital behind me."[32]

The week after she suspended publication of her *Washington*, Field returned to Newport to contest her aunt's will in a celebrated trial. Cornelia Riddle Sanford had died of breast cancer on August 1, 1894, and within a week her last will and testament was filed in the local Newport probate court. Whereas the will, originally filed in 1891, bequeathed most of her estate to Field, a codicil executed in October 1893 conferred on Field only some castoff clothing, the furniture in her third-story room at Edna Villa, and a few paintings. Aunt Corda's caretaker Alla Newton, on the other hand, received "all the wardrobe, household linen, silverware, . . . pictures and furniture in several rooms," her jewelry, including her wedding ring, "contents of the stable" at Edna Villa, including carriages, and the furniture in her New York apartment. The codicil also removed Field as the executor of the will.[33] Though Cornelia Sanford had received about $110,000 during the final decade of her life from a trust fund her husband had left her, all but a few thousand dollars had disappeared. The ownership of Edna Villa was never in dispute: Milton Sanford had willed his real estate, including the cottage, to two of his other nieces with the proviso that his wife could live in the Newport home until her death.[34] (The house was sold at auction the following year, at the height of the economic depression, for only about $18,000.) Still, Field was outraged by what she believed to be the domination of her aunt by Alla Newton, whom she considered a "designing woman." Newton had prevented Field from visiting her aunt alone during the last years of her life,[35] "a clear case of undue influence over a brilliant and attractive woman, whose cruel physical suffering of twenty years had weakened her will and made her a prey to her environment."[36] Having been left out of her uncle's will when he died in 1883, Field wanted to protest her virtual omission from her aunt's will as a matter of principle, even if the value of the estate was modest.[37] She also wished "to vindicate my character" from the suggestion that she had been disowned by her aunt in favor of "an attendant who had been her keeper in an insane asylum and who left the asylum" to care for her.[38] Her cousin George Riddle later admitted that he had reluctantly joined the suit—he called it "a wrangle over pots and pans"—because he "did not want any contest that would bring his aunt's insanity before the public."[39]

The trial of *Kate Field et al. vs. Probate Court of Newport* lasted an entire week, April 28 to May 4, 1895. It attracted crowds of onlookers eager to catch a glimpse of Field. The contestants claimed that Cordelia Sanford "was insane and was entirely under the influence of her attendant" when she signed the codicil and that Newton "effected the increase of her salary and practically got possession of Mrs. Sanford's property either before or after her death." According to Field, Newton "had entire control of my aunt's income" during the last eleven years of her life.[40] The physician who treated Cordelia Sanford in the 1870s and early 1880s testified that he considered her "hopelessly insane" after 1873. One of the servants at Edna Villa testified that she saw Mrs. Sanford copy in her own handwriting a will Newton had given her for that purpose and that it included "bequests to colleges, because if [Newton] received everything Mrs. Sanford's relatives would object." A neighbor testified that he often saw "delicacies" and "wine and liquors" on the dinner table at Edna Villa. It seems, too, that Cordelia Sanford and Newton vacationed together in Florida and California and toured Europe "at Mrs. Sanford's expense" and that twice a year Newton shipped Cordelia's newest clothes to her sister in Vermont. Field testified that her aunt was incompetent to change her will and she was not cross-examined on the point. The lawyers for the court, however, called other physicians to testify that Cordelia Sanford was sane when the codicil was drawn.[41] In the end, by a vote of eight to four in favor of the court, the jury failed to reach a verdict and so the will was effectively sustained.[42] As Field wrote Stedman, she had been "in Newport contesting a will. Jury disagreed of course because my claim was righteous. My cousin refuses to join me in a second trial and I am forced thereby to let crime triumph. Such is life."[43]

So at the age of fifty-six, otherwise unemployed, Field accepted an offer to become a roving correspondent for the *Chicago Times-Herald*. Published by Herman H. Kohlstaat, a pro-tariff Republican who favored Hawaiian annexation, the *Times-Herald* was a distant third in the competition among Chicago papers behind the venerable *Tribune* and the upstart *Inter-Ocean*. At the very least, Field's name added luster to its columns. Between May and July, she contributed a thrice-weekly column from Washington, with occasional sidebars from Harper's Ferry; Hot Springs, Virginia; and New-port. In one of her first pieces for the *Times-Herald*, she reported on the funeral of her friend Walter Gresham, the secretary of state, in the East Room of the White House. Field was, in fact, the last person to leave the room. She waited "until all had gone and then looked my last on the face" of her friend before the casket was closed.[44]

On July 25, she headed to Chicago, where she remained more than a month. She devoted her column during these weeks to such local issues as sewerage, civic transportation, and fares on the Illinois Central rail-road, as if she was reluctant to tackle larger questions of public policy. Two days before leaving Chicago, she dined with her old friend Eugene Field. "How I envy you" her proposed trip west, he told her. "I'd sacrifice both my big ears to go."[45] Finally, in late August she lit out for the territories. She planned to travel at least as far as Hawaii. "I am much in need of rest," she explained, and so she hankered for a vacation in "the little South Sea republic. I selected Hawaii as the place for my recreation rather than Europe, because I think I shall find more to interest me there at this time. I have never been farther west than Alaska." She weighed the possibility of a trip "round the world before I stop."[46]

Field sent the *Times-Herald* a total of fifteen essays during the two weeks she spent in Colorado on her way across the continent, visiting several towns along the rim of the Rockies as well as the mining camps of Cripple Creek, Victor, and Leadville. "My journey from Chicago was over the Chicago, Burlington and Quincy railroad, one of the best managed systems in the country, I should say, judging by the civility of the employees, the comfort I experienced, the excellence of the roadbed, and the punctuality of the arrivals," she reported on September 1. "I actually reached Denver ahead of time." She registered at the Brown Palace, "one of the finest hotels in this or any country," and marveled at the growth of the city since her first visit in 1883. "The progress Denver has made within my recollection of a dozen years is marvelous," she reported. "Fully 200 houses are building in Denver," she noted. "The private houses going up or already built on and about Capitol Hill are a revelation to people used to the monotonous rows of New York and Philadelphia. Most of them stand in the center of gardens or turfed grounds, and are spacious in size, individual in character and excellent in design." Her first questions to the citizens of Colorado were about woman suffrage, which had been approved the year before. "Good women worked like beavers to wrest Colorado from populism," she crowed, and "all admit that woman suffrage has done no harm." The Women's Club of Denver—with annual dues of only five dollars and nearly three hundred members—had already founded twenty free kindergartens.[47]

She remained in Denver less than a week before railing south. "I look out upon Pike's Peak and the Garden of the Gods as upon old friends," she wrote from the Antlers Hotel at Colorado Springs on September 6. "I want to mount a good horse, scamper over the mesas and climb the mountains."

She was also "amazed at the transformation" of the Springs over the years, with its swelling population and new development—fine schoolhouses, a college, twenty-five miles of trolley, a country club "where golf and tennis and racing and ball matches have their day," and the Casino of Broadmoor, "an excellent bit of architecture" unlike any structure in either Newport or Bar Harbor. The repeal of the Sherman Silver Purchase Act and the demonetization of silver after the Panic of '93 had little long-term effect in Colorado because gold had been discovered on the southwestern slopes of the Peak in 1890. The local chamber of commerce had also been instrumental in preserving "for the recreation of the people the gorges and waterfalls that are the joy of this region" and the floodplain that supplied water to Colorado Springs.[48]

Predictably, Field also took the opportunity to tweak the Colorado Springs city fathers for their foolhardy prohibition of saloons. Instead, as she observed, "drugstores do a thriving business under cover of medicine and grog shops move beyond the city limits, where there is none to make them afraid. The main street of Colorado City, two miles away, is dedicated to rum." Human nature "won't be made virtuous by statute," so "even in this well-regulated, law-abiding, highly intelligent community prohibition does not prohibit." This brand of "morality doesn't agree with my kind of Christianity," Field concluded, "but if Colorado Springs is satisfied I presume it is none of my business."[49]

Two days later she took the Midland Terminal train up the mountain to spend the next month inspecting the gold mining operations on Pike's Peak. With a population of thirty thousand, Cripple Creek was an archetypal boomtown. Gold production in the district had increased exponentially, from $200,000 in 1891 to $600,000 in 1892. Despite the economic depression, production in 1893 had exceeded two million dollars. Despite a half-year labor strike in 1894, output that year "very nearly reached $4,000,000." Production in 1895 was projected to be about ten million dollars, with the yield in the month of July alone amounting to $850,000. "At this rate of increase," Field asked, "and with a gold bearing tract thirty square miles in area, six miles long, and five miles wide, who shall say what may happen with veins that go beyond the porphyry?" So long as the miners did not strike again: in June 1894, after a 130-day walkout to protest a wage offer of three dollars per ten-hour working day, the Cripple Creek miners belonging to the Western Federation of Miners won a guaranteed wage of three dollars per eight-hour day. Much as she sided with Pullman in the railway strike the year before, however, Field sympathized more with the mining companies and owners such as W. S. Stratton and T. C. Parrish than with the laborers, and she thought the Cripple Creek strike had been "ill-advised." Not that she believed the miners uncouth or criminal. Though she had recently read that Cripple Creek was "the toughest town on earth," she walked its streets without fear or reservation. "The difference between an old city and a pioneer camp is that the city covers up its iniquity and relegates it to certain districts, whereas the camp hides nothing under a bushel," she wrote. "So long as I acted like a lady I am sure I'd be treated like one. As a class miners are generous and kind and have a great deal of chivalry burning in their hearts."[50]

In late September she took the train five hours uphill to Gillett, then rode on horseback past Bull Hill and Altman to Victor. There, outfitted in rubber boots, coat, and gloves, she descended into the famous Isabella Mine, which alone produced some fifteen million dollars in gold between the mid-1890s and the 1940s. Deep in the bowels of the mountain and accompanied by the superintendent, Field saw "rumbling cars, filled with dirty ore that yields goodness knows how much gold to the ton" and lonely miners "breaking off they know not what, working by the light of a tallow dip for hours at a time, and saying, with a smile, that they like their work." She was hauled by steam engine back to the surface in the ore-bucket. "Now that I have been down one gold mine," she confessed, "I am willing to let other people go down all the rest, high grade and low grade, foreign and native. A sorrier spectacle than I present I do not care to gaze upon." Still, she conceded, the discovery of gold had brought a semblance of civilization to the region. According to a state survey in October 1893, Victor consisted of nothing more than a name, two shanties, two tents, and grazing land. Now it "boasts a church, brick hotel, business blocks, a newspaper, sampling and reduction works and saloons galore," as well as two railroads, four thousand residents, and several mining companies with a total payroll of twenty thousand dollars per month. Field thought Stratton a beneficent employer because all of the work in his Independence mine was "done by means of air drills" rather than shovels and dynamite. "No miner's candle satisfies Mr. Stratton," she added. "The Independence is lighted by electricity all the way down."[51] Would that were the standard of worker safety.

On September 12, after returning to Colorado Springs, Field took the new cogwheel railroad to the summit of Pike's Peak. "Little did I imagine in 1883 when passing the summer in Manitou and making unavailing attempts to ascend Pike's Peak that twelve years later I should reach the top of the great white mountain with as much ease as if the distance had been ironed out flat," she gloated. Not that the station-house at the summit merited a mention, nor that the "thirteen acres of boulders that form the summit" were enchanting. But she could see for three hundred miles in any direction and she was awed by the grandeur of the view. "I do not marvel that savages hold mountains sacred and never intrude on their solemnity," she mused. "I do not marvel that Christ went up into a high mountain to commune with the Father."[52]

Field left Colorado Springs on September 14, paused briefly in Leadville, and stopped the next day in Glenwood Springs, "one of the loveliest resorts in this or any other country." She registered at the Colorado Hotel, which offered its residents both hot springs and electric lights. The town was situated "at the confluence of two mountain streams, the Roaring Fork and the Grand River," with the hotel "on the north branch of the Grand, with the hot springs in its grounds. A pretty garden and wondrous fountain adorn the façade. At all points of the compass mountains arise to tempt the sportsman and the tramp, and cañons bid the artist and poet to celebrate their charms. To the east white-capped Mount Sopris towers above all, and for twenty miles the cañon of the Grand is indescribable."

On September 16 she continued to Grand Junction, where she spent the weekend and again marveled at the civic progress since she last visited. With over ninety thousand acres under irrigation, the town had become an agricultural center, sending east annually the equivalent of no fewer than two hundred railcars "laden with fruit grown on the Great American Desert!"[53]

By the end of September Field had reached Salt Lake City, where she renewed old friendships with Judge Goodwin and others. But, as ever, she refused to pander to the Mormon priesthood. She repeated her criticism of the LDS church even as she expressed her sympathy for its rank-and-file members. "I have been accused of maligning the Mormon people," she insisted. "It is false. The arrows that I have shot from my bow for the past eleven years have been directed at leaders that I believed to be as human as inhumane, as selfish and scheming as is possible for men to be in this generation." Still, she found social conditions in Zion dramatically changed from her first visit in 1883: "Today Mormons and gentiles shake hands" and "speak from the same platform. . . . I am glad."[54]

Field tarried in Salt Lake City for two months, her trip to Hawaii delayed by a quarantine of the islands caused by a cholera epidemic there. During these months, she attended the sixty-sixth semiannual Mormon conference, and her reaction was the same as to the fifty-fourth conference in 1883: "The sum total of three days' talk from inspired prophets is that God's chosen people will inherit everything here and hereafter provided they are good children and do exactly as they are told. They can't expect to go to heaven if they refuse to buy sugar that tastes of the beet and dare to think for themselves."[55] Field was also in Utah for the vote to approve a new state constitution. "I am doing what I can to prevent statehood," she wrote Stoddard on October 28, a week before the election on November 5, "but I shall not succeed, for both parties are playing into the hands of the Mormons."[56] She was surprised, however, by the landslide of approval. "With a majority of 25,000 in favor of the adoption of the constitution there can be little doubt that President Cleveland will accept the situation," she conceded in the *Times-Herald*. "We can, therefore, assume with tolerable safety that Utah will soon be the forty-fifth star in the union." Though she had lost the long fight against statehood, she remained optimistic that the next generation of Mormons would not be so easily "corralled" as their elders. "Priest-ridden to the verge of imbecility," young Mormons "are beginning to taste blood, as it were, and they like it," she declared. "They have been told to do their own thinking, and they are jumping at the chance."[57]

As soon as she heard two days after the election that the port of Honolulu had reopened, she left Utah for San Francisco, a journey by train of only thirty-six hours, and registered at the Occidental Hotel. "My departure for the islands has been delayed six months," she explained to a reporter for the *San Francisco Chronicle*—four months in Washington due to

18. Drawing of Kate Field at reception in San Francisco, captioned "Reception at the Press Club in Kate Field's Honor." *San Francisco Chronicle,* 13 November 1895, 16.

illness and "business matters," two months in Utah while she waited for the cholera epidemic in Hawaii to abate. "If the fates are willing," however, "I will sail on the next steamer."[58] She visited a few friends—she later referred to the "feasts on Nob Hill" where she was entertained.[59] While in the city, she met with the notorious "sugar king" Claus Spreckels,[60] who opposed Hawaiian annexation because he feared it would destroy the contract labor system on the plantations, particularly the hiring of Asian workers. He may have been the only prominent anti-annexationist with whom she ever spoke. The Press Club of San Francisco hosted a reception for her attended by over a hundred and fifty San Franciscans in the afternoon of November 12.[61] "When I last saw Kate Field in San Francisco," the editor Rounseville Wildman reminisced, "I thought I had never seen her look so well."[62] Finally, on November 14, Field embarked from the Port of San

Francisco for Hawaii aboard the steamer *Mariposa*. Among her fellow passengers was Fanny Stevenson, the wife of Robert Louis Stevenson. Field's "greatest care," the *San Francisco Examiner* reported, seemed to be "securing a stateroom" aboard the ship and "her chief regret was that she had to change from a deck-room to one inside the cabin." Still, she told the *Examiner* that "her visit to San Francisco," however brief, "had been an exceedingly enjoyable one."[63] Habitually seasick, she joked as soon as the ship reached deep water that the person who had christened the "pacific" ocean ought to be forgiven.[64]

13

Hawaii and Home

FIELD ARRIVED IN HONOLULU A WEEK LATER, and over the next four months she sent a total of thirty-five travel letters from Oahu to the *Chicago Times-Herald*—in effect a series of snapshots of the short-lived Republic of Hawaii between the end of the monarchy in 1893 and its annexation by the United States in 1898. Lorrin A. Thurston, whom Field had met in Washington in the summer of '93 when he was a member of the Annexation Committee, had invited her to stay at his home, but Field wisely declined. "I think that I ought not to commit myself to either party in the beginning," she explained.[1] She was determined to maintain at least the appearance of objectivity on the issue she had been sent to investigate.

In truth, Field's pro-annexation opinions were fully formed as early as January 1891. Upon the death of King Kalakaua, as she argued in her *Washington,* the islands "ought to be purchased" (though from whom Field failed to make clear) much as Louisiana had been bought from France and Alaska from Russia because they were "worth far more to the United States than to their present possessors or to any other foreign powers." The islands "are ours by the trend of trade."[2] Not only were native Hawaiians "not fit to rule the loveliest islands of the Pacific," she declared after the bloodless revolution that deposed Liluokalani in January 1893, they were "the outer gate to our golden West and belong to us by manifest destiny." Field worried that "if we don't annex Hawaii, Great Britain will." She was alarmed that over the previous twelve years Britain had "annexed nearly four hundred islands in the Pacific."[3] She blamed the queen "for her own overthrow," insisting that the revolution had been sparked by her attempt to seize "more power" through a coup d'état (or, more banally, by dismissing the Wilcox cabinet and proposing a new constitution that strengthened the monarchy). On the surface Field was a proponent of Hawaiian "home rule," much as she championed home rule in Ireland, though in fact she expected that such a policy would soon lead to peaceful annexation of the islands by the United States.[4] More specifically, in August 1893 Field lauded the provisional government of President Sanford Dole, cousin of James Dole, the founder of the Hawaiian Pineapple Company, later the Dole Food Company. The government of the Republic "is constituted of the best material in the country, both for honorable character and business ability," she averred. A year later, she was even more emphatic in her praise for the provisional government. "President Dole and his advisers have proved their capacity," she crowed. "Their knowledge of what best suits the strangely-mixed population of the islands should be accepted on general principles." To be sure, her support of the Dole administration was grounded in her conventional racial opinions. The native Hawaiian population was falling at the rate of about a thousand per year, and she believed it simply a matter of time before they would become "practically extinct." In any event, Field hailed President Grover Cleveland's reluctant recognition of the Republic of Hawaii, a territory she asserted had been "planted in the Pacific by the sons of our own soil," in August 1894.[5] Formal diplomatic recognition of the Republic, she thought, was another step toward its annexation.

In short, Field sided with the expansionists or colonialists in the debate over Hawaii long before the aborted 1895 counterrevolution led by Robert Wilcox and long before she sailed for Honolulu. Kohlstaat may have hired her to express her opinions from the islands, but he already knew what her opinions were. She was not employed to defame the former queen in order to justify annexation. She was perfectly capable of maligning the "putrid monarchy"[6] on her own. While she was not exactly a paid propagandist for the white ruling class in Hawaii, what she reported from the islands would have been little different had she been.

On November 22, 1895, the day after her arrival, Field was interviewed in her room at the Hawaiian Hotel in Honolulu by a reporter for the *Pacific Commercial Advertiser,* a local daily paper owned and published by Thurston. Asked to state her position on annexation, Field hedged: "I have an opinion—everyone has, but I do not intend that it shall influence me in my letters to the *Times-Herald*. I will blot it out, so to speak, and form a new opinion after I have visited among the people." Asked about a clause in the annexation treaty that would permit Chinese laborers to continue to immigrate to Hawaii, she sided with the opponents of "Chinese cheap labor": "I do not see how it could be arranged." With the passage of the Chinese Exclusionary Act of 1892, she asked, "how could the Government discriminate in favor of an island possession?" Field hoped annexation and enforcement of the Exclusionary Act would halt Asian immigration. On only one point was she unequivocal: her advocacy of a telegraph cable between Hawaii and the mainland[7]—a project that was completed seven years later.

She began her "investigation" into the social and political status of Hawaii and its inhabitants almost immediately. While she had promised to keep an open mind until she had "visited among the people," her "new opinion" on annexation turned out to be indistinguishable from her old one. From the first she insinuated that the islands should belong to the United States. Her first view from her hotel her first morning in Honolulu was of "our good ship *Bennington*, of the blessed white squadron." Everyone who called on her was "either born in New England or born here of New England parents. I seek in vain for natives." Four days later she attended the annual meeting of the Sugar Planters' Association, composed of "a very intelligent body of businessmen," all of them of European descent, the vast majority of them in favor of annexation. "The orgies of Kalakaua were detrimental to good government," one of the members of the association told her. "Liluokalani showed her hand by throwing out the Wilcox cabinet." A week to the day after her arrival, she celebrated Thanksgiving in Honolulu much as she celebrated the holiday in Boston: by eating a turkey dinner, then watching a parade. "Commanded by an American skilled in his profession," the marching troops consisted of eight companies—four American, one Irish-American, one Portuguese, one German, and one native Hawaiian. "Thus is Hawaii becoming Americanized," Field concluded, "even unto the tooting of tin horns, turkey and cranberry sauce." Scarcely ten days into her planned months-long "investigation," she already had concluded that "restoration of the monarchy is impossible" and that "the dominant elements here are American and want annexation to the United States."[8] She had solicited an audience with Liluokalani, recently released from her prison in Iolani Palace to house arrest in Washington Place, through partisans of both the deposed monarchy and the provisional government, albeit to no avail. Meanwhile, she arranged to interview Sanford Dole in his office on December 10.

Two different versions of this interview exist—the version Field afterwards submitted to Dole for his approval, a copy of which survives among the Field papers at the Boston Public Library, and the version actually published in the *Chicago Times-Herald*.[9] In the former, Dole refuses to answer Field's questions about the future of the Japanese and African American minorities in Hawaii. When she asks whether the rights of "the native women and the half-white women" could be protected legally "when annexation came," Dole replies that "[y]ou cannot legislate in social matters. It is a matter of sentiment." He also concedes that since the bloodless revolution in January 1893 "we have disfranchised a good many people here who are ignorant and thriftless, men whose votes are not only no benefit but a great menace to representative government." Nor does he apologize: "Plantation laborers cannot vote. They ought not to vote; they are too ignorant as a rule." (Apparently it *is* possible to "legislate in social matters.") Dole also alleges without either elaborating or citing evidence that "there is a filibustering crowd" of fortune-hunters eager to invade the islands; that is, he argues for the right of the provisional government to defend the Republic. None of these comments appears in Field's published record of the interview.

Instead, the published interview emphasizes the favorable business climate in Hawaii after the revolution and the likelihood of eventual annexation. Halfway through the interview, according to the unpublished transcript, Dole declared that "[o]ur sole policy is annexation to the United States." In the published version, however, Dole begins the interview with this statement. Field also asks Dole, "What form of annexation would best meet your desire?" According to the transcript, he merely replies, "It is very difficult to answer that question. Of course the most satisfactory thing would be to be a State; but that is out of the question at present." In the published version, however, his answer is much more detailed:

It is very difficult to answer that question. A territorial form of government as the basis of American territories without modification would not be very suitable. Probably the best thing would be to have a government which would be a gradual development from our present system, federal authorities, of course, having jurisdiction over federal matters, such as a federal custom-house, federal courts, federal post office, etc., and our own government not limited by the law of the United States in regard to territories.

"The last year of the monarchy," Dole insisted, "had a disturbing effect on business" because of the "anxiety" it fostered. Now, however, the prospects for the next sugar crop "are very favorable indeed."

Like all of Field's letters to the *Times-Herald,* this interview with President Dole was widely reprinted across the United States.[10] "I've written a dozen letters for publication," she wrote Whiting on December 25, "but only one of them has national importance,—an interview with President Dole." Kohlstaat editorialized that the interview was nothing less than "a communication to the congress, President, and people of the United States" of "a proposal by the government of Hawaii to come into the union and a definition of the terms upon which entry would be agreeable to the republic" transmitted through Field's agency. Similarly, the Honolulu *Pacific Commercial Advertiser,* Thurston's newspaper, suggested in late January 1896 that Field's "interview with President Dole has done more to set this Government before the American people in its true light than anything that has thus far been written."[11]

Field spent the remainder of December and the first days of the New Year in social activities that dovetailed with her pro-annexation agenda. "As I'm here for politics," she admitted to Whiting, "I'm obliged to study the history and the people" of the islands even when she was at leisure. She partied with the officers of the gunboat *Bennington,* including its commander (later admiral) George W. Pigman, and together they raised "several hundred dollars to be expended in Christmas gifts to the lepers who are segregated on the island of Molokai fifty miles away."[12] She performed "The Spanish Muleteer's Song," accompanied with castanets, from her musical monologue at Kaumakapili Church in Honolulu on December 14 to help raise more money for the lepers, and she even helped to deliver the gifts personally. She attended holiday receptions at the offices of the American and British legations,[13] and on Christmas Eve she dined at the home of Dr. John Strayer McGrew, who had immigrated from Ohio to Hawaii twenty-nine years before. On Christmas Day she dined at the home of President Dole, and in a subsequent letter to the *Times-Herald* she again attested to his noble character: "I have never, in any country, met a man so full of the milk of human kindness, so fair in his estimate of those who oppose the republic, so averse to making capital for his cause by using the power he undoubtedly possesses." She attended an open house on New Year's Day hosted by Dole in the throne room of the executive building, the very room in the former royal palace where the queen's trial had been held in 1893, and afterwards a tea on the grounds of the nearby Pacific Tennis Club.[14] She also read several books to supplement her research, including Isabella Bird's *The Hawaiian Archipelago* (1875), Laura F. Judd's *Honolulu: Sketches of Life* (1880), and Georges Sauvin's *Un royaume polynésien* (1893).

Over the next few weeks Field quickened the pace of her work. She interviewed a veritable Who's Who of Anglo-Hawaiian annexationists: Colonel Zeph S. Spalding, owner of Kealia plantation and the Makee Sugar Company on Kauai; the missionary F. W. Damon, brother of the finance minister; the Hawaiian attorney general William Owen Smith, another member of the Committee on Safety; Albert F. Judd, chief justice of the Supreme Court, who explained how the new constitution of the Republic protected the rights of native Hawaiians; the local railroad magnate Benjamin F. Dillingham, who believed that annexation by the United States would both "advance our material interests" and "insure peace" among the many factions of people on the islands; Oliver P. Emerson, secretary of the Hawaiian board of missions; and Professor W. D. Alexander, former principal of Oahu College and author of *A Brief History of the Hawaiian People* (1891). In late February she attended a lecture by William R. Castle, the ex–Hawaiian minister to the United States and like Thurston a member of both the Committee on Safety and the Annexation Committee. While in the United States, Castle had urged American farmers to immigrate to Hawaii to cultivate sugar cane and coffee. Field heartily endorsed the idea, albeit with a xenophobic tint: "Unless the character of immigration is radically changed, these islands will soon swarm with Japanese.

White men will be driven out, natives will be stamped out and the United States will have themselves to thank for the dangerous advance of an aggressive people, whose cheap labor defies competition. Annexation alone can rescue Hawaii from Japan." Elsewhere she concluded, "The most intelligent and far-seeing planters want annexation" and "the greatest need of Hawaii is small farmers" who might institute a system of profit-sharing with their workers like the plan recently adopted on the Ewa sugar plantation near Honolulu.[15]

Three days after Castle's talk, Field delivered her Dickens lecture at the Kaumakapili Church, with proceeds benefiting the local kindergarten association.[16] During her myriad investigations into conditions during her first months in Hawaii, in short, Field mostly mingled with people of her own race and class. Despite her repeated professions of objectivity, she made little effort to meet and interview native Hawaiians or royalists sympathetic to the deposed queen.

Still, she did not entirely ignore the more traditional topics of travel articles in her correspondence with the *Times-Herald*. In one letter, she described the effects of an earthquake that shook the islands on December 9, the evening before she interviewed Dole in his office, and in two others she detailed the logistical advantages of the cable that would expedite communications among the major islands and with the mainland. By chance, she met the former queen Liluokalani on December 13 while on a visit to the royal cemetery, an event she did not write up until three weeks later, after the holiday receptions with her friends in the provisional government. Technically still under house arrest, Liluokalani modestly declined Field's request for a photograph at the tomb of her father, and in response Field testified to her "great dignity of manner" and "charming voice." In other articles she gossiped about the eccentricities of the late king ("'Died of Mumm's Extra Dry' might have been inscribed on Kalakaua's coffin with no little reason") and the success of mixed marriages between Chinese men and native women. At an auction to dispose of some royal relics, Field bought "Kamehameha III's solid silver gravy spoon, as long as a swan's neck," and a helmet given to Kalakaua by the Emperor Franz Josef of Austria.[17]

Field was also prescient in recognizing the strategic importance of Pearl Harbor, "ceded to us twenty years ago" as a condition of the reciprocity trade agreement of 1875 "and never utilized from that day to this. It is such a landlocked harbor as does not exist in any other part of the globe." She inspected the harbor on December 28 with officers from the *Bennington* and "spoke highly of its natural location for harbor defense." "Eight miles long, five miles wide and forty feet deep," she insisted, "Pearl Harbor offers every facility for an unrivalled naval station." It might "long since have been transformed into an impregnable naval station" but for the "stupidity" of the American government. "Twenty miles of wharfage could be built were Uncle Sam bent upon making a magnificent naval station in the middle of the Pacific."[18]

Field mailed the last of her travel letters to the *Chicago Times-Herald* on March 24 and she sailed for the big island to continue her "investigations" the same day. She planned to remain there at least a month, as she wrote Whiting, "going around it and visiting the volcano." She readily allowed that she had underestimated the difficulty of her research. "Anyone who thinks these islands can be seen quickly and intelligently reckons without a host of problems," she admitted. "The [major] islands are eight in number" and she planned to "visit at least three more," first Hawaii, then Maui and Kauai. After "the worst sea voyage I ever took," Field arrived in Hilo on Wednesday, March 25, "but now [that] I'm in this strange land among natives, I'm very glad I came." She set off on horseback for Kilauea on Saturday, March 28, a distance of only about forty miles, but "as the journey must be made in the saddle and will take several days," she wrote Whiting, "you can imagine I'm as far from it as Omaha is from N.Y."[19] She spent a week at the Volcano House on the crater rim of Kilauea before returning to Hilo to reconnoiter and plan a longer trip around the island.

She wrote her friends in Honolulu on April 23 that she intended to travel around the big island, "stopping overnight at the houses of planters or natives." As the *Pacific Commercial Advertiser* reported, "Miss Field has been deeply interested in the sights and sounds of the outside districts, and does not anticipate returning to Honolulu before the 1st of June."[20] She left Hilo on April 25 accompanied by Anna Paris, the proprietor of a small hotel in Kailua. She had decided to forego a visit to Mauna Loa, which had recently erupted, until she was "ready to leave this island. It looks as if I might remain several months longer," as she wrote Whiting. "Then what will happen I don't know. Japan? I can't say. I live from day to day and think as little as possible of the future." In company with Henry Lyman and his sister Sarah, grandchildren of two of the earliest Christian missionaries to the islands, she stopped at the home of Rufus Lyman in Paahau. En route north she also toured the Rycroft and Wight coffee plantations[21] before pausing in Waimea. On May 3 she rode twenty-five miles to Kohala.

> It was the most awful ride of my life, equal to seventy-five miles on a level road. Imagine a hurricane and rain, up and down hills, more or less steep, at the foot of Mouna Kea (white), which is really 14,000 feet high. The rain and wind set in after we started, and, as the journey had to be made, we went on. Had the weather been cold it would have been a blizzard, but in this latitude there are no blizzards. Several times I thought I would be blown off the horse. However, we pulled through, but my horse is very tired, and I must wait until it is fit to travel.

From Kohala on May 4 she sent her first letter to Kohlstaat in six weeks—a private one not intended for publication:

> Merely to sit down in Honolulu and pretend to know about these islands is absurd, and no Hawaiian would give a penny for my opinion did I not do what I am doing, nor would the people and congress of the United States. . . . I can't tell you how gratified the islanders are that I am roughing it for their benefit. Remember that there are no roads and no hotels. I was loaned an easy mare in Hilo, who has brought me 100 miles in ten days. I have traveled from plantation to plantation of sugar and coffee and been well treated by whites of American or British birth. I am guided by the local police, who are natives, and I see as many of the Hawaiians as possible. I address the natives as an American whenever invited, and make friends for my country and annexation.

As usual, Field believed that camping out and the fresh air were invigorating. "Though some of the travel is very hard," she insisted to Kohlstaat, "the trip will do me a lot of good physically."[22] She also began to reach out to natives of the islands after leaving Oahu. To be sure, she befriended them from selfish motives—she wanted to convert them to her political views—but at least she no longer associated only with people who already shared them.

She spent over a week in Kohala while she and her horse recuperated from the ardors of the trip, and on May 12 she delivered her Dickens lecture there from memory.[23] She left a day or two later for Kona, sixty miles distant over lava beds. Upon her arrival at Anna Paris' hotel in Kailua on May 16 she was exhausted and feverish from the journey but she refused to rest. The next day she rode another ten miles to Henry Greenwell's farm near Kaawaloa.[24] There she collapsed and, alarmed by her symptoms, she finally agreed to return to Honolulu before her condition worsened. After writing letters all morning, in the afternoon of May 18 she was carried from the beach to a reserved stateroom aboard the offshore steamer *Hall*. According to the purser of the *Hall*, she had been "riding too hard," and Field apparently agreed. "I am only tired all out," she insisted. "Riding all sorts of horses (for my own got a sore back), and tramping over their lava beds and looking into the condition of these natives. . . . Yes, I am too tired to do any more just now." She was nursed by two members of the Amherst College Eclipse Expedition that was en route to Japan: the physician Vanderpoel Adriance and Mabel Loomis Todd, wife of Amherst astronomer David Todd, coeditor with Thomas Wentworth Higginson of Emily Dickinson's verse, and lover of Dickinson's brother Austin. Todd initially did not think that Field's condition was life-threatening. "Lack of proper food and attention, a severe cold contracted through exposure to varying temperatures at different altitudes, and general fatigue had left obvious traces on her pale face," she noted.[25]

But Adriance's diagnosis of her condition was dire. Field in fact was suffering from acute pneumonia. About 5 P.M. on May 18 she left her stateroom and went on deck of the *Hall*, though Adriance ordered her back to bed. He sat by her side all night and administered stimulants. About 2 A.M. her condition worsened, and early in the morning of May 19 he told Todd "that he had been fighting for her life ever since she came on board, obstinate pneumonia his antagonist. With little hope, from the first, of conquering, he had continued to give her stimulants on the chance of sustaining the slight strength remaining. He thought she must have had the disease for several days, while still exposed to constant hard riding and all

temperatures." Todd broke the sad news to her "that in all human prob-
ability she must die before another sunset. Miss Field listened in almost a
dazed way at first. Then she said,—'Yes, yes—give me time.' She lay back
for a moment in strange stupor, while I quietly waited." Field dictated a
letter or two before slipping into unconsciousness. She rallied occasionally when Todd spoke to her, "but it was evident that she was rapidly dying,
and her breathing became very labored." The captain of the *Hall* pushed
its speed to the limit in order to reach Honolulu before her death. "As we
passed Maui," Todd recalled, Field "suddenly opened her eyes and looked
out. The cliffs are bold and rugged, and the mountains very impressive,
with cloud-shadows chasing over them, and between island and steamer lay
a bright blue strip of white-capped sea. 'Oh, how beautiful!' she exclaimed,
and for a moment her eyes brightened clearly." An hour or two later she
tried to converse with Todd.[26]

> "What did you say was the name of your expedition, and what are you
> going for?"
> "The Amherst eclipse expedition," I replied, "and we go to Japan to
> observe a total eclipse of the sun August 9th."
> "The Amherst eclipse expedition," she said brightly; and those were
> her last words on earth. She simply slept more and more soundly.[27]

The *Hall* arrived in Honolulu harbor at about 1 P.M. on May 19, well
ahead of schedule, and a detail of sailors from the frigate USS *Adams* carried Field on a stretcher to the nearby home of J. S. McGrew on Hotel
Street near the harbor, where she had dined on Christmas Eve scarcely four
months before. Todd gathered Field's scattered belongings, including her
saddle, riding-whip, "walking shoes all scratched and scarred with rough
lava," and a copy of Charles Warren Stoddard's *Hawaiian Life,* and took
them to McGrew's cottage. There Field died peacefully an hour later.[28]

Without a cable between the islands and the mainland, the news of
Field's death was telegraphed by Thurston to Yokohama, Japan, and from
there to Kohlstaat in Chicago. Field's funeral on May 20 at the Central
Union Church in Honolulu was a virtual reunion of annexationists. Her
pallbearers included McGrew and two members of the Committee on

Safety: Lorrin Thurston and James Castle. Also in attendance were President Dole, Chief Justice Judd, Associate Justice Walter F. Frear, and three other members of the Committee: Minister of Foreign Affairs Henry E. Cooper, President of the Senate William C. Wilder, and the rancher and politician James S. McCandless. The U.S. consul Albert S. Willis also attended the funeral and arranged for Field's body to be embalmed and placed in the family vault in the Nuuanu cemetery of John H. Paty, a partner in the Bank of Bishop and Company.[29] Predictably, Paty was an annexationist too. In his obituary, Kohlstaat praised his ostensible "hireling" and editorialized that her letters from Hawaii had been "accepted universally as the first frank, comprehensive and trustworthy accounts, wholly disinterested, that have come from the islands. Keen of observation, alert to pursuit of truth, her pen vivid, these letters in the columns of the *Times-Herald* constitute the case of Hawaii for annexation."[30] Even after her death, Field's reputation was invoked to serve the cause.

Field was an advocate of cremation, though she rarely mentioned the subject publicly. She once told an interviewer that as "a small girl" she had "insisted on having the grave of a dear friend reopened, and the shock I received on seeing that face I shall never forget." Field almost certainly referred to her insistence on disinterring her mother's body so that she could look upon her face when she returned from England in August 1872. In any case, she resolved on the spot "that I would never permit myself to add to the earth's poisonous material." Elsewhere she declared she was a "cremationist because I believe cremation is not only the healthiest and cleanest, but the most poetical way of disposing of the dead." Who would prefer "loathsome worms to ashes?" She joined the New York Cremation Society in 1885, and in her will she provided "for the cremation of my body in such terms as no friend or foe of mine would think of disregarding, even after I am dead."[31]

Unfortunately, her will was not found at the Shoreham Hotel in Washington until the September following her death,[32] and even more unfortunately there was no crematorium in Hawaii. The Press Club of San Francisco raised a small fund to pay the cost of shipping Field's body to the mainland,[33] and in December 1896 it was removed from the crypt where it had been sealed in Honolulu and returned to San Francisco for cremation.[34] Adolph Sutro and James Phelan, the mayor and mayor-elect of San Francisco, attended the memorial ceremony, and President and Mrs. Cleveland sent a wreath of roses.[35] The ashes were sent across the continent to Field's cousin George Riddle, her nearest surviving relative. Lilian Whiting hosted a memorial for Field in her rooms at the Brunswick Hotel on Boylston Avenue in Boston on January 9, 1897, and her ashes were buried in Mount Auburn cemetery in Cambridge, between the graves of her parents, the next day. Riddle, the undertaker, and a reporter were the only people present when the urn was lowered into the grave.[36]

The rumor soon circulated that Field had died penniless.[37] In fact, her estate was estimated in October 1896 at $12,000, "more than enough," according to Whiting, to provide "for every claim upon it."[38] Her estate was not so much contested as was her legacy. Whiting took the locket containing a few wisps of Elizabeth Barrett Browning's hair.[39] In August 1897, she gave the letter Poe had written Joe Field in 1847 to Stedman, claiming that Kate had instructed her to do so from the spirit world. For the record, Stedman still owned the letter at his death eleven years later, when it was sold at auction by the Anderson Gallery in New York for $490.[40] The morocco-bound manuscript is located today in the Huntington Library in San Marino, California. Field willed Vedder's painting of her in Florence in 1860 to the Boston Museum of Fine Arts, and her executors honored the bequest. The painting was sold at auction in 1926 and since lost.[41] Field willed Millet's painting of her to the St. Louis Museum of Fine Arts and, since the museum's demise, it too has been lost. She willed a drawing by Gainsborough to John E. Searles of New York in payment of $1,000 he had invested in her weekly, and she bequested the remaining sketches in her "Landor album" to the New York stockbroker S. V. White, from whom she had once borrowed $500.[42] To the end of her life, Whiting treasured the copy of Stoddard's *Hawaiian Life* that Field read as she was dying. Stoddard later stated that he had "held that very copy" of his book. "Lilian let me hold it for a time in her rooms at the Brunswick, Boston. It gave me a strange thrill that I did not recover from for some time."[43]

Though her life was eventually lost in a biographical blind spot, Field was never forgotten by her friends, nor by an occasional enemy. "I believe she did more good than all the fanatics in the world," Stoddard reminisced. "She was mighty good to me."[44] Jeanette Gilder, who owed her start in journalism to Field, recalled her as a "brilliant, kind woman. . . . How brilliant the world knows—how kind is known only to her friends."[45] Laurence Hutton remembered her at length:

> She was a curious admixture of sentiment and assurance. She was an indefatigable worker, quick and ready with her pen and her tongue. She was blessed with a good deal of practical common-sense, and yet she did many foolish things. She made many warm friends, and she antagonized friends whom she could not afford to lose. She was ambitious, self-assertive, and self-advertising; but she was the soul of honesty and honor. She had a feminine side, with all her masculinity and angularity, and there was a gentleness and sweetness about her which the world did not suspect. She was bitterly treated, but I never heard her speak bitterly. She fought a hard fight against the world, and she fought it alone. She never hit a man when he was down, and she never hit a false blow. She said what she thought, without regard to the ultimate effect of her speech upon herself. She had a good deal of tact, and yet sometimes she was utterly tactless. She was a staunch friend, and never a cruel enemy. She made many mistakes. She had a hard life and not a very successful one; but she never lost her self-respect, and she never forfeited the respect of those who have known her.[46]

Then again, Mark Twain compared her in his sketch "Villagers of 1840–3" (1897) to "a loud vulgar beauty" or "one of the earliest chipper and self-satisfied and idiotic correspondents of the back-country newspapers."[47]

Whiting claimed to communicate with Field for years after her death, usually through the medium Leonora Piper, for the first time on October 24, 1896.[48] Whiting even published a book based upon ostensible conversations and a two-hundred-page letter Field sent her from beyond the grave. The book did not contain a single new biographical detail. Instead, according to Whiting, "I begged her to take up the story from the moment of her conscious waking in the other life," and she told me

> that her first consciousness in the other world was that of standing on the floor in the room in which her body lay. Her father and mother were

beside her; and her mother, calling her by name, said, "Come, my child, have no fear," and she then went away with them and joined other near relatives. . . . "I live in a house with my father and mother. My brother is here. He is grown up now, and is a man. I read and study and cultivate my mind. I hear beautiful music and noble lectures, and enjoy art in the drama and in paintings. I lecture and my audiences are far more intelligent and clear-headed than they were in your world. I can travel without any fatigue, and, as I have told you, the sensation of flying through the air is delicious."[49]

However reassuring such a pretty picture may be, Field hardly would have approved of it. She discussed the notion of immortality in a piece published in the *Boston Traveller* in 1882, and she harbored neither hope nor expectation of eternal life. "The ambition that thirsts for immortality," she wrote, is "beneath contempt. Shakespeare wrote plays for his theater because he was compelled to write them, not because of posterity—an animal, I'll wager, he never dreamed of. The only noble ambition is the noble desire to be fully one's self, to act out one's whole nature." On her part, "I do not hanker after posterity; I only desire to be myself, and if I like to do more than one thing I see no crime in gratifying a desire that certainly injures no one else. I'd rather do a little practical good in my lifetime than wield anything less than the greatest which isn't me."[50] More than any other American woman of her generation, Kate Field heeded her calling, spread her gospel of noble deeds, and deserves to be resurrected from the footnote.

NOTES | BIBLIOGRAPHY | INDEX

Notes

ABBREVIATIONS

BA	*Boston Advertiser*
BC	*Boston Courier*
BE	*Brooklyn Eagle*
BG	*Boston Globe*
BH	*Boston Herald*
BJ	*Boston Journal*
BP	*Boston Post*
BPL	Kate Field Collection, Boston Public Library
BT	*Boston Transcript*
CH	*Chicago Herald*
CT	*Chicago Tribune*
CT-H	*Chicago Times-Herald*
KF	Kate Field
KFW	*Kate Field's Washington*
MHS	Missouri Historical Society
MiamiU	Miami University of Ohio
NOP	*New Orleans Picayune*
NYG	*New York Graphic*
NYH	*New York Herald*
NYTimes	*New York Times*
NYTrib	*New York Tribune*
PJ	*Providence Journal*
SR	*Springfield Republican*
WP	*Washington Post*

PREFACE

1. *KFW,* 1 Jan. 1890, 1–3; "KF Dead," *NYTrib,* 31 May 1896, 7; "KF's Work Over," *CT,* 31 May 1896, 6.

2. "A Woman's Opinion," *San Diego Sun,* 14 Feb. 1888, 5.

3. Lilian Whiting, *Kate Field: A Record* (Boston: Little, Brown, 1899), 210; Kate Phillips, *Helen Hunt Jackson* (Berkeley: Univ. of California Press, 2003), 96, 307–8.

4. See Gary Scharnhorst, "Kate Field: A Primary Bibliography," *Resources for American Literary Study* 29 (2004): 141–63.

1. BEGINNINGS

1. Roberta Florence Brinkley, *Nathan Field, the Actor-Playwright* (New Haven: Yale Univ. Press, 1928), 36.

2. John E. Sunder, ed. *Matt Field on the Santa Fe Trail* (Norman: Univ. of Oklahoma Press, 1960), xvii; "Home Rule in Ireland," *KFW,* 3 Dec. 1890, 362.

3. "The Late Mrs. J. M. Field," *NYTrib,* 19 June 1871, 5.

4. Fritz Oehlschlaeger, ed. *Old Southwest Humor from the St. Louis Reveille, 1844–1850* (Columbia: Univ. of Missouri Press, 1990), 6; William G. B. Carson, *The Theatre on the Frontier* (Chicago: Univ. of Chicago Press, 1932), 2.

5. "Straws," *NOP,* 17 July 1840, 2; "Are Bicycles Immoral?" *KFW,* 11 Apr. 1894, 225.

6. *NYTrib,* 19 June 1871, 5.

7. Sol Smith, *Theatrical Journey Work* (Philadelphia: Peterson, 1854), 180.

8. "Edwin Booth," *KFW,* 14 June 1893, 372.

9. W. R. Alger, *Life of Edwin Forrest* (Philadelphia: Lippincott, 1877), 99, 106, 110, 537.

10. James E. Murdoch, *The Stage* (1880; rpt. New York: Blom, 1969), 124.

11. Carolyn J. Moss, ed. *Kate Field: Selected Letters* (Carbondale: Southern Illinois Univ. Press, 1996), 80.

12. Carson, *Theatre on the Frontier,* 246.

13. *NYG,* 21 Nov. 1874, 161.

14. *NOP,* 9 Jan. 1840, 2; 10 Jan. 1840, 2; 5 May 1840, 2.

15. "Pacific Railroad Celebration," *St. Louis Missouri Republican,* 6 July 1851, 2.

16. *NOP,* 7 May 1840, 2; 8 May 1840, 2.

17. "To Mrs. Straws," *NOP,* 15 July 1840, 2; 17 July 1840, 2; 31 Oct. 1840, 2.

18. Whiting, *A Record,* 13.

19. "Straws," *NOP,* 21 July 1841, 2; "Boz," *NOP,* 15 Dec. 1841, 2.

20. Eugene R. Page, ed., *Metamora and Other Plays* (Princeton: Princeton Univ. Press, 1941), 238.

21. *St. Louis Reveille,* 1 Feb. 1849, 2.

22. "Fugitive Slave Rows," *St. Louis Reveille,* 4 Oct. 1850, 2.

23. *NOP*, 12 Apr. 1840, 2.

24. "A Wish," *St. Louis Reveille*, 25 Dec. 1847, 2.

25. Arthur Quinn, *Edgar Allan Poe* (New York: Appleton-Century, 1941), 488.

26. John Ward Ostrom, ed., *The Letters of Poe* (New York: Harvard Univ. Press, 1948), 318–20.

27. Bernard De Voto, *Mark Twain's America* (Boston: Little, Brown, 1932), 252; Walter Blair, *Native American Humor* (San Francisco: Chandler, 1960), 155, 156.

28. Whiting, *A Record*, 14.

29. *Mobile Register*, 24 Dec. 1850, 2; 13 June 1851, 2.

30. Moss, *Selected Letters*, 80.

31. "Mr. Joseph M. Field," *NOP*, 22 Dec. 1855, afternoon ed., 2; *NOP*, 31 Jan. 1856, 1.

32. *Omaha Republican*, 23 Mar. 1887, 5; "Ecce Homo," *St. Louis Reveille*, 21 Sept. 1847, 1.

33. "Are Public Schools a Fraud?" *KFW*, 8 Feb. 1893, 81.

34. Whiting, *A Record*, 20, 34; KF file in the MHS. Though the original volumes have been lost, many excerpts from the diaries survive in Whiting's biography of KF.

35. Whiting, *A Record*, 32, 50, 64, 97; "Robert Browning: A Few Unpublished Letters," *KFW*, 13 May 1891, 298; "Letter from Boston," *NOP*, 3 Dec. 1855, 3.

36. "Thank You Very Much," *KFW*, 2 Sept. 1891, 163.

37. Eliza Field to Sol Smith, 22 Mar. 1856 (MHS); "Joseph Burnett," *KFW*, 19 Sept. 1894, 179; Whiting, *A Record*, 34, 49, 52, 53, 59, 60, 62, 76; *Saturday Evening Gazette*, 12 June 1858, 2.

38. Eliza Field to Sol Smith, 22 Mar. 1856 (MHS).

39. KF to Noah Ludlow, 12 and 19 June 1857 (MHS).

40. KF to Sol Smith, 9 Sept. 1856 (MHS).

41. Whiting, *A Record*, 61–69.

42. Ibid., 68–77.

43. KF to Noah Ludlow, 16 Sept. 1858 (MHS).

44. Eliza Field to Noah Ludlow, 24 Oct. 1858 (MHS).

2. FLORENCE

1. Whiting, *A Record*, 85–86, 89–90, 93; "Letter from Straws, Jr.," *BC*, 17 Mar. 1859, 1.

2. "Letter from Straws, Jr.," *BC*, 25 Apr. 1859, 1.

3. "Letter from Straws, Jr.," *BC*, 27 June 1859, 1.

4. "Letter from Straws, Jr.," *BC*, 30 May 1859, 1; 8 June 1859, 1; 4 July 1859, 1.

5. *BT*, 2 Apr. 1860, 4; 10 Apr. 1860, 2.

6. "Letter from Straws, Jr.," *BC*, 27 June 1859, 1; 18 June 1859, 1.

7. "Letter from Straws, Jr.," *BC*, 1 Sept. 1859, 1.

8. "Letter from Florence," *NOP*, 1 Sept. 1859, 1; 8 July 1860, 1.

9. Whiting, *A Record*, 98, 99; "KF Dead," *BP*, 31 May 1896, 6.

10. "Letter from Italy, *NOP*, 26 Feb. 1860, 10; 19 Feb. 1860, 10; 8 Apr. 1860, 10.

11. Whiting, *A Record*, 100, 122; Eliza Field to Sol Smith, 16 Jan. 1860 (MHS).

12. Edward C. McAleer, "Isa Blagden to Kate Field," *Boston Public Library Quarterly* 3 (1951): 210.

13. Frances Power Cobbe, *Italics* (London: Trübner, 1864), 397–98.

14. Whiting, *A Record*, 116.

15. "Modern Art in Florence," *BT*, 6 July 1860, 1; Whiting, *A Record*, 100; Regina Soria, *Elihu Vedder* (Rutherford, N.J.: Fairleigh Dickinson Univ. Press, 1970), 30.

16. Elihu Vedder, *Digressions of V* (Boston: Houghton Mifflin, 1910), 149.

17. Whiting, *A Record*, 101.

18. "Chain of Personals," *BT*, 21 June 1860, 1.

19. "English Authors in Florence," *Atlantic Monthly* 14 (Dec. 1864): 665–66.

20. Scott Lewis, *The Letters of Elizabeth Barrett Browning to Her Sister Arabella* (Waco, Tex.: Wedgestone Press, 2002), 2:410.

21. Whiting, *A Record*, 94.

22. "Letter from Straws, Jr.," *BC*, 28 July 1859, 1.

23. Whiting, *A Record*, 95.

24. "Mrs. Browning's Essays on the Poets," *Christian Examiner* 75 (July 1863): 40–41.

25. "Ruskin to Mrs. Browning," *KFW*, 10 Oct. 1894, 228; Edward C. McAleer, *Dearest Isa: Robert Browning's Letters to Isa Blagden* (Austin: Univ. of Texas Press, 1951), 41, 43.

26. "Elizabeth Barrett Browning," *Atlantic Monthly* 8 (Sept. 1861): 372.

27. Whiting, *A Record*, 105; Philip Kelley, *The Browning Collections: A Reconstruction* (Waco, Tex.: Armstrong Browning Library, 1984), 393.

28. "Foreign Correspondence of the Transcript," *BT*, 4 Feb. 1860, 2; 24 Feb. 1860, 2.

29. "Letter from Italy," *NOP*, 19 Feb. 1860, 3; 22 July 1860, 1.

30. Lilian Whiting, *A Study of Elizabeth Barrett Browning* (Boston: Little, Brown, 1899), 187–87; Whiting, *A Record*, 115.

31. Whiting, *A Record*, 101.

32. "The Last Days of Walter Savage Landor," *Atlantic Monthly* 17 (June 1866): 695.

33. Whiting, *A Record*, 103, 104, 121; Kelley, *The Browning Connections*, 226.

34. "Last Days," *Atlantic Monthly* 17 (June 1866): 695.

35. "Robert Browning: A Few Unpublished Letters," *KFW*, 13 May 1891, 298–99.

36. "Elizabeth Barrett Browning," *Atlantic Monthly* 8 (Sept. 1861): 373.

37. *New Orleans Times-Democrat*, 20 Jan. 1895, 17; *BG*, 6 Jan. 1890, 5.

38. *Baylor Bulletin* 35 (Dec. 1932): 29.

39. "Robert Browning: A Few Unpublished Letters," 299.

40. Whiting, *A Record*, 106–7, 110.

41. "Last Days," *Atlantic Monthly* 17 (Apr. 1866): 385.

42. *Baylor Bulletin* 35 (Dec. 1932): 37.

43. Whiting, *A Record,* 129, 132; "Last Days," *Atlantic Monthly* 17 (June 1866): 691; 17 (Apr. 1866): 387.

44. Whiting, *A Record,* 132–33; Moss, *Selected Letters,* 156–57.

45. "Last Days," *Atlantic Monthly* 17 (May 1866): 545.

46. Whiting, *A Record,* 133, 382; "KF's Work Over," *CT,* 31 May 1896, 6.

47. "Letter from Italy," *NOP,* 26 Feb. 1860, 10; 8 Apr. 1860, 10.

48. Whiting, *A Record,* 124–25.

49. "From New York," *SR,* 22 June 1864, 2.

50. Whiting, *A Record,* 190.

51. "Forty to Twenty," *Appleton's,* ns 2 (June 1877): 563–64.

52. Whiting, *A Record,* 193–94.

53. "Letter from Italy," *NOP,* 16 Dec. 1860, 12; 18 July 1860, 1; 7 Sept. 1860, 1.

54. "Letter from Straws, Jr.," *BC,* 4 July 1859.

55. "Letter from Florence," *NOP,* 5 Aug. 1860, 6.

56. "Foreign Correspondence of the Transcript," *BT,* 13 Apr. 1860, 2.

57. "Letter from Italy," *NOP,* 30 Dec. 1860, 11; 8 Aug. 1860, 1; 22 June 1861, 1.

58. Whiting, *A Record,* 112, 129, 131.

59. Whiting, *A Record,* 134–38; Moss, *Selected Letters,* 26–30.

60. McAleer, "Isa Blagden to KF," 212.

61. Whiting, *A Record,* 134–43; Moss, *Selected Letters,* 26–30.

62. Whiting, *A Record,* 140–43; Moss, *Selected Letters,* 29–30.

63. "Elizabeth Barrett Browning," *Atlantic Monthly* 8 (Sept. 1861): 368–76; Alfred Habegger, *"My Wars Are Laid Away in Books": The Life of Emily Dickinson* (New York: Random House, 2001), 700.

64. KF to Mrs. Chaflin, 29 June 1863 (Hayes Presidential Center, Fremont, Ohio).

65. "From New York," *SR,* 20 Jan. 1866, 1; "New York," *CT,* 22 May 1867, 2.

66. *Saturday Review,* 31 March 1860, 402–4.

67. "Essays on the Poets," *Christian Examiner* 75 (July 1863): 24–43.

68. McAleer, *Dearest Isa,* 167–68, 173.

69. "Last Days," *Atlantic Monthly* 17 (June 1866): 700.

3. INTERREGNUM

1. KF Collection file 783 (BPL).

2. M.C.F., "An Appeal in Behalf of the Discharged Soldiers' Home," *BT,* 26 Sept. 1862, 1.

3. "What Northern Women Ask of the Government," *Boston Commonwealth,* 20 Dec. 1862, 1; 3 Jan. 1863, 1–2; 10 Jan. 1863, 1–2; 24 Jan. 1863, 1–2; and 31 Jan. 1863, 1–2.

4. Whiting, *A Record,* 123.

5. N. John Hall, ed., *Letters of Anthony Trollope* (Stanford, Calif.: Stanford Univ. Press, 1983), 127, 171, 175, 192, 509; "Anthony Trollope on America," *Continental Monthly* 2 (Sept. 1862): 302–14.

6. Michael Sadlier, *Anthony Trollope: A Commentary* (Boston: Houghton Mifflin, 1927), 210; James Pope-Hennessey, *Anthony Trollope* (Boston: Little, Brown, 1971), 219; R. H. Super, *The Chronicler of Barsetshire* (Ann Arbor: Univ. of Michigan Press, 1988), 355; C. P. Snow, *Trollope* (London: Macmillan, 1975), 117, 127, 118; Victoria Glendinning, *Anthony Trollope* (New York: Knopf, 1992), 316.

7. "Letter from Straws, Jr.," *BC*, 30 May 1859, 1.

8. "English Authors in Florence," 660–72.

9. Whiting, *A Record*, 183; Hall, *Letters of Anthony Trollope*, 433, 437, 438; Zoltán Haraszti, "Kate Field and the Trollope Brothers," *More Books: Being the Bulletin of the BPL* 2 (July 1927): 132.

10. Anthony Trollope, *An Autobiography* (1883; rpt. Berkeley: Univ. of California Press, 1947), 262.

11. Vedder, *Digressions of V*, 190.

12. Soria, *Elihu Vedder*, 38; Vedder, *Digressions of V*, 242, 245.

13. Gary Scharnhorst, "Whitman and Kate Field," *Walt Whitman Quarterly Review* 23 (Summer/Fall 2005): 49–52.

14. Vedder, *Digressions of V*, 245, 246.

15. "Death of KF," *NYH*, 31 May 1896, 10.

16. Whiting, *A Record*, 357.

17. Ripley to KF, 24 Feb. and 9 Mar. 1864 (BPL).

18. Scrapbook in the KF Collection (BPL).

19. *SR*, 16 Apr. 1864, 2; 30 Apr. 1864, 2; 6 Apr. 1864, 1; *BJ Supplement*, 20 Apr. 1864, 1.

20. "From New York," *SR*, 22 June 1864, 2; 4 July 1864, 1; 29 July 1865, 6; Soria, *Elihu Vedder*, 45.

21. "From New York," *SR*, 29 Mar. 1865, 1.

22. "The Drama," *NYTrib*, 1 Feb. 1867, 4.

23. "From New York," *SR*, 13 May 1865, 1.

24. "From New York," *SR*, 28 Feb. 1866, 2; *NYH*, 8 Dec. 1872, 7; Moss, *Selected Letters*, 75.

25. "The Season at Newport," *BJ*, 29 Aug. 1864, 4.

26. "KF's Letter," *CT-H*, 22 Sept. 1895, 30.

27. "From Newport," *BP*, 16 Aug. 1865, 1; "A Voice from Newport," *KFW*, 27 July 1892, 52; "Life at Newport," *BJ*, 20 Aug. 1864, 4.

28. "The Season at Newport," *BJ*, 7 Sept. 1865, 4.

29. "Newport on Wheels," *SR*, 24 Aug. 1864, 2; 7 Sept. 1864, 4.

30. *SR*, 22 Nov. 1864, 2; 12 Apr. 1865, 2; 28 June 1865, 6; 29 July 1865, 6; 20 June 1866, 1; *BA*, 26 July 1865, 2.

31. "The New York Women in Council," *SR*, 21 May 1864, 2.

32. "What Some Good Bostonians Saw at the Bowery," *BA,* 10 Feb. 1865, 2.

33. "'Class Day' at Harvard," *SR,* 29 June 1864, 1; 13 May 1865, 1.

34. McAleer, *Dearest Isa,* 211.

35. "From New York," *SR,* 22 Nov. 1864, 2; 8 Feb. 1865, 2; 20 Jan. 1866, 1; "An Esthetic View of Boston's Fourth," *SR,* 9 July 1864, 1.

36. "A Side View of Solemn Things," *BA,* 9 May 1865, 2.

37. *SR,* 3 May 1865, 1; 11 May 1865, 2.

38. Bowles to KF, 4 May [1865] (BPL).

39. George S. Merriam, *The Life and Times of Samuel Bowles* (New York: Century, 1885), 2:74.

40. "In the Beginning," *KFW,* 1 Jan. 1890, 2.

41. "The Lesson of the Hour," *SR,* 3 May 1865, 1; 7 Mar. 1866, 2.

42. M. A. DeWolfe Howe, *Memories of a Hostess* (Boston: Atlantic Monthly Press, 1922), 259–61.

43. Winter to KF, 15 Sept. 1866 (BPL).

44. "Ristori," *NYTrib,* 20 Sept. 1866, 5; 15 Nov. 1866, 4; 15 Oct. 1866, 6.

45. William Winter to KF, 7 Oct. 1866 (BPL).

46. *SR,* 23 Oct. 1867, 1.

47. Moss, *Selected Letters,* 176.

48. "From New York," *CT,* 17 July 1867, 2; 21 Aug. 1867, 2; 15 Sept. 1867, 2; "The Watering Places," *NYTrib,* 31 July 1867, 2; Soria, *Elihu Vedder,* 53–54.

49. John Paul, "Letter from New York," *SR,* 29 May 1867, 4.

50. *BE,* 23 Apr. 1867, 4; 31 May 1867, 4.

4. NEW YORK AND NEW ENGLAND

1. "New York Gossip," *CT,* 6 Oct. 1867, 2.

2. Whiting, *A Record,* 170; "Charles Dickens," *NYTrib,* 3 Dec. 1867, 1.

3. *BT,* 8 Jan. 1868, 1.

4. "Charles Dickens," *St. Louis Missouri Republican,* 1 Mar. 1871, 2; Gary Scharnhorst, "Kate Field's 'An Evening with Charles Dickens': A Reconstructed Lecture," *Dickens Quarterly* 21 (June 2004): 71–89.

5. Mark Twain, *Autobiography* (New York: Harper, 1924), 1:157.

6. "Charles Dickens," *NYTrib,* 3 Dec. 1867, 1; 13 Dec. 1867, 4.

7. "Charles Dickens and KF," *BT,* 24 Oct. 1890, 3.

8. Whiting, *A Record,* 149, 175; Annie Field to KF, 10 Jan. 1868 (BPL).

9. "Charles Dickens and KF," *BT,* 24 Oct. 1890, 3.

10. Whiting, *A Record,* 175.

11. "Charles Dickens and KF."

12. "A Chat with KF," *Baltimore Gazette,* 3 May 1880, 4.

13. Rev. of *Pen Photographs, BT,* 6 Mar. 1868, 1; *Putnam's* 11 (May 1868): 643–44; *Independent,* 12 Mar. 1868, 6.

14. J. R. Osgood to KF, 17 Feb. 1868 (BPL).

15. Whiting, *A Record,* 178.

16. Kate Field, *Pen Photographs* (Boston: Loring, 1868), 33.

17. "Some Letters to Mr. J. R. Osgood," *Critic,* 29 June 1895, 484.

18. Whiting, *A Record,* 179.

19. "Some Letters to Mr. J. R. Osgood."

20. Hall, *Letters of Anthony Trollope,* 448.

21. Jane C. Croly, *Sorosis: Its Origin and History* (New York: Little and Co., 1886), 12 and passim; "Sorosis," *SR,* 2 May 1877, 2; *BE,* 17 Apr. 1868, 2.

22. Croly, *Sorosis,* 13.

23. Moss, *Selected Letters,* 39; Annie Fields to KF, 18 May 1868 (BPL).

24. Osgood to KF, 25 May 1868 (BPL).

25. Moss, *Selected Letters,* 39.

26. "The New England Women's Club," *Woman's Advocate* 1 (Jan. 1869): 25–33; Joel Myerson and Daniel Shealy, eds., *Journals of Louisa May Alcott* (Boston: Little, Brown, 1989), 167; Whiting, *A Record,* 201.

27. *Mad on Purpose,* trans. by KF from the Italian of Giovanni Carlo Cosenza (New York: Gray and Green, 1868).

28. "Criticism and the Drama," *Beadle's* 2 (Nov. 1866): 442.

29. "An Amusement Critique," *NYTrib,* 29 Apr. 1873, 2.

30. "Church and Theatre," *NYTrib,* 29 Mar. 1875, 3; *KFW,* 30 Mar. 1895, 205.

31. "Dramatic Criticism," *Echo,* 17 Apr. 1875, 1; *NYG,* 27 Nov. 1874, 193.

32. Higginson to KF, 6 Nov. 1867 (BPL).

33. Hall, *Letters of Anthony Trollope,* 429.

34. Higginson to KF, 4 Nov. 1867 (BPL).

35. "The Wisdom of Masks," *Public Spirit* 2 (Feb. 1868): 393–96.

36. Winter to KF, 27 Sept. 1868 (BPL).

37. Whiting, *A Record,* 184–85, 211; KF to Howells, 13 Nov. 1870 (BPL).

38. Henry James, *The Portrait of a Lady* (1881; rpt. New York: Library of America, 1985), 242 and passim; "KF and Her Critics," *NYG,* 23 Nov. 1874, 193.

39. "From Boston," *SR,* 21 Nov. 1868, 2; 1 Feb. 1869, 2; "The Radical Club and Woman," *SR,* 23 Nov. 1868, 2; Moss, *Selected Letters,* 37; *New York Evening Mail,* 1 May 1869, 1; Whiting, *A Record,* 98, 202, 23, 207; Henry James to KF, 9 Dec. 1868 (BPL).

40. *Planchette's Diary* (New York: Redfield, 1868), 5–6, 11, 13, and passim.

41. Whiting, *A Record,* 195; *BT,* 7 Nov. 1868, 2.

42. *BT,* 27 Nov. 1868, 2; *Philadelphia Press,* 8 Dec. 1868, 2; *Galaxy* 7 (Jan. 1869): 137; Winter to KF, 6 Nov. 1868 (BPL).

43. Hall, *Letters of Anthony Trollope,* 431.

44. Osgood to KF, 11 June 1868 (BPL).

45. Annie Fields diary entry for 1 Jan. 1869 (Massachusetts Historical Society).

46. Whiting, *A Record,* 198; Moss, *Selected Letters,* 48.

47. "Why People Lecture," *KFW,* 29 June 1892, 413.

48. "Landor's Preferences among Italian Poets," *Echo,* 14 Apr. 1875, 2.

49. Hall, *Letters of Anthony Trollope,* 709.

50. KF to Ludlow, 3 July 1869 (MHS).

51. "Miss KF in Brooklyn," *New York Evening Mail,* 4 May 1869, 3.

52. "From Boston," *SR,* 16 Mar. 1869, 2; *BA,* 16 Mar. 1869, 1.

53. Henry James to KF, 31 Mar. 1869 (BPL).

54. Annie Fields diary entry for 1 Apr. 1869 (Massachusetts Historical Society).

55. Whiting, *A Record,* 211; "Crumbs of Boston Culture," *NYG,* 22 Nov. 1884, 167.

56. Whiting, *A Record,* 217; Whipple, *BT,* 1 Apr. 1869, 2; Edward King, *SR,* 3 Apr. 1869, 3; *Newport News,* 7 Apr. 1869, 2.

57. "Boston," *NYTimes,* 18 Apr. 1869, 3.

58. John B. Pickard, ed., *The Letters of John Greenleaf Whittier* (Cambridge, Mass.: Belknap, 1975), 3:193.

59. "Woman in the Lyceum," *Newton Journal,* 24 Apr. 1869, 2.

60. Moss, *Selected Letters,* 42.

61. *NYTimes,* 4 May 1869, 5; *NYTrib,* 4 May 1869, 5; *SR,* 5 May 1869, 4; *New York World,* 4 May 1869, 5; *Independent,* 6 May 1869, 4; *BE,* 4 May 1869, 2.

62. E. L. Godkin, "Woman in the Lyceum," *Nation,* 13 May 1869, 371.

63. *Scribner's* 5 (Apr. 1873): 746–47.

64. Moss, *Selected Letters,* 126.

65. "Miss KF's Lecture," *New York Evening Mail,* 11 May 1869, 2; *SR,* 30 June 1869, 2.

66. *NYTrib,* 11 May 1869, 4; Winter to KF, 11 May 1869 (BPL); Moss, *Selected Letters,* 43.

67. KF to Reid, 30 June 1869 (MiamiU); Moss, *Selected Letters,* 76.

68. Reid to KF, 29 Sept. 1869 (BPL).

69. KF to Reid, 6 Apr. 1869 (MiamiU).

70. Moss, *Selected Letters,* 47.

71. "Odds and Ends of the Peace Jubilee," *NYTrib,* 23 June 1869, 2.

72. G.W.S., "The Dangers of the City," *New York World,* 18 June 1869, 1.

73. Moss, *Selected Letters,* 47.

74. "A New Old Firm," *SR,* 14 Dec. 1868, 2.

75. "In and Out of the Woods," *Atlantic Almanac for 1870* (Boston: Field, Osgood, 1869), 50 and passim.

76. *NYTrib,* 3 Sept. 1869, 2; "Among the Adirondacks," *NYTrib,* 12 Aug. 1869, 2.

77. KF to Reid, 6 Aug. 1869 (MiamiU).

78. Ralph L. Rusk, ed., *Letters of Ralph Waldo Emerson* (New York: Columbia Univ. Press, 1939), 6:91–92.

79. *NYTrib,* 18 Nov. 1869, 4, 5.

80. "Saratoga Seen with the Naked Eye," *NYTrib,* 12 Aug. 1869, 1–2.

81. "Saratoga Seen with Another Eye," *NYTrib,* 21 Aug. 1869, 2.

82. Reid to KF, 12 Aug. 1869; 9 Sept. 1869; 29 Sept. 1869 (BPL).

83. Moss, *Selected Letters,* 51.

84. Reid to KF, 29 Sept. 1869 (BPL).

85. KF to Reid, 17 Aug. 1869 (MiamiU).

86. "A Newport Experience," *NYTrib,* 30 Aug. 1869, 5.

87. KF to Reid, 31 Aug. 1869 (MiamiU).

88. Reid to KF, 9 Sept. 1869 (BPL).

89. "Newport in Summer," *Independent,* 30 Sept. 1869, 1.

5. AT LARGE

1. Lin Salamo et al., eds., *Mark Twain's Letters 1872–1873* (Berkeley: Univ. of California Press, 1997), 539.

2. KF to Mr. Mumford, 28 July 1870 (New York Univ).

3. Whiting, *A Record,* 213.

4. "Among the Adirondacks," *CT,* 8 Feb. 1870, 4.

5. KF to Reid, 9 Nov. 1870 (MiamiU).

6. Kate Field, *Hap-Hazard* (Boston: Osgood, 1873), 11.

7. *New York Evening Mail,* 14 Feb. 1870, 1; advertising brochure for KF's lectures (Alderman Library, Univ. of Virginia).

8. *New Haven Journal and Courier,* 6 Jan. 1870, 2; *Buffalo Courier,* 12 Jan. 1870, 2.

9. *BJ,* 21 Oct. 1869, 2; *BA,* 21 Oct. 1869, 1; *Troy Times,* 22 Dec. 1869, 2.

10. *Boston Commonwealth,* 20 Nov. 1869, 2.

11. *St. Paul Pioneer,* 20 Feb. 1870, 4.

12. Whiting, *A Record,* 227; *BE,* 30 Mar. 1870, 1.

13. *Boston Commonwealth,* 9 Apr. 1870, 2.

14. "Daly's Grand Opera House," *NYH,* 4 May 1873, 5.

15. "Fechter as Hamlet," *Atlantic Monthly* 26 (Nov. 1870): 558.

16. *SR,* 10 Nov. 1870, 3.

17. KF to Mr. Guild, 15 Oct. 1882 (Massachusetts Historical Society).

18. KF to Whitelaw Reid, 14 May 1870 (MiamiU).

19. William C. DeVane, ed., *New Letters of Robert Browning* (New Haven: Yale Univ. Press, 1950), 196.

20. Moss, *Selected Letters,* 58; *SR,* 4 July 1870, 3.

21. KF to Reid, 20 Aug. 1870 (MiamiU).

22. Margery Deane, "Letter from Newport," *New York Evening Post,* 12 Aug. 1870, 2.

23. "John Paul at Newport," *NYTrib,* 2 Sept. 1870, 2.

24. Deane, "Letter from Newport," 2.

25. KF to Reid, 20 Aug. 1870 (MiamiU).

26. "In Memoriam," *KFW,* 22 Aug. 1894, 113; KF file in the MHS.

27. KF to Reid, 5 Oct. 1870 (MiamiU).

28. *BE,* 10 June 1870, 1; *Philadelphia Press,* 22 Sept. 1870, 4.

29. Scharnhorst, "KF's 'An Evening with Dickens.'"

30. "A Sharp Episcopal Criticism on KF," *BE,* 18 Feb. 1871, 2.

31. Whiting, *A Record,* 228.

32. KF to Reid, 18 Nov. 1870 (MiamiU).

33. KF to Reid, 16 Feb. 1871 (MiamiU).

34. *NYTrib,* 7 Dec. 1870, 5.

35. Moss, *Selected Letters,* 66.

36. Whiting, *A Record,* 232.

37. Moss, *Selected Letters,* 74.

38. *NYH,* 14 Feb. 1871, 4; 10 Apr. 1871, 7; 1 May 1871, 8.

39. KF to Reid, 5 Feb. 1871; 30 Mar. 1871; 16 Apr. 1871 (MiamiU).

40. Moss, *Selected Letters,* 75, 90.

41. Victor Fischer et al., eds., *Mark Twain's Letters 1870–1871* (Berkeley: Univ. of California Press, 1995), 291, 322, 324, 549.

42. "KF on Charles Dickens," *Buffalo Courier,* 31 Jan. 1871, 2; Moss, *Selected Letters,* 69.

43. *Ironton Register,* 9 Feb. 1871, 3; Moss, *Selected Letters,* 88.

44. *BG,* 22 Nov. 1885, 9.

45. *Autobiography of Mark Twain* (New York: Harper, 1959), 1:151.

46. *Indianapolis Journal,* 8 Feb. 1871, 4.

47. KF to Reid, 16 Feb. 1871 (MiamiU).

48. KF to Reid, 30 Mar. 1871 (MiamiU); Moss, *Selected Letters,* 76.

49. *NYTimes,* 27 Mar. 1871, 2; *NYTrib,* 5 Jan. 1872, 2.

50. Annie Fields diary entry for 27 Apr. 1871 (Massachusetts Historical Society).

51. *BT,* 18 Mar. 1871, 2.

52. KF to Reid, 30 Mar. 1871 (MiamiU).

53. Moss, *Selected Letters,* 78–79.

54. G.W.S., "Transatlantic Steamships," *NYTrib,* 5 Aug. 1871, 5.

55. Moss, *Selected Letters,* 80, 81; Whiting, *A Record,* 259.

56. Whiting, *A Record,* 257.

57. KF to Reid, 6 Sept. 1871 (MiamiU).

58. McAleer, *Dearest Isa,* 359.

59. Whiting, *A Record,* 266–67; McAleer, "Isa Blagden to KF," 217.

60. DeVane, *New Letters of Robert Browning,* 201–2.

61. McAleer, *Dearest Isa,* 361, 364; KF to Reid, 6 Sept. 1871; 28 July 1871 (MiamiU).

62. "Robert Browning: A Few Unpublished Letters," 298–99.

63. Moss, *Selected Letters*, 82.

64. "Sir Charles Dilke," *KFW*, 27 July 1892, 50.

65. Whiting, *A Record*, 292.

66. *SR*, 11 Aug. 1871, 4; Whiting, *A Record*, 274; KF to Reid, 28 July 1871 (MiamiU).

67. KF to Reid, 28 July 1871 (MiamiU).

68. "KF's 'Pen Photographs' in England," *Every Saturday*, 30 Dec. 1871, 631.

69. *SR*, 18 Aug. 1871, 4.

70. N[ora] P[erry], "Newport Correspondence," *PJ*, 21 Sept. 1871, 1.

71. KF to Reid, 28 July 1871 (MiamiU).

72. Moss, *Selected Letters*, 93.

73. KF to Reid, 6 Sept. 1871; 28 July 1871 (MiamiU).

74. *BE*, 12 Oct. 1871, 1; *National Standard*, 11 Nov. 1871, 1.

75. Paris *American Register*, 21 Oct. 1871, 1.

76. Moss, *Selected Letters*, 98.

77. "George Eliot Dead," *NYTrib*, 24 Dec. 1880, 5; Moss, *Selected Letters*, 96.

78. G. H. Lewes to KF, n.d. (BPL).

79. Paris *American Register*, 5 Oct. 1872, 3.

80. "A Chat with KF," *Baltimore Gazette*, 3 May 1880, 4; "George Eliot Dead."

81. Field, *Hap-Hazard*, 242.

82. McAleer, *Dearest Isa*, 373; Moss, *Selected Letters*, 96.

83. KF to Reid, 2 Feb. 1872 (MiamiU); Whiting, *A Record*, 281; Moss, *Selected Letters*, 92–94.

84. KF to Reid, 20 Feb. 1872; 6 Apr. 1872 (MiamiU); Whiting, *A Record*, 312–13, 315; Hall, *Letters of Anthony Trollope*, 589.

85. Moss, *Selected Letters*, 85.

86. Lewes to KF, 1 Apr. 1872 (BPL).

87. DeVane, *New Letters of Robert Browning*, 207–8; McAleer, *Dearest Isa*, 378.

88. London *Daily News*, 6 May 1872, 2; London *Times*, 6 May 1872, 1; *Examiner*, 11 May 1872, 479.

89. G.W.S., "Miss KF on the London Platform," *NYTrib*, 22 May 1872, 6; *BG*, 24 May 1872, 2.

90. *NYG*, 3 May 1877, 440.

91. L.C.M., "Boston," *NYTrib*, 10 Oct. 1872, 6.

92. George Eliot to KF, 21 May 1872 (BPL); "George Eliot Dead."

93. "KF at a London Banquet," *Woman's Journal*, 10 Aug. 1872, 254.

94. "Miss KF on the London Platform," *NYTrib*, 22 May 1872, 6.

95. Whiting, *A Record*, 284–86, 291; Paris *American Register*, 8 June 1872, 1.

96. KF to Reid, 12 June 1872 (MiamiU).

97. Field, *Hap-Hazard*, 198–206; "A Fourth at Ems," *KFW*, 13 July 1892, 18–20.

98. *BG*, 21 Aug. 1872, 5.

99. KF to Reid, 12 Sept. 1872; 17 Oct. 1872 (MiamiU).

6. "FREE LANCE"

1. KF to Reid, 20 Oct. 1872 (MiamiU).

2. Moss, *Selected Letters,* 104.

3. *NYTrib,* 5 Dec. 1872, 1.

4. Moss, *Selected Letters,* 107.

5. KF to Reid, 18 Nov. 1872 (MiamiU).

6. KF to Hay, 17 Jan. 1873; 14 Feb. 1873 (Brown).

7. *Saturday Evening Gazette,* 2 Jan. 1875, 1; S.H.M. Byers, *Twenty Years in Europe* (Chicago: Rand, McNally, 1900), 111; *BE,* 1 May 1875, 4.

8. Whiting, *A Record,* 322.

9. *NYH,* 10 Nov. 1872, 7; 2 Dec. 1872, 4; 19 Jan. 1873, 5.

10. Enclosure in letter to Reid, 10 Nov. 1872 (MiamiU).

11. Moss, *Selected Letters,* 60.

12. Carl Weber, *The Rise and Fall of James Ripley Osgood* (Waterville, Maine: Colby College Press, 1959), 98.

13. L.C.M., "Boston," *NYTrib,* 10 Oct. 1872, 6.

14. "Lectures and Meetings," *NYTrib,* 20 Dec. 1872, 5.

15. L.C.M., "Boston," *NYTrib,* 12 June 1873, 6.

16. Fuller Walker, "Literary Notices," *Woman's Journal,* 5 July 1873, 216; *New York Evening Mail,* 7 July 1873, 1; *BG,* 14 Aug. 1873, 2; *Overland Monthly* 14 (Dec. 1873): 584–85; *Christian Union,* 3 Sept. 1873, 188.

17. Roy Jenkins, *Sir Charles Dilke* (London: Collins, 1965), 81.

18. Fitz-Mac, "KF," *Denver Rocky Mountain News,* 8 Nov. 1891, 11.

19. "The Summer Resorts," *NYTrib,* 14 May 1873, 2.

20. "Miss Field Heard," *Newport News,* 1 May 1895, 3.

21. "On the Ocean Wave," *NYTrib,* 28 June 1873, 3.

22. Salamo et al., *Mark Twain's Letters,* 375.

23. "Receiving the Shah," *NYTrib,* 9 July 1873, 4–5.

24. Hall, *Letters of Anthony Trollope,* 591.

25. "Alfred Tennyson," *KFW,* 12 Oct. 1892, 226.

26. Whiting, *A Record,* 306–7.

27. Hall, *Letters of Anthony Trollope,* 589.

28. Whiting, *A Record,* 308.

29. "Receiving the Shah."

30. "The Shah at Windsor," *NYTrib,* 1 July 1873, 1.

31. "Why Fresh Fields Should Turn to Pastures New," *BE,* 6 Aug. 1873, 2.

32. Rpt. "The Eagle and Miss Field," *BE,* 12 Aug. 1873, 3.

33. "Railway Traveling in England," *SR*, 7 Jan. 1874, 3.

34. G.W.S., "American Tourists," *BG*, 20 Aug. 1873, 2.

35. Whiting, *A Record*, 316.

36. "Ten Days in Spain," *NYTrib*, 1 Jan. 1874, 2; 23 Feb. 1874, 3.

37. "Ten Days in Spain," *NYTrib*, 7 Jan. 74, 3.

38. "Ten Days in Spain," *NYTrib*, 31 Jan. 1874, 3.

39. "Ten Days in Spain," *NYTrib*, 23 Feb. 1874, 3; 23 Mar. 1874, 3.

40. "Ten Days in Spain," *NYTrib*, 9 May 1874, 3.

41. Whiting, *A Record*, 319.

42. G.W.S., "American Tourists."

43. L.C.M., "Boston," *NYTrib*, 21 Nov. 1874, 8.

44. Whiting, *A Record*, 293; Edward Mather, "KF's New Departure," *Bay State Monthly* 3 (Nov. 1885): 429.

45. "Boston," *NYTrib*, 21 Nov. 1874, 8; *BT*, 3 Dec. 1874, 6; Whiting, *A Record*, 496.

46. G.W.S., "American Tourists."

47. "Charles Bradlaugh," *Cincinnati Commercial*, 17 Nov. 1873, 1–2.

48. *Albany Evening Journal*, 11 Feb. 1871, 2; KF to Reid, 5 Feb. 1871 (MiamiU).

49. "Republican Notes on England," *St. Louis Missouri Republican*, 20 Sept. 1874, 8.

50. "Current Topics in London," *NYG*, 3 May 1877, 440.

51. *BT*, 3 Dec. 1874, 6.

52. KF to Stedman, 4 Sept. 1876 (Butler Library, Columbia Univ.); Moss, *Selected Letters*, 125.

53. L.C.M., "Boston," *NYTrib*, 1 June 1874, 8.

54. Moss, *Selected Letters*, 111; *NYH*, 26 June 1874, 7.

55. "Miss Field's Readings," *NYTrib*, 26 June 1874, 4.

56. Winter to KF, 29 June 1874 (BPL).

57. KF to W. H. Huntington, 1 June 1874 (Baylor).

58. "Miss KF—The Scarlet Letter," *NYTrib*, 28 Aug. 1874, 4.

59. "KF and Her Critics."

60. "Books, Authors, and Art," *SR*, 7 July 1874, 3.

61. KF to Stedman, 17 Nov. 1874 (Butler Library, Columbia Univ.).

62. KF file (MHS).

63. *Saturday Evening Gazette*, 21 Nov. 1874, 2; *NYH*, 15 Nov. 1874, 12.

64. Whiting, *A Record*, 326.

65. Moss, *Selected Letters*, 112.

66. *New York Clipper*, 21 Nov. 1874, 270; *NYTimes*, 15 Nov. 1874, 7; *BT*, 11 Jan. 1875, 3; *Baltimore American Supplement*, 21 Nov. 1874, 1; *New York World*, 15 Nov. 1874, 5; *New York Evening Post*, 16 Nov. 1874, 2; *NYG*, 16 Nov. 1874, 113.

67. "Booth's Theater—Masks and Faces—Miss KF," *NYTrib*, 16 Nov. 1874, 5.

68. Moss, *Selected Letters*, 112; "KF and Her Critics," *NYG*, 27 Nov. 1874, 193.

69. "Our New York Letter," *Baltimore American Supplement,* 21 Nov. 1874, 1.

70. *Cincinnati Commercial,* 4 July 1876, 5.

71. "KF and Her Critics," *NYG,* 27 Nov. 1874, 193; Moss, *Selected Letters,* 112.

72. "Miss Field's Debut," *NYTrib,* 18 Nov. 1874, 5.

73. Whiting, *A Record,* 326–27.

74. KF to Stedman, 8 Dec. 1874 (Butler Library, Columbia Univ.).

75. "Colonel Sellers," *Hartford Courant,* 12 Jan. 1875, 2.

76. "Col. Sellers Last Night," *Hartford Courant,* 13 Jan. 1875, 2.

77. "The Gilded Age," *SR,* 14 Jan. 1875, 6.

78. KF to Jeanette Gilder, 14 Jan. 1875 (Alderman Library, Univ. of Virginia).

79. "Miss KF in the Country," *NYTrib,* 19 Jan. 1875, 5.

80. Karl Kiralis, "Two Recently Discovered Letters: Mark Twain on Kate Field," *Mark Twain Journal* 20 (Summer 1980): 1.

81. "The Gilded Age," *Newark Advertiser,* 26 Jan. 1875, 2.

82. *BT,* 10 Feb. 1875, 6.

83. "Gabrielle, or A Night's Hazard," KF Collection file 1496 (BPL).

84. "The Opera Box," KF Collection file 1491 (BPL).

85. "Providence Opera House," *PJ,* 24 Mar. 1875, 2.

86. KF to "dear friend," 3 Apr. 1875 (Alderman Library, Univ. of Virginia).

87. KF to Laurence Hutton, 22 May 1877 (Princeton).

88. *Cleveland Leader,* 6 May 1875, 8; 7 May 1875, 8; *Cleveland Plain Dealer,* 6 May 1875, 1.

89. "KF and Her Critics," *Cleveland Leader,* 24 June 1875, 6; Whiting, *A Record,* 336.

90. *NYG,* 10 June 1875, 774; *NYTrib,* 10 June 1875, 6; *NYTimes,* 10 June 1875, 6; *BE,* 21 June 1875, 2.

91. KF to Stedman, 23 Nov. 1874 (Butler Library, Columbia Univ.).

92. "Departures for Europe," *NYTimes,* 27 June 1875, 12.

93. Moss, *Selected Letters,* 116–17.

7. ENGLAND

1. Moss, *Selected Letters,* 116.

2. "English Topics," *Louisville Courier-Journal,* 27 Aug. 1875, 3; 29 Dec. 1875, 2.

3. Moss, *Selected Letters,* 119, 135; KF to Stedman, 9 Feb. 1876 (Butler Library, Columbia Univ.).

4. KF to Stedman, 17 June 1876 (Butler Library, Columbia Univ.).

5. Soria, *Elihu Vedder,* 111.

6. KF to Stedman, 17 June 1876 (Butler Library, Columbia Univ.).

7. "Current Topics in London," *NYG,* 3 May 1877, 440.

8. KF to Stedman, 5 Oct. 1875 (Butler Library, Columbia Univ.).

9. Moss, *Selected Letters,* 117.

10. "Miss Dickinson Must Follow KF's Example," *BG*, 12 May 1876, 4.

11. *NYTrib*, 3 Dec. 1875, 4.

12. William Baker and William M. Clarke, eds., *The Letters of Wilkie Collins* (New York: St. Martin's, 1999), 2:404.

13. G.W.S., "London Letter," *NYTrib*, 15 Jan. 1876, 3.

14. KF to Stedman, 7 Aug. 1875; 9 Feb. 1876; 19 May 1876 (Butler Library, Columbia Univ.); Moss, *Selected Letters*, 120.

15. Moss, *Selected Letters*, 122.

16. M.D.C., "London Letter," *Cincinnati Commercial*, 10 May 1876, 2.

17. "Personal," *NYTrib*, 16 May 1876, 4; 2 May 1876, 4.

18. G.W.S., "Personal," *NYTrib*, 12 May 1876, 4.

19. *NYH*, 30 Apr. 1876, 5; Moss, *Selected Letters*, 121.

20. G.W.S., "The London Stage," *NYTrib*, 3 June 1876, 3.

21. *Cincinnati Commercial*, 25 May 1876, 5; Philadelphia *Forney's Sunday Chronicle*, 11 June 1876, 1.

22. *CT*, 19 Nov. 1876, 13.

23. KF to Stedman, 11 Oct. 1876 (Butler Library, Columbia Univ.).

24. "Caught Napping," *KFW*, 29 Jan. 1890, 79–82.

25. "Very Private Theatricals," *NYG*, Christmas edition 1877, 3.

26. *NYTrib*, 18 Apr. 1877, 4.

27. KF to William Moy Thomas, 14 Mar. 1877 (Rochester).

28. Kate Field, *Extremes Meet* (New York: Wheat and Cornett, 1878), 91.

29. *Examiner*, 17 Mar. 1877, 342; Moss, *Selected Letters*, 131–32; *NYTrib*, 30 Mar. 1877, 4; *Theatre*, 27 Mar. 1877, 97.

30. KF to Frederick Stedman, 31 Mar. 1877 (Butler Library, Columbia Univ.).

31. KF to Stedman, 31 May 1877 (Butler Library, Columbia Univ.); KF to Laurence Hutton, 7 Apr. 1877 (Princeton); *NYTrib*, 23 Apr. 1877, 4.

32. "Current Topics in London," *NYG*, 3 May 1877, 440.

33. "Theatrical Gossip," *NYH*, 18 Mar. 1877, 9; *NYTrib*, 4 Apr. 1877, 4.

34. M.D.C., "London Letter," *Cincinnati Commercial*, 2 Apr. 1877, 5.

35. KF to Stedman, 31 Mar. 1877 (Butler Library, Columbia Univ.); Moss, *Selected Letters*, 133.

36. *Theatre*, 17 July 1877, 340.

37. Moss, *Selected Letters*, 139.

38. G.W.S., "Gen. Grant in England," *NYTrib*, 21 June 1877, 1.

39. "The Glorious Fourth and So Forth," *Truth*, 12 July 1877, 52–53.

40. Philadelphia *Forney's Sunday Chronicle*, 9 Sept. 1877, 1.

41. "The Pierrepont and Badeau Receptions to General Grant," *Truth*, 14 June 1877, 755.

42. Moss, *Selected Letters*, 135.

43. "KF's Travels," Philadelphia *Forney's Sunday Chronicle*, 11 Nov. 1877, 1.

44. *Truth,* 1 Nov. 1877, 531–32; 6 Dec. 1877, 684–85; Moss, *Selected Letters,* 137.

45. "KF," *PJ,* 19 Jan. 1881, 4.

46. KF papers, file 843 (BPL).

47. Moss, *Selected Letters,* 132

48. "Crossing the Channel," *Truth,* 27 Sept. 1877, 386.

49. "London Gossip," *Truth,* 18 Apr. 1878, 503.

50. Moss, *Selected Letters,* 137.

51. "Through the Looking Glass," *Whitehall Review,* 10 Nov. 1877, 520.

52. *History of Bell's Telephone* (London: Bradbury, Agnew, 1878), 14–17; Whiting, *A Record,* 348–49; *Theatre,* ns 1 (Aug. 1878): 33.

53. Moss, *Selected Letters,* 138, 140; "The Telephone," London *Times,* 16 Nov. 1877, 3–4; Whiting, *A Record,* 250.

54. "The American Telephone," *NYH,* 4 Feb. 1878, 2; "The Telephone at Court," London *Times,* 16 Jan. 1878, 9.

55. Whiting, *A Record,* 359.

56. Ibid., 351–52.

57. "The American Telephone."

58. *Hartford Courant,* 20 Mar. 1878, 1.

59. KF to Stedman, 14 Mar. 1878 (MiamiU); Joseph Hatton, ed. *Reminiscences of J. L. Toole* (London: Routledge, 1892), 269.

60. "George Eliot Dead."

61. "The Newest Books," *Whitehall Review,* 9 Mar. 1878, 402.

62. "The American Telephone."

63. "Sharp as Steel / KF was Brainy and Beautiful," *BG,* 1 June 1896, 6.

64. KF to Winter, 7 June 1878 (Folger); "Sharp as Steel."

65. *NYTrib,* 6 June 1878, 5.

66. "The Shakespeare Memorial," *NYG,* 20 Feb. 1879, 751.

67. *Theatre,* 29 May 1878, 279; "The Shakespeare Memorial."

68. Moss, *Selected Letters,* 145, 146; KF to Stedman, 7 June 1878 (Butler Library, Columbia Univ.).

69. KF to E. F. Smyth Piggott, 21 June 1878 (Folger).

70. G.W.S., "Anglo-American Topics," *NYTrib,* 8 June 1878, 5.

71. KF to Stedman, 27 June 1878 (Butler Library, Columbia Univ.).

72. *NYTimes,* 23 May 1878, 1; *NYH,* 28 May 1878, 7.

73. Moss, *Selected Letters,* 148.

74. KF to Stedman, 7 June 1878 (Butler Library, Columbia Univ.).

75. "Apropos of the Divine William," *Truth,* 2 May 1878, 569.

76. *CH,* 15 June 1893, 13; KF to Hutton, 20 Jan. 1879 (Princeton).

77. *Truth,* 18 July 1878, 86; 8 Aug. 1878, 169–70; 15 Aug. 1878, 197–98.

78. *SR,* 3 Aug. 1878, 8; "What the World Says," London *World,* 28 Aug. 1878, 12.

79. *Truth,* 22 Aug. 1878, 227–28; 3 Oct. 1878, 395.

80. Whiting, *A Record,* 371; KF to Hutton, 1 Sept. 1878 (Princeton); *SR,* 5 Oct. 1878, 8.

81. *Philadelphia Press,* 5 Nov. 1878, 4; *NYTimes,* 7 Nov. 1878, 3.

82. KF to Hutton, 20 Jan. 1879 (Princeton); *NYTrib,* 27 Jan. 1879, 4.

83. "The Shakespeare Memorial"; Whiting, *A Record,* 366.

84. Hall, *Letters of Anthony Trollope,* 770.

85. Moss, *Selected Letters,* 147.

86. "On the Banks of the Avon," *NYTimes,* 8 May 1879, 5; *NYTrib,* 8 May 1879, 5.

87. *NYTrib,* 12 May 1879, 4.

88. "On the Banks of the Avon"; "William Shakespeare," *CT,* 25 Apr. 1879, 12.

89. *NYTimes,* 5 Sept. 1879, 3; "Miss KF," *NYTrib,* 1 Oct. 1879, 5.

90. Moss, *Selected Letters,* 154.

91. KF to Stedman, 22 Oct. 1879 (Butler Library, Columbia Univ.).

92. "Life at a Water-Cure," *Truth,* 23 Oct. 1879, 518–19.

93. *BE,* 28 Nov. 1879; *NYTrib,* 8 Dec. 1879, 4.

8. NEW YORK REDUX

1. Soria, *Elihu Vedder,* 144, 146, 167; *Newport News,* 29 Apr. 1895, 5; 1 May 1895, 3.

2. *NYTrib,* 16 Jan. 1880, 4.

3. *SR,* 20 Nov. 1879, 4; *BG,* 29 Feb. 1880, 3.

4. "Don't!" *KFW,* 2 Apr. 1890, 221.

5. *BP,* 11 Mar. 1880, 3; *BA,* 11 Mar. 1880, 1; *Boston Traveller,* 11 Mar. 1880, 3; *BG,* 11 Mar. 1880, 4.

6. N[ora] P[erry], "Boston," *PJ,* 15 Mar. 1880, 6.

7. Whiting, *A Record,* 386.

8. *NYTrib,* 21 Apr. 1880, 4.

9. *Baltimore American,* 28 Apr. 1880, 2; *WP,* 1 May 1880, 2; *Troy Times,* 15 May 1880, 3.

10. "The Poe Memorial Performance," *NYTrib,* 12 Feb. 1881, 4.

11. "KF's Suitor," *PJ,* 21 Jan. 1881, 1.

12. KF to Reid, 2 Aug. 1870; 16 Sept. 1870 (MiamiU).

13. *BE,* 16 July 1872, 1; 12 Oct. 1874, 1.

14. *NYG,* 15 Aug. 1876, 305.

15. "KF," *Cincinnati Commercial,* 20 Dec. 1877, 4.

16. "A Naughty, Fascinating Editor," *BE,* 16 Sept. 1883, 8.

17. Moss, *Selected Letters,* 12, 87; Charles Warren Stoddard, "Kate Field: Cosmopolite," *National Magazine* 23 (Jan. 1906): 370; Whiting, *A Record,* 414.

18. "Plays and Actors," *NYTimes,* 10 Apr. 1881, 9.

19. *NYG,* 27 Feb. 1880, 852; *NYTrib,* 1 Mar. 1880, 5.

20. KF to Lizzie Boott, 12 Apr. [1880] (Barnard).

21. KF to John Hay, 27 Apr. [1880] (Brown).

22. *CT-H*, 22 May 1895, 6; *BE*, 20 Mar. 1881, 3; *NYG*, 3 June 1882, 668; Moss, *Selected Letters*, 163.

23. *NYTrib*, 10 June 1880, 4; *Harper's Weekly*, 26 June 1880, 403.

24. "Personal and General," *Denver Republican*, 14 Nov. 1891, 4.

25. "KF's Society," *NYTimes*, 12 Apr. 1882, 8.

26. *NYTimes*, 7 Mar. 1880, 7; 12 Mar. 1880, 3; 31 Mar. 1880, 2; *BT*, 10 Mar. 1880, 4.

27. *Elmira Advertiser*, 15 Mar. 1880, 4.

28. Pulbrook, "The Ladies' Dress Association," *NYTrib*, 23 May 1880, 5.

29. *NYTrib*, 30 May 1880, 5; 10 June 1880, 4; 27 Oct. 1880, 4.

30. "An Anglo-American Feast," *NYTimes*, 21 July 1882, 3.

31. "London Stage Gossip," *NYG*, 19 Aug. 1880, 361.

32. "A Talk with Bradlaugh," *NYTrib*, 25 July 1880, 2.

33. "A Realistic View of the Passion Play at Ober-Ammergau," *PJ*, 19 Jan. 1881, 1.

34. *NYTimes*, 13 Oct. 1880, 2; 23 Oct. 1880, 10.

35. "Cooperative Dress Reform," *NYTrib*, 12 Jan. 1881, 5.

36. "Trouble in Cooperation," *NYTrib*, 15 May 1881, 2.

37. Moss, *Selected Letters*, 161.

38. "Suing for a Fair Divide," *BE*, 15 May 1881, 3.

39. *NYG*, 18 May 1881, 578.

40. "Mr. Pulbrook Goes Home," *NYTimes*, 15 May 1881, 10.

41. "Current Events," *BE*, 3 June 1881, 2.

42. KF to Stedman, 17 Aug. 1881 (Butler Library, Columbia Univ.).

43. *NYTrib*, 23 May 1881, 5; "Trouble in Cooperation."

44. Moss, *Selected Letters*, 161, 163; "KF's Enterprise Fails," *BG*, 28 Dec. 1882, 1.

45. KF to Stedman, 15 Dec. 1881 (Butler Library, Columbia Univ.).

46. KF to Hutton, 11 Aug. [1881] (Princeton).

47. KF to C. C. Buel, 8 Jan. 1883 (MHS).

48. "The Closed Association," *NYTimes*, 29 Dec. 1882, 8.

49. "KF's Society," *NYTimes*, 12 Apr. 1882, 8.

50. "KF's Society"; *NYG*, 9 Oct. 1882, 701.

51. KF to Jeanette Gilder, 27 May 1882 (Alderman Library, Univ. of Virginia).

52. "Lady Habberton's 'Rational Gown,'" *Our Continent*, 12 Apr. 1882, 142.

53. *BE*, 27 Dec. 1882, 2; 24 Mar. 1881, 2; Whiting, *A Record*, 402.

54. Moss, *Selected Letters*, 169; *Boston Traveller*, 20 June 1882, 2.

55. Whiting, *A Record*, 411–12.

56. KF to Stedman, 13 July 1882 (Butler Library, Columbia Univ.).

57. KF to C. C. Buel, 8 Jan. 1883 (MHS).

58. Moss, *Selected Letters*, 171.

59. "The Closed Association."

60. Whiting, *A Record*, 415–16.

61. *BE*, 27 Dec. 1882, 2; 28 Dec. 1882, 2; "The Closed Association."

62. KF to Stedman, 12 Jan. 1883 (Butler Library, Columbia Univ.); Moss, *Selected Letters*, 171.

63. KF to "Dear Madam," 22 May 1883 (MHS).

64. KF to C. C. Buel, 8 Jan. 1883 (MHS).

65. Vezin to KF, 21 Dec. 1881 (BPL).

66. "Oscar Wilde Feasting," *NYH*, 12 Jan. 1882, 10.

67. Moss, *Selected Letters*, 164; Richard Ellmann, *Oscar Wilde* (New York: Knopf, 1988), 161.

68. Lloyd Lewis and Henry Justin Smith, *Oscar Wilde Discovers America* (New York: Harcourt, Brace, 1936), 44.

69. "The English Renaissance," *NYTrib*, 10 Jan. 1882, 2.

70. "How Mr. Wilde Spent Yesterday," *New York World*, 12 Jan. 1882, 4.

71. "Oscar Wilde Feasting," 10.

72. *NYG*, 11 Jan. 1882, 486.

73. *Denver Republican*, 21 July 1883, 8; *Denver Rocky Mountain News*, 29 July 1883, 12.

74. "A Reception to the Aesthete," *Philadelphia Press*, 17 Jan. 1882, 2.

75. Moss, *Selected Letters*, 164–65.

76. "Wilde Questioning," *BJ*, 30 Jan. 1882, 2.

77. "Knee-Breeches—Why Not?" *Our Continent*, 1 Mar. 1882, 47; 8 Mar. 1882, 63.

78. *NYTimes*, 24 Sept. 1882, 14; *BG*, 10 Sept. 1882, 3.

79. "KF," *PJ*, 19 Jan. 1881, 4.

80. "Books About the Stage," *Nation*, 16 Nov. 1882, 427.

81. Brander Matthews, *These Many Years* (New York: Scribner's, 1917), 246–47.

82. "KF in Utah," *BH*, 27 Jan. 1884, 13.

83. Whiting, *A Record*, 319.

9. ZION

1. Moss, *Selected Letters*, 70.

2. Helen Hunt Jackson to KF, 23 Apr. 1874 (BPL).

3. "Intercepted Letters," *Truth*, 5 Sept. 1878, 279.

4. Moss, *Selected Letters*, 173; Whiting, *A Record*, 422; "Debs Dictator," *KFW*, 11 July 1894, 17.

5. Whiting, *A Record*, 422; Slason Thompson, *Life of Eugene Field* (New York: Appleton, 1927), 82.

6. "KF," *Denver Tribune*, 21 July 1883, 4; *Denver Times*, 21 July 1883, 4; *Denver Republican*, 21 July 1883, 4.

7. "KF," *Alaska Free Press*, 23 July 1887, 4.

8. *Denver Times,* 30 July 1883, 2; "The Age of Appreciation," *Denver Tribune,* 29 July 1883, 4.

9. *Denver Tribune,* 1 Aug. 1883, 4; *Denver Republican,* 1 Aug. 1883, 1; "KF," *Denver Times,* 2 Aug. 1883, 2; 3 Aug. 1883, 4.

10. Moss, *Selected Letters,* 174.

11. Whiting, *A Record,* 420; *Denver Republican,* 3 Aug. 1883, 5; *Denver Tribune,* 3 Aug. 1883, 4; *Denver Times,* 3 Aug. 1883, 2.

12. "Miss Field Heard," *Newport News,* 1 May 1895, 1; Moss, *Selected Letters,* 176.

13. *Colorado Springs Daily Gazette,* 5 Aug. 1883, 1.

14. "KF's Letter," *CT-H,* 22 Sept. 1895, 30.

15. "Miss Field's Monologue," *Colorado Springs Daily Gazette,* 11 Aug. 1883, 1.

16. *Castle Rock Journal,* 29 Aug. 1883, 3. I am indebted to Herbert Edwards of the Palmer Lake Historical Society for identifying this source. See also Whiting, *A Record,* 421.

17. "Leaves from My Diary," *KFW,* 23 Mar. 1892, 179.

18. "KF's Letter," *CT-H,* 19 Sept. 1895, 8.

19. KF to Laurence Hutton, 25 Nov. 1883 (Princeton).

20. "An Evening with Dickens," *Grand Junction News,* 20 Oct. 1883, 2.

21. *BE,* 26 Mar. 1885, 2; *Salt Lake Tribune,* 16 Oct. 1883, 4.

22. "KF in Utah," *BH,* 27 Jan. 1884, 12.

23. *Salt Lake Tribune,* 21 Oct. 1883, 4; 4 Nov. 1883, 4.

24. *NYG,* 3 Dec. 1883, 244; *Kansas City Times,* 5 Mar. 1887, 8.

25. Whiting, *A Record,* 428.

26. *Ogden Standard Examiner,* 6 Mar. 1884, 1; *Deseret Evening News,* 10 July 1885, 4; "Miss KF," *Salt Lake Tribune,* 22 Feb. 1885, 5; "KF's Letter," *CT-H,* 23 Oct. 1895, 10.

27. "KF in Utah," *BH,* 6 Apr. 1884, 20; "A Polygamic Craze," *BH,* 15 June 1884, 14.

28. Moss, *Selected Letters,* 176.

29. "KF in Utah," *BH,* 20 Apr. 1884, 14; "Kate and the Mormons," *CT,* 6 June 1886, 15.

30. KF to E. C. Stedman, 19 May 1884 (Butler Library, Columbia Univ.).

31. "KF in Utah," *BH,* 14 May 1884, 2.

32. "Muchly Married Women," *Cincinnati Enquirer,* 8 Feb. 1886, 4.

33. "A Mormon Martyr," *BH,* 8 June 1884, 12.

34. "KF in Utah," *BH Supplement,* 2 June 1884, 1.

35. KF to Andrew P. Peabody, 17 Jan. 1885 (Massachusetts Historical Society).

36. "KF's Lecture," *Boston Traveller,* 21 Nov. 1884, 1.

37. *Ogden Standard Examiner,* 20 June 1884, 2.

38. "KF," *Salt Lake Tribune,* 19 June 1884, 2; 27 Nov. 1885, 2.

39. Moss, *Selected Letters,* 184.

40. "KF's Letter," *CT-H,* 18 Nov. 1895, 12.

41. *BG,* 15 Nov. 1884, 5.

42. *St. Louis Missouri Republican,* 10 July 1884, 4; KF to Hay, 27 July 1884 (Brown).

43. KF to Stedman, 11 Sept. 1884 (Butler Library, Columbia Univ.).

44. *BT*, 11 Dec. 1884, 8; "Crumbs of Boston Culture," *NYG*, 2 Jan. 1885, 447.

45. "KF's New Lectures," *BH*, 16 Nov. 1884, 16.

46. "Her Crazy Quilt," *NYG*, 6 Feb. 1884, 718.

47. Moss, *Selected Letters*, 190.

48. Whiting, *A Record*, 448–49.

49. *Omaha World-Herald*, 12 Oct. 1891, 8; KF to Thomas Gregg, 22 Apr. 1886 (MHS).

50. "The Forty-Fifth Star," *KFW*, 25 July 1894, 49.

51. "Crumbs of Boston Culture," *NYG*, 8 Aug. 1884, 279.

52. *Philadelphia Evening Bulletin*, 15 Nov. 1884, 5.

53. *Boston Traveller*, 19 Nov. 1884, 1; *NYG*, 22 Nov. 1884, 167; Whiting, *A Record*, 430.

54. KF to Mrs. Kimball, 18 Dec. 1884 (West Virginia).

55. *Boston Traveller*, 19 Nov. 1884, 1; *BG*, 23 Nov. 1884, 13.

56. "KF's Letter," *CT-H*, 28 May 1895, 6.

57. *Salt Lake Tribune*, 17 Feb. 1885, 4; 22 Feb. 1885, 5; Whiting, *A Record*, 447; *NYTimes*, 5 Mar. 1885, 2.

58. "The Mormon Monster," *Evansville Courier*, 21 Jan. 1886, 4.

59. *BG*, 23 Nov. 1884, 13; Moss, *Selected Letters*, 188; "KF," *Los Angeles Times*, 13 Apr. 1888, 8.

60. "Crimes Committed in Utah," *NYTimes*, 22 Nov. 1885, 7.

61. "How to Crush Polygamy," *NYTrib*, 22 Nov. 1885, 7.

62. "Men and Women," *KFW*, 22 Jan. 1890, 66–67.

63. KF to Laurence Hutton, 1 Feb. 1884 (Princeton).

64. Moss, *Selected Letters*, 175–76, 181.

65. "An Awful Confession," *Chicago Inter-Ocean*, 18 July 1885, 15.

66. "Crimes Committed in Utah," *NYTimes*, 22 Nov. 1885, 7.

67. "Mormonism," *CT*, 19 Jan. 1886, 2.

68. *Boston Traveller*, 24 Feb. 1886, 2; *NYTimes*, 21 Oct. 1886, 5; Whiting, *A Record*, 437.

69. "Marshalltown," *Iowa State Register*, morning ed., 25 Sept. 1886, 2.

70. "Honor to Fairchild," *Minneapolis Tribune*, 31 Aug. 1886, 4.

71. "KF's Welcome," *Salt Lake Weekly Tribune*, 5 May 1887, 3.

72. "Miss KF," *Salt Lake Tribune*, 8 Sept. 1886, 2.

73. Thompson, *Life of Eugene Field*, 82; *Chicago Evening News*, 27 Sept. 1886, 2.

74. "KF," *Boston Traveller*, 26 Feb. 1886, 2.

75. Whiting, *A Record*, 442.

76. "Miss Field Scolds the President," *BE*, 6 June 1886, 2.

77. *Salt Lake Tribune*, 25 Jan. 1885, 2; *BE*, 6 Apr. 1885, 4.

78. *Ogden Standard Examiner*, 20 Nov. 1886, 4.

79. *Boston Traveller*, 26 Feb. 1886, 2; *NYTimes*, 28 Feb. 1886, 4; 11 Apr. 1886, 14.

80. Eugene Field, *Chicago Daily News*, 25 Feb. 1887, 2.

81. Moss, *Selected Letters,* 179.

82. *BG,* 15 Nov. 1884, 5.

83. "The 'News' on KF," *Salt Lake Tribune,* 5 Dec. 1886, 2.

84. *Ogden Standard Examiner,* 5 May 1885, 2; 6 May 1886, 2; 18 Dec. 1886, 2; Leonard J. Arrington, *Kate Field and J. H. Beadle: Manipulators of the Mormon Past* (Salt Lake City: Univ. of Utah Press, 1971), 5, 12.

85. *Utah Journal,* 8 Nov. 1884.

86. *BG,* 6 Sept. 1890, 4; "Woman Suffrage in South Carolina," *KFW,* 6 Apr. 1895, 210.

87. "KF," *Boston Traveller,* 26 Feb. 1886, 2.

88. "Preparing for Easter," *NYTimes,* 11 Apr. 1886, 14.

89. "KF's Opinion," *WP,* 16 May 1886, 5.

90. *Salt Lake Tribune,* 2 Dec. 1886, 1; 17 Dec. 1886, 1; *Riverside Daily Press,* 27 Mar. 1888, 3.

91. *Salt Lake Tribune,* 1 Nov. 1891, 2; "The Forty-Fifth Star," 49.

92. KF to Hutton, 25 Sept. 1890 (Princeton).

93. *Salt Lake Weekly Tribune,* 5 May 1887, 6; "KF's Career," *CT-H,* 1 June 1896, 6.

10. OUT WEST

1. Whiting, *A Record,* 448.

2. *Atchison Daily Globe,* 22 Mar. 1887, 4.

3. "Miss KF's Lecture," *Denver Republican,* 13 Apr. 1887, 5.

4. Whiting, *A Record,* 422.

5. *Salt Lake Tribune,* 1 May 1887, 6; 11 May 1887, 4; 19 May 1887, 4.

6. Whiting, *A Record,* 462; "KF's Letter," *CT-H,* 18 Oct. 1895, 11.

7. Moss, *Selected Letters,* 187.

8. *Portland Oregonian,* 1 July 1887, 3.

9. *Juneau Alaska Free Press,* 23 July 1887, 1.

10. Morgan B. Sherwood, *Exploration of Alaska* (New Haven: Yale Univ. Press, 1965), 71.

11. "A Trip to Southeastern Alaska," *Harper's Weekly,* 8 Sept. 1888, 683.

12. Ernest Gruening, *The State of Alaska* (New York: Random House, 1954), 74.

13. "KF in Alaska," *Portland Oregonian,* 27 July 1887, 2.

14. "Hills of Gold," *BE,* 11 Nov. 1890, 1; "A Trip to Southeastern Alaska."

15. Whiting, *A Record,* 453.

16. *Juneau Alaska Free Press,* 16 July 1887, 3.

17. "Alaska's Natives," *San Francisco Chronicle,* 1 Sept. 1887, 6.

18. "KF Dead," *BP,* 31 May 1896, 6.

19. Moss, *Selected Letters,* 197.

20. "Kate Fieldisms," *San Francisco Chronicle,* 9 Oct. 1887, 12.

21. Moss, *Selected Letters,* 198.

22. "Despised Alaska," KF Collection file 1497 (BPL).

23. "A Trip to Southeastern Alaska"; Sherwood, *Exploration of Alaska,* 109, 120.

24. "A Trip to Southeastern Alaska."

25. Moss, *Selected Letters,* 197–98.

26. "Ten Years' Acquaintance with Alaska," *Harper's Monthly* 55 (Nov. 1877): 802.

27. "Our Ignorance of Alaska," *North American Review* 149 (July 1889): 78–90.

28. KF to Laurence Hutton, 25 Feb. 1888; 2 Mar. 1888 (Princeton); Moss, *Selected Letters,* 199.

29. "Miss KF," *San Diego Bee,* 8 Feb. 1888, 8.

30. "KF," *San Diego Union,* 8 Feb. 1888, 8.

31. *San Diego Sun,* 9 Feb. 1888, 4; *San Diego Union,* 9 Feb. 1888, 8.

32. Whiting, *A Record,* 456–57.

33. *San Diego Bee,* 10 Feb. 1888, 5; *Daily San Diegen,* 10 Feb. 1888, 8.

34. KF to Sarah B. Cooper, 13 Feb. 1888 (MHS).

35. "Coronado," *Coronado Mercury,* 14 Feb. 1888, 2.

36. "KF by Telephone," *San Diego Bee,* 20 Feb. 1888, 1.

37. "Under Mexican Skies," *Coronado Mercury,* 16 Feb. 1888, 2.

38. "A Glimpse of Lower California," *KFW,* 25 Nov. 1891, 346–48.

39. KF to Hutton, 25 Feb. 1888 (Princeton).

40. "Miss Field's Return," *San Diego Bee,* 3 Mar. 1888, 4; "KF by Telephone," *San Diego Bee,* 20 Feb. 1888, 1; "Miss KF," *San Diego Sun,* 1 Mar. 1888, 5.

41. KF to Hutton, 25 Feb. 1888 (Princeton); "Ensenada," *San Diego Bee,* 25 Feb. 1888, 5.

42. "Miss KF," *San Diego Sun,* 1 Mar. 1888, 5; "Miss Field's Return."

43. "A Glimpse"; "Miss Field's Return."

44. "Exit Kalakaua: What Next?" *KFW,* 28 Jan. 1891, 49.

45. "A Glimpse"; "Miss Field's Return"; "Miss Field on San Diego," *San Diego Bee,* 25 Mar. 1888, 4.

46. "From Lower California," *San Diego Bee,* 2 Mar. 1888, 5.

47. KF to Hutton, 2 Mar. 1888 (Princeton).

48. *San Diego Sun,* 6 Mar. 1888, 1; *San Diego Union,* 18 Mar. 1888, 4.

49. *San Diego Bee,* 9 Mar. 1888, 8.

50. *San Diego Union,* 23 Mar. 1888, 5.

51. "Miss Field on San Diego," *San Diego Bee,* 25 Mar. 1888, 4.

52. "A Glimpse."

53. "Experiences with Prohibitionists," *KFW,* 8 Jan. 1890, 26.

54. *Riverside Daily Press,* 30 Mar. 1888, 3.

55. Moss, *Selected Letters,* 199; KF to Hutton, 4 Jan. 1888; 16 Apr. 1888 (Princeton); "KF," *Los Angeles Times,* 13 Apr. 1888, 8; 15 Apr. 1888, 2.

56. "Pullman Passengers," *Los Angeles Times,* 28 Apr. 1888, 2.

57. "California as I Saw It," *San Francisco Examiner* special issue, 4 June 1893, 29; "San Rafael and the Golden State," *Harper's Weekly,* 26 Jan. 1889, 70.

58. "Leaves from My Diary," *KFW*, 4 May 1892, 275.

59. John Muir, ed. *Picturesque California* (New York: Dewing, 1888), 257–76.

60. *NYTrib*, 12 Aug. 1888, 11.

11. WASHINGTON

1. "The New York Women in Council," *SR*, 21 May 1864, 2.

2. "Gossip from New York," *CT*, 3 Nov. 1867, 2.

3. "Holly Tree Inns," *NYTrib*, 15 Apr. 1874, 2.

4. KF to Mary Anthony, 9 May 1869 (BPL).

5. "Church and Theater," *NYTrib*, 29 Mar. 1875, 3.

6. "Another Critic Gone Wrong," *KFW*, 14 Feb. 1894, 100.

7. "The Intemperance of Prohibition," *WP*, 23 Mar. 1889, 2.

8. "Woman Against Woman," *BP*, 15 Apr. 1889, 8.

9. "KF's Lecture," *BP*, 13 Apr. 1889, 4; Moss, *Selected Letters*, 195.

10. "Rum in Alaska," *KFW*, 26 Feb. 1890, 137–39.

11. "KF," *San Diego Union*, 9 Feb. 1888, 8.

12. "Howard's Gossip," *BG*, 11 July 1889, 4; "California as I Saw It"; Moss, *Selected Letters*, 201.

13. "Theatrical Themes," *Salt Lake Tribune*, 30 Dec. 1888, 4.

14. "Wines in Washington," *BG*, 23 Dec. 1888, 4.

15. *NYTrib*, 24 Mar. 1889, 9.

16. KF to Jeanette Gilder, 26 Apr. 1889 (Radcliffe).

17. "Theatrical Themes."

18. "Women on Wine," *BG*, 13 Apr. 1889, 8.

19. "Mrs. Foster on KF," *NYTrib*, 28 July 1889, 5; Moss, *Selected Letters*, 200.

20. "Pennsylvania's Vote Today," *NYTimes*, 18 June 1889, 1; *KFW*, 29 Apr. 1891, 265.

21. "KF on Prohibition," *NYTrib*, 26 July 1889, 7.

22. "KF's New Paper," *St. Louis Post-Dispatch*, 17 Nov. 1889, 27.

23. "Incubus, Farewell!" *KFW*, 28 May 1890, 346.

24. "Miss Field's Experience," *NYTrib*, 17 July 1889, 4.

25. "Your Hand, Dr. Rainsford," *KFW*, 8 June 1892, 353.

26. "Women as Politicians," *St. Louis Post-Dispatch*, 3 Nov. 1889, 26.

27. P. J. and C. W. Townsend III, eds., *Milo Adams Townsend and Social Movements of the Nineteenth Century* <bchistory.org/beavercounty/booklengthdocuments/Amilobooks/title.html>

28. *KFW*, 20 June 1894, 385; "Mrs. Stanton and KF," *Woman's Journal*, 21 July 1894, 231.

29. "KF in Utah," *BH*, 24 Feb. 1884, 14; *NYTimes*, 29 Dec. 1895, 23.

30. KF to E. C. Stedman, 4 Dec. 1875 (Butler Library, Columbia Univ.).

31. Whiting, *A Record*, 467–68.

32. "KF's Beliefs," *NYTimes*, 1 Dec. 1889, 4.

33. Moss, *Selected Letters*, 201.

34. *BG*, 6 Jan. 1890, 5; 18 May 1890, 21; *Louisville Courier-Journal*, 4 June 1893, 18; Whiting, *A Record*, 382.

35. Whiting, *A Record*, 470.

36. "The Girl Who Thinks She Can Write," *Youth's Companion*, 8 Sept. 1892, 447.

37. "In the Beginning," *KFW*, 1 Jan. 1890, 2.

38. *NYTimes*, 4 Aug. 1890, 5.

39. Gary Scharnhorst, *Charlotte Perkins Gilman: A Bibliography* (Metuchen, N.J.: Scarecrow, 1985), 59 and passim.

40. Denise D. Knight, ed. *The Diaries of Charlotte Perkins Gilman* (Charlottesville: Univ. Press of Virginia, 1994), 2:416.

41. Moss, *Selected Letters*, 221; Hutton, "The Literary Life," *Critic* 45 (1904): 429.

42. "A Puglistic Carnival" and "The Language of the Ring," *KFW*, 14 Sept. 1892, 162–63.

43. Stoddard, "Kate Field: Cosmopolite," 367.

44. Moss, *Selected Letters*, 209.

45. Ibid., 213.

46. KF to Hutton, 25 Sept. 1890 (Princeton); KF to Hugh McCulloch, 30 Apr. 1891 (Indiana).

47. KF to Anna C. L. Botta, 9 Feb. 1890 (West Virginia); L. R., "Women in Washington," *New York Star*, 2 Mar. 1890, 10; Moss, *Selected Letters*, 212.

48. Quoted in "The Tongue," *Ogden Standard Examiner*, 1 Jan. 1891, 4.

49. Fitz-Mac, "KF," *Denver Rocky Mountain News*, 8 Nov. 1891, 11.

50. A flyer enclosed with *KFW*, 1 Jan. 1890; Moss, *Selected Letters*, 207; "The Washington's Mail Bag," *KFW*, 8 Apr. 1891, 231; *KFW*, 23 Mar. 1895, 179–80.

51. "Prattle," *San Francisco Examiner*, 7 Aug. 1892, 6; 16 Apr. 1893, 6; 23 Apr. 1893, 6; Ignas K. Skrupskelis and Elizabeth M. Berkeley, eds., *The Correspondence of William James* (Charlottesville: Univ. Press of Virginia, 1999), 7:168–69.

52. Gertrude Atherton, *Adventures of a Novelist* (New York: Liveright, 1932), 185; for example, "Concerning Brains," *Woman's Journal*, 18 Feb. 1893, 50; "Lawrence Barrett," *SR*, 29 Mar. 1891, 6:3; "A Mormon Ruse—Beware!" *Salt Lake Tribune*, 2 Aug. 1891, 9; and "The New Massachusetts," *NOP*, 6 Sept. 1891, 2; KF to Mr. St. John, 1 Nov. 1894 (New York Univ.); *BE*, 28 May 1893, 4.

53. "Very Faithfully Recorded," *KFW*, 23 Sept. 1891, 212.

54. *BG*, 20 Mar. 1893, 4.

55. "From New York," *SR*, 22 Nov. 1864, 2.

56. "Sixteen Thousand Needy People," *KFW*, 25 Jan. 1893, 49.

57. "Moses in Mississippi," *KFW*, 8 Oct. 1890, 1; *The Autobiography of W.E.B. Du Bois* (New York: International Pub., 1968), 147.

58. "Frederick Douglass Still Lives," *KFW*, 2 Mar. 1895, 129.

59. "Broad as the Atlantic," *Minneapolis Tribune*, 20 Sept. 1891, 14.

60. "Society for Self-Preservation," *KFW*, 12 Oct. 1892, 225.

61. "It Seems to Me That—," *KFW*, 19 Mar. 1890, 190.

62. *BE*, 1 Oct. 1892, 4; "Liberty Island for the People," *KFW*, 14 May 1890, 313–15.

63. *KFW*, 25 Mar. 1891, 181; 9 Nov. 1892, 291; 29 Mar. 1893, 195.

64. *KFW*, 14 May 1890, 313–14; 21 May 1890, 331; 11 June 1890, 378–79; 10 Dec. 1890, 373; Moss, *Selected Letters*, 212.

65. "In Honor of the Victory," *NYTimes*, 4 Apr. 1891, 5.

66. Moss, *Selected Letters*, 206.

67. "Vandalism in Yosemite Park," *KFW*, 12 Feb. 1890, 105–6; Whiting, *A Record*, 74.

68. *NYTimes*, 14 Feb. 1890, 4; "A Commendable Plea," *BH*, 14 Feb. 1890, 4.

69. *KFW*, 22 Oct. 1890, 259; 31 Dec. 1890, 433.

70. "Glory Halleluha! Free Art Possible," *KFW*, 2 Apr. 1890, 218.

71. "KF's Dilemma," *NYTimes*, 15 Dec. 1891, 1.

72. "Art Must Be Free," *Denver Rocky Mountain News*, 12 Nov. 1891, 3.

73. "What They Say About Free Art," *KFW*, 9 Apr. 1890, 245–46.

74. "KF on Art," *Boston Traveller*, 29 Mar. 1890, 4.

75. Laura Stedman et al., eds., *Life and Letters of Edmund Clarence Stedman* (New York: Moffat, Yard, 1910), 544.

76. "Art Must Be Free."

77. Ibid.

78. *Denver Republican*, 9 Nov. 1891, 2; *Denver Times*, 9 Nov. 1891, 4; "KF's Letter," *CT-H*, 23 Oct. 1895, 10.

79. *Denver Times*, 12 Nov. 1891, 1; *Denver Republican*, 12 Nov. 1891, 5.

80. "Miss KF's Reply," *Denver Rocky Mountain News*, 15 Nov. 1891, 12.

81. "A Discussion on Free Art," *Colorado Springs Daily Gazette*, 18 Nov. 1891, 1.

82. "Health and Art in Colorado Springs," *KFW*, 16 Dec. 1891, 405.

83. *KFW*, 25 Nov. 1891, 345–48; *Pueblo Chieftain*, 17 Nov. 1891, 4.

84. *St. Louis Post-Dispatch*, 5 Dec. 1891, 4.

85. "Plea for Free Art," *CT*, 10 Dec. 1891, 1; "The Senseless Art Duty," *CT*, 11 Dec. 1891, 4.

86. "KF's Dilemma"; "What Women Wear," *Chicago Inter-Ocean*, 15 Dec. 1891, 2.

87. *NYTimes*, 7 Jan. 1892, 8; "Leaves from My Diary," *KFW*, 9 Mar. 1892, 146–47.

88. "The Press Clubs in Chicago," *Ogden Standard Examiner*, 8 Jan. 1892, 1.

89. "Home from San Francisco," *NYTimes*, 1 Feb. 1892, 2.

90. "Leaves from My Diary," *KFW*, 16 Mar. 1892, 161–62.

91. "Leaves from My Diary," *KFW*, 6 Apr. 1892, 211–12.

92. "Salt Lake City," *KFW*, 11 Nov. 1891, 309.

93. "California as I Saw It."

94. KF to ?, 16 Jan. 1892 (New York Univ.).

95. "A New Chinese Wall," *KFW*, 13 Apr. 1892, 225.

96. "A Minister Extraordinary!" *KFW*, 13 May 1891, 297.

97. "California as I Saw It."

98. Charlotte Perkins Gilman, *The Living of Charlotte Perkins Gilman* (New York: Appleton-Century, 1935), 136.

99. "KF's Letter," *CT-H*, 26 Oct. 1895, 6.

100. "A Democratic Indigestion," *KFW*, 17 Feb. 1892, 98.

101. "Art Must Be Free"; KF to Mr. Stone, 14 Apr. 1892 (Newberry).

102. "National Art Association," *Harper's Weekly*, 14 May 1892, 459; Whiting, *A Record*, 487; KF to Phoebe Hearst, 9 Feb. 1892 (Berkeley).

103. "Kate in the Pulpit," *CH*, 5 June 1893, 3.

104. "A National Academy of Art," *NYTimes*, 16 July 1892, 9.

105. "Pleas for Free Art," *NYTimes*, 19 May 1892, 4.

106. "Art Is Free!" *KFW*, 5 Sept. 1894, 145; *NYTimes*, 29 Nov. 1894, 1.

107. Whiting, *A Record*, 514; "What the Papers Said," *KFW*, 5 Dec. 1894, 367.

108. "Rum in Alaska," *KFW*, 26 Feb. 1890, 137–39.

109. "Education in Alaska," *KFW*, 26 Mar. 1890, 201–2.

110. "A Week of Parades," *KFW*, 19 Oct. 1892, 242–43.

111. KF to Hutton, 11 Jan. 1888 (Princeton).

112. "Alaska Must Go to the Fair," *KFW*, 24 Dec. 1890, 414.

12. CHICAGO AND BEYOND

1. "KF's Views," *CH*, 31 May 1893, 1.

2. "Of Newspaperwomen," *CT*, 27 May 1893, 5.

3. "To Hear KF," *CH*, 1 June 1893, 9; "A Talk," in *The Congress of Women*, ed. Mary K. O. Eagle (Chicago: American Publishing, 1894), 77–79; *KFW*, 11 Jan. 1893, 17.

4. Whiting, *A Record*, 504.

5. "A Talk," 77–79; "The Woman's Building," *KFW*, 8 Nov. 1893, 291; "KF's Views," *CH*, 31 May 1893, 1.

6. "To Hear KF," *CH*, 1 June 1893, 9.

7. "The Mistakes of the Fair," *KFW*, 21 June 1893, 385–87.

8. "KF's Charge," *CH*, 13 June 1893, 13.

9. "Pleads for Open Gates," *CT*, 5 June 1893, 3; "KF's Views," *CH*, 31 May 1893, 1.

10. "On to the Great Fair," *CH*, 4 June 1893, 1.

11. "Buffalo Bill and Royalty," *KFW*, 19 July 1893, 33.

12. *CH*, 2 June 1893, 1; 6 June 1893, 9; 22 June 1893, 9.

13. "Helping to Fulfill KF's Last Wish," *San Francisco Examiner*, 9 Aug. 1896, 8.

14. "KF Talks Out in Meeting," *BE*, 24 Sept. 1893, 8.

15. "Prurient Prudery," *KFW*, 1 June 1892, 339.

16. KF to Phoebe Hearst, 27 Aug. 1893 (Berkeley).

17. Moss, *Selected Letters*, 219.

18. *The Drama of Glass* (Toledo, Ohio: Libby Glass, 1894), 23, 28, 24, 39.

19. *BG*, 28 Jan. 1893, 4; "Miss KF," *BE*, 7 Apr. 1895, 24.

20. Whiting, *A Record*, 501.

21. *New Orleans Times-Picayune*, 10 Sept. 1893, 16; *Chicago Inter-Ocean*, 14 Oct. 1893, 10; 15 Oct. 1893, 31.

22. *NYTimes*, 13 Nov. 1893, 1; Whiting, *A Record*, 503; *KFW*, 22 Nov. 1893, 321–22.

23. "KF's Appeal," *Chicago Inter-Ocean*, 11 Aug. 1895, 7.

24. "My Mailbag," *KFW*, 16 Mar. 1895, 162–64.

25. "Will the Chinese Go?" *KFW*, 24 May 1893, 321.

26. "KF's Lecture," *Cairo Weekly Citizen*, 13 Dec. 1894, 1.

27. *KFW*, 28 June 1891, 25; *NYTrib*, 8 July 1891, 6; "Can You Cook?" *Impress*, 27 Oct. 1894, 3.

28. Moss, *Selected Letters*, 230; KF to Lydia Avery Coonley, 28 Nov. 1893 (Alderman Library, Univ. of Virginia); Whiting, *A Record*, 508.

29. "Women in Washington," *NYTrib*, 29 Apr. 1895, 7.

30. Ella W. Peattie, "A Word with the Women," *Omaha World-Herald*, 28 Apr. 1895, 8; W. J. McGee, "Memorial of KF," *Records of the Columbia Historical Society* 1 (1897): 172–76; Rounseville Wildman, "The Death of KF," *Overland Monthly*, ns 28 (July 1896): 126–27.

31. KF to Laurence and Eleanor Hutton, 29 May 1895 (Princeton).

32. *Honolulu Pacific Commercial Advertiser*, 20 May 1896, 1, 3.

33. *Newport News*, 9 Aug. 1894, 5; 1 May 1895, 6.

34. "KF in a New Role," *NYTimes*, 17 Sept. 1894, 9.

35. "Was She Sane?" *Newport News*, 3 May 1895, 3, 6; 1 May 1895, 3.

36. "KF's Letter," *CT-H*, 12 May 1895, 17.

37. "Women in Washington," *NYTrib*, 29 Apr. 1895, 7.

38. "KF's Letter," *CT-H*, 12 May 1895, 17.

39. "Was She Sane?"

40. "KF's Letter," *CT-H*, 12 May 1895, 17.

41. "Was She Sane?"; "Servant's Ears Open," *BG*, 30 Apr. 1895, 12.

42. "The Jury Disagreed," *Newport News*, 6 May 1895, 8.

43. KF to Stedman, 21 June 1895 (Baylor).

44. "KF's Letter," *CT-H*, 3 June 1895, 6; *Ogden Standard Examiner*, 29 May 1895, 1.

45. "KF's Letter," *CT-H*, 20 Dec. 1895, 6.

46. "Going to Honolulu," *Salt Lake Deseret Evening News*, 26 Aug. 1895, 1; Moss, *Selected Letters*, 28.

47. "KF's Letter," *CT-H*, 14 Sept. 1895, 8; 18 Sept. 1895, 6.

48. "KF's Letter," *CT-H*, 22 Sept. 1895, 30; 19 Sept. 1895, 8; 22 Sept. 1895, 30.

49. "KF's Letter," *CT-H*, 21 Sept. 1895, 8.

50. "KF's Letter," *CT-H*, 25 Sept. 1895, 6; 1 Oct. 1895, 8.

51. "KF's Letter," *CT-H*, 3 Oct. 1895, 6; 27 Sept. 1895, 6; 1 Oct. 1895, 8; 7 Oct. 1895, 6.

52. "KF's Letter," *CT-H*, 10 Oct. 1895, 10.

53. "KF's Letter," *CT-H*, 5 Oct. 1895, 8; 13 Oct. 1895, 8.

54. "KF's Letter," *CT-H*, 5 Nov. 1895, 10; 14 Oct. 1895, 6.

55. "KF's Letter," *CT-H*, 26 Oct. 1895, 6.

56. Stoddard, "Kate Field: Cosmopolite," 371.

57. "KF's Letter," *CT-H*, 16 Nov. 1895, 14; 30 Oct. 1895, 8.

58. Whiting, *A Record*, 533; "Miss KF Arrives," *San Francisco Chronicle*, 9 Nov. 1895, 8.

59. "KF's Letter," *CT-H*, 15 Dec. 1895, 36.

60. "Death of a Noted American Writer," *Honolulu Pacific Commercial Advertiser*, 20 May 1896, 3.

61. "Honored by Women Writers," *San Francisco Examiner*, 13 Nov. 1895, 16.

62. Wildman, "The Death of KF," 126.

63. "Noted Women on Board," *San Francisco Examiner*, 15 Nov. 1895, 16.

64. "KF's Letter," *CT-H*, 18 Dec. 1895, 6.

13. HAWAII AND HOME

1. "The Hawaiian Kingdom," *KFW*, 9 Aug. 1893, 86–87; Stoddard, "Kate Field: Cosmopolite," 371.

2. *KFW*, 28 Jan. 1891, 49; 16 Dec. 1891, 407–8.

3. "Annex Hawaii," *KFW*, 8 Feb. 1893, 81; 23 Feb. 1895, 114.

4. "Welcome, Hawaii!" *KFW*, 22 Feb. 1893, 113.

5. "The Hawaiian Kingdom," *KFW*, 9 Aug. 1893, 86–87; 15 Aug. 1894, 97.

6. "State Secret Out," *CT-H*, 7 Jan. 1896, 1.

7. "KF's Opinion," *Honolulu Pacific Commercial Advertiser*, 23 Nov. 1895, 1.

8. "KF in Hawaii," *CT-H*, 19 Dec. 1895, 6; 22 Dec. 1895, 26; 26 Dec. 1895, 9; 28 Dec. 1895, 11.

9. Rare Book and Manuscript Room, BPL (MS 1139); "Dole at the Door," *CT-H*, 30 Dec. 1895, 1–2.

10. For example, "The Hawaiian President," *Salt Lake Tribune*, 30 Dec. 1895, 5; "KF's Letter," *CT-H*, 22 Feb. 1896, 10.

11. Moss, *Selected Letters*, 232; "A Letter with a History," *CT-H*, 4 Jan. 1896, 8.

12. Moss, *Selected Letters*, 232–33.

13. *Honolulu Pacific Commercial Advertiser*, 16 Dec. 1895, 1; 6 Dec. 1895, 1; 24 Dec. 1895, 3.

14. "KF's Letter," *CT-H*, 19 Jan. 1896, 24; 20 Jan. 1896, 9; 8 Feb. 1896, 10; Moss, *Selected Letters*, 232.

15. "KF's Letter," *CT-H*, 11 Jan. 1896, 14; 20 Jan. 1896, 9; 9 Feb. 1896, 24; 1 Mar. 1896, 15, 19; 2 Mar. 1896, 9; 11 Apr. 1896, 9; 12 Apr. 1896, 40; 22 Feb. 1896, 10; 9 Mar. 1896, 9.

16. "An Evening with Dickens," *Honolulu Pacific Commercial Advertiser*, 26 Feb. 1896, 1.

17. "KF in Hawaii," *CT-H*, 3 Jan. 1896, 6; 31 Dec. 1895, 6; 11 Jan. 1896, 14; 26 Jan. 1896, 35; 22 Feb. 1896, 10; 15 Mar. 1896, 14; 21 Mar. 1896, 10.

18. "KF's Letter," *CT-H*, 16 Mar. 1896, 9; "Viewed Pearl Lochs," *Honolulu Pacific Commercial Advertiser*, 30 Dec. 1895, 5.

19. Moss, *Selected Letters*, 233–34.

20. "KF Interested," *Honolulu Pacific Commercial Advertiser*, 27 Apr. 1896, 1.

21. Whiting, *A Record*, 545, 549.

22. "KF's Demise," *CT-H*, 31 May 1896, 1.

23. "KF in Kohala," *Honolulu Pacific Commercial Advertiser*, 15 May 1896, 6.

24. "KF's Last Illness," *NYTimes*, 15 June 1896, 12.

25. Mabel Loomis Todd, *Corona and Coronet* (Boston: Houghton Mifflin, 1898), 101–3.

26. Ibid.

27. Ibid.

28. Ibid.

29. "KF Is Laid at Rest," *Honolulu Pacific Commercial Advertiser*, 21 May 1896, 1.

30. "Death of KF," *CT-H*, 31 May 1896, 40.

31. "Miss KF," *Salt Lake Tribune*, 22 Feb. 1885, 5; Stoddard, "Kate Field: Cosmopolite," 371; *NYTimes*, 27 Aug. 1896, 9.

32. "KF's Will," *BG*, 4 Sept. 1896, 12.

33. "Helping to Fulfill KF's Last Wish," *San Francisco Examiner*, 9 Aug. 1896, 8.

34. "The Body of KF," *NYTimes*, 23 Dec. 1896, 5.

35. "Last Honors to KF," *BG*, 28 Dec. 1896, 1.

36. "Surrounded by Flowers," *BG*, 10 Jan. 1897, 4; *NYTimes*, 11 Jan. 1897, 1.

37. *BG*, 3 Aug. 1896, 4; *NYTimes*, 1 Aug. 1896, 2.

38. "KF Not in Debt," *BG*, 17 Aug. 1896, 2; *NYTimes*, 2 Oct. 1896, 1.

39. "KF and Landor," *NYTimes Saturday Review of Books*, 19 Nov. 1898, 782.

40. "Poe MSS," *NYTimes*, 25 Jan. 1911, 7.

41. "William Black and KF," *NYTimes*, 24 Dec. 1898, BR 872; Soria, *Elihu Vedder*, 280.

42. Isabel Moore, *Talks in a Library with Laurence Hutton* (New York: Putnam's, 1905), 384; Moss, *Selected Letters*, 135.

43. Stoddard to Dewitt Miller, Oct. 1908 (Huntington).

44. Ibid.

45. Jeanette L. Gilder, *The Tomboy at Work* (New York: Doubleday, Page, 1904), 107.

46. Moore, *Talks in a Library*, 382–83.

47. Dahlia Armon and Walter Blair, eds., *Huck Finn and Tom Sawyer Among the Indians and Other Unfinished Stories* (Berkeley: Univ. of California Press, 1989), 98.

48. "From a Spirit," *BG,* 13 Nov. 1899, 4; "Lilian Whiting, Says She Talked with Kate Field in the Spirit World," *NYH,* 12 Nov. 1899, 4:2.

49. Lilian Whiting, *After Her Death: The Story of a Summer* (Boston: Roberts Bros., 1897), 152–53.

50. "KF," *Boston Traveller,* 28 Sept. 1882, 2.

Bibliography

Alger, W. R. *Life of Edwin Forrest.* Philadelphia: Lippincott, 1877.

Armon, Dahlia, and Walter Blair, eds. *Huck Finn and Tom Sawyer Among the Indians and Other Unfinished Stories.* Berkeley: Univ. of California Press, 1989.

Arrington, Leonard J. *Kate Field and J. H. Beadle: Manipulators of the Mormon Past.* Salt Lake City: Univ. of Utah Press, 1971.

Atherton, Gertrude. *Adventures of a Novelist.* New York: Liveright, 1932.

Baker, William, and William M. Clarke, eds. *The Letters of Wilkie Collins.* New York: St. Martin's, 1999.

Blair, Walter. *Native American Humor.* San Francisco: Chandler, 1960.

Brinkley, Roberta Florence. *Nathan Field, the Actor-Playwright.* New Haven: Yale Univ. Press, 1928.

Carson, William G. B. *The Theatre on the Frontier.* Chicago: Univ. of Chicago Press, 1932.

Cobbe, Frances Power. *Italics.* London: Trübner 1864.

Croly, Jane C. *Sorosis: Its Origin and History.* New York: Little and Co., 1886.

De Voto, Bernard. *Mark Twain's America.* Boston: Little, Brown, 1932.

Deane, Margery "Letter from Newport." *New York Evening Post,* 12 Aug. 1870.

DeVane, William C., ed. *New Letters of Robert Browning.* New Haven: Yale Univ. Press, 1950.

Ellmann, Richard. *Oscar Wilde.* New York: Knopf, 1988.

Fischer, Victor, et al., eds. *Mark Twain's Letters 1870–1871.* Berkeley: Univ. of California Press, 1995.

Fitz-Mac. "KF." *Denver Rocky Mountain News,* 8 Nov. 1891.

Gilder, Jeanette L. *The Tomboy at Work.* New York: Doubleday, Page, 1904.

Gilman, Charlotte Perkins. *The Living of Charlotte Perkins Gilman.* New York: Appleton-Century, 1935.

Glendinning, Victoria. *Anthony Trollope.* New York: Knopf, 1992.

Habegger, Alfred. *My Wars Are Laid Away in Books: The Life of Emily Dickinson*. New York: Random House, 2001.

Hall, N. John, ed. "Anthony Trollope on America." *Continental Monthly*. Sept. 1862.

————, ed. *Letters of Anthony Trollope*. Stanford, Calif.: Stanford Univ. Press, 1983.

Haraszti, Zoltán. "Kate Field and the Trollope Brothers." *More Books: Being the Bulletin of the BPL*. July 1927.

Hatton, Joseph, ed. *Reminiscences of J. L. Toole*. London: Routledge, 1892.

Howe, M. A. DeWolfe. *Memories of a Hostess*. Boston: Atlantic Monthly Press, 1922.

James, Henry. *The Portrait of a Lady*. New York: Library of America, 1985.

Jenkins, Roy. *Sir Charles Dilke*. London: Collins, 1965

Kelley, Philip. *The Browning Collections: A Reconstruction*. Waco, Tex.: Armstrong Browning Library, 1984.

"KF Dead." *BP*, 31 May 1896.

Kiralis, Karl. "Two Recently Discovered Letters: Mark Twain on Kate Field." *Mark Twain Journal*. Summer 1980.

Knight, Denise D., ed. *The Diaries of Charlotte Perkins Gilman*. Charlottesville: Univ. Press of Virginia, 1994.

"Letter from Boston." *NOP*, 3 Dec. 1855.

"Letter from Florence." *NOP*, 1 Sept. 1859.

"Letter from Florence." *NOP*, 8 July 1860.

"Letter from Italy." *NOP*, 19 Feb. 1860.

"Letter from Italy." *NOP*, 26 Feb. 1860.

"Letter from Italy." *NOP*, 8 Apr. 1860.

"Letter from Straws, Jr." *BC*, 1 Sept. 1859.

"Letter from Straws, Jr." *BC*, 17 Mar. 1859.

"Letter from Straws, Jr." *BC*, 18 June 1859.

"Letter from Straws, Jr." *BC*, 25 Apr. 1859.

"Letter from Straws, Jr." *BC*, 27 June 1859

"Letter from Straws, Jr." *BC*, 28 July 1859.

"Letter from Straws, Jr." *BC*, 30 May 1859.

"Letter from Straws, Jr." *BC*, 4 July 1859.

"Letter from Straws, Jr." *BC*, 8 June 1859.

Lewis, Lloyd, and Henry Justin Smith. *Oscar Wilde Discovers America*. New York: Harcourt, Brace, 1936.

Lewis, Scott. *The Letters of Elizabeth Barrett Browning to Her Sister Arabella*. Waco, Tex.: Wedgestone Press, 2002.

Mather, Edward. "KF's New Departure." *Bay State Monthly*. Nov. 1885.

Matthews, Brander. *These Many Years*. New York: Scribner's, 1917.

McAleer, Edward C. "Isa Blagden to Kate Field." *Boston Public Library Quarterly* 3 (1951): 210-20.

———. *Dearest Isa: Robert Browning's Letters to Isa Blagden*. Austin: Univ. of Texas Press, 1951.

McGee, W. J. "Memorial of KF." *Records of the Columbia Historical Society*. 1897.

Merriam, George S. *The Life and Times of Samuel Bowles*. New York: Century, 1885.

Moore, Isabel. *Talks in a Library with Laurence Hutton*. New York: Putnam's, 1905.

Moss, Carolyn J., ed. *Kate Field: Selected Letters*. Carbondale: Southern Illinois Univ. Press, 1996.

Murdoch, James E. *The Stage*. New York: Blom, 1969.

Myerson, Joel, and Daniel Shealy, eds. *Journals of Louisa May Alcott*. Boston: Little, Brown, 1989.

Oehlschlaeger, Fritz, ed. *Old Southwest Humor from the St. Louis Reveille, 1844–1850*. Columbia: Univ. of Missouri Press, 1990.

Ostrom, John Ward, ed. *The Letters of Poe*. New York: Harvard Univ. Press, 1948.

P[erry], N[ora]. "Boston." *PJ*. 15 Mar. 1880.

———. "Newport Correspondence." *PJ*. 21 Sept. 1871.

Page, Eugene R., ed. *Metamora and Other Plays*. Princeton, N.J.: Princeton Univ. Press, 1941.

Paul, John. "Letter from New York." *SR*, 29 May 1867.

Peattie, Ella W. "A Word with the Women." *Omaha World-Herald*. 28 Apr. 1895.

Phillips, Kate. *Helen Hunt Jackson*. Berkeley: Univ. of California Press, 2003.

Pickard, John B., ed. *The Letters of John Greenleaf Whittier*. Cambridge, Mass.: Belknap, 1975.

Pope-Hennessey, James. *Anthony Trollope*. Boston: Little, Brown, 1971.

Quinn, Arthur. *Edgar Allan Poe*. New York: Appleton-Century, 1941.

"Robert Browning: A Few Unpublished Letters" *KFW*, 13 May 1891.

Rusk, Ralph L., ed. *Letters of Ralph Waldo Emerson*. New York: Columbia Univ. Press, 1939.

Sadlier, Michael. *Anthony Trollope: A Commentary*. Boston: Houghton Mifflin, 1927.

Salamo, Lin, et al., eds. *Mark Twain's Letters 1872–1873*. Berkeley: Univ. of California Press, 1997.

Scharnhorst, Gary. "Kate Field's 'An Evening with Charles Dickens': A Reconstructed Lecture." *Dickens Quarterly*. June 2004.

———. "Whitman and Kate Field." *Walt Whitman Quarterly Review*. Summer/Fall 2005.

———. *Charlotte Perkins Gilman: A Bibliography*. Metuchen, N.J.: Scarecrow, 1985.

———. "Kate Field: A Primary Bibliography." *Resources for American Literary Study* 29 (2004).

Sherwood, Morgan B. *Exploration of Alaska*. New Haven: Yale Univ. Press, 1965.

Skrupskelis, Ignas K., and Elizabeth M. Berkeley, eds. *The Correspondence of William James*. Charlottesville: Univ. Press of Virginia, 1999.

Smith, Sol. *Theatrical Journey Work*. Philadelphia: Peterson, 1854.

Snow, C. P. *Trollope*. London: Macmillan, 1975.

Soria, Regina. *Elihu Vedder*. Rutherford, N.J.: Fairleigh Dickinson Univ. Press, 1970.

Stedman, Laura, et al., eds. *Life and Letters of Edmund Clarence Stedman*. New York: Moffat, Yard, 1910.

Stoddard, Charles Warren. "Kate Field: Cosmopolite." *National Magazine* 23 (Jan. 1906): 361–72.

Sunder, John E., ed. *Matt Field on the Santa Fe Trail*. Norman: Univ. of Oklahoma Press, 1960.

Super, R. H. *The Chronicler of Barsetshire*. Ann Arbor: Univ. of Michigan Press, 1988.

Thompson, Slason. *Life of Eugene Field*. New York: Appleton, 1927.

Townsend, Charles Walker III, and Peggy Jean Townsend, eds. *Milo Adams Townsend and Social Movements of the Nineteenth Century*. <bchistory.org\beavercounty\ booklengthdocuments\Amilobooks\title.html>

Trollope, Anthony. *An Autobiography*. Berkeley: Univ. of California Press, 1947.

Twain, Mark. *Autobiography*. New York: Harper, 1924.

Vedder, Elihu. *Digressions of V*. Boston: Houghton Mifflin, 1910.

Walker, Fuller. "Literary Notices." *Woman's Journal*, 5 July 1873.

Weber, Carl. *The Rise and Fall of James Ripley Osgood*. Waterville, Me.: Colby College Press, 1959.

Whiting, Lilian. *Kate Field: A Record*. Boston: Little, Brown, 1899.

Wildman, Rounseville. "The Death of KF." *Overland Monthly*, July 1896.

Index